Gold Cloths of Sumatra

Indonesia's Songkets from Ceremony to Commodity

Gold Cloths of Sumatra

Indonesia's Songkets from Ceremony to Commodity

Susan Rodgers, Anne Summerfield and John Summerfield

KITLV • PRESS

2007

IRIS AND B. GERALD CANTOR ART GALLERY

College of the Holy Cross ▪ Worcester, Massachusetts

KITLV Press
Koninklijk Instituut voor Taal-, Land- en Volkenkunde
(Royal Netherlands Institute of Southeast Asian and Caribbean Studies)
P.O. Box 9515
2300 RA Leiden
The Netherlands
website: www.kitlv.nl
e-mail: kitlvpress@kitlv.nl

Iris and B. Gerald Cantor Art Gallery
College of the Holy Cross
One College Street
Worcester, Massachusetts 01610-2395
website: www.holycross.edu

All inquiries about the sale of this volume should be directed to KITLV Press

KITLV is an institute of the Royal Netherlands Academy of Arts and Sciences (KNAW)

ISBN 978 90 6718 312 3

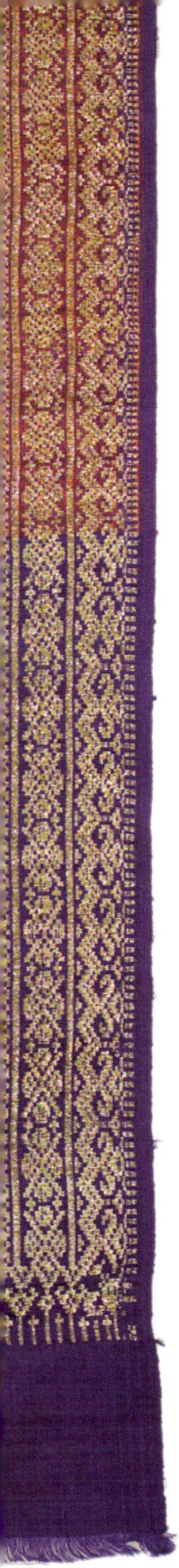

TABLE OF CONTENTS

Gold Cloths of Sumatra

Indonesia's Songkets from Ceremony to Commodity

by Susan Rodgers, Anne Summerfield and John Summerfield

Acknowledgments

1. Introduction 1
Susan Rodgers

2. Sumatra's songkets: Not a fragile tradition 10
Susan Rodgers

3. Songkets within Indonesian textile worlds 26
Susan Rodgers

4. What lies behind a songket textile? 46
Anne Summerfield and John Summerfield

5. Commerce and creativity: Sumatran songket business families, marketing and innovation in contemporary songket weaving 62
Susan Rodgers

6. Biographied textiles 84
Susan Rodgers, Anne Summerfield and John Summerfield

List of References 132

Photography credits, textile collections 137

MAP 2

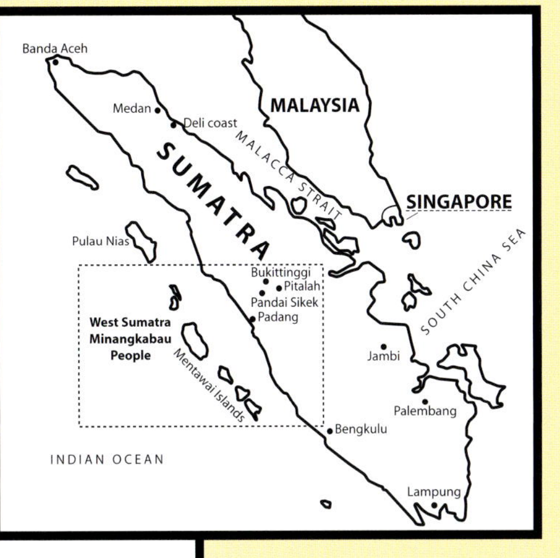
Banda Aceh
Medan
Deli coast
MALAYSIA
MALACCA STRAIT
SUMATRA
SINGAPORE
Pulau Nias
SOUTH CHINA SEA
Bukittinggi
Pitalah
Pandai Sikek
Padang
West Sumatra
Minangkabau
People
Mentawai Islands
Jambi
Palembang
Bengkulu
INDIAN OCEAN
Lampung

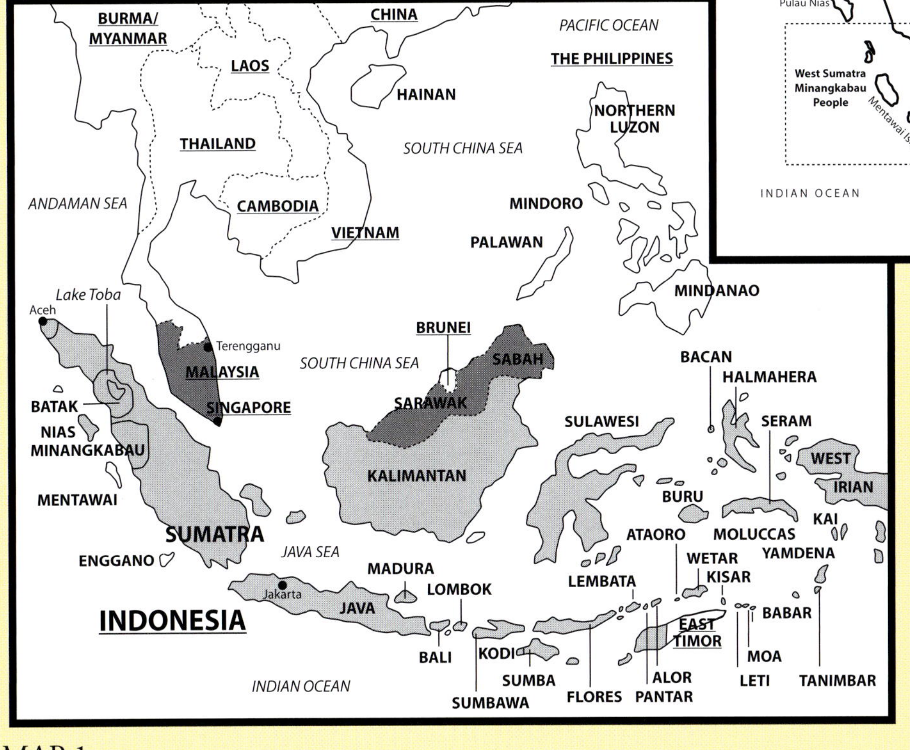
BURMA/
MYANMAR
CHINA
PACIFIC OCEAN
LAOS
THE PHILIPPINES
HAINAN
NORTHERN
LUZON
THAILAND
SOUTH CHINA SEA
ANDAMAN SEA
CAMBODIA
MINDORO
VIETNAM
PALAWAN
MINDANAO
Lake Toba
Aceh
Terengganu
BRUNEI
SABAH
MALAYSIA
SOUTH CHINA SEA
BACAN
HALMAHERA
BATAK
SINGAPORE
SARAWAK
SULAWESI
SERAM
NIAS
MINANGKABAU
WEST
IRIAN
KALIMANTAN
MENTAWAI
BURU
KAI
SUMATRA
ATAORO
MOLUCCAS
YAMDENA
JAVA SEA
ENGGANO
WETAR
MADURA
KISAR
LEMBATA
LOMBOK
Jakarta
INDONESIA
JAVA
BABAR
EAST
TIMOR
BALI
KODI
MOA
SUMBA
ALOR
INDIAN OCEAN
LETI
TANIMBAR
FLORES
PANTAR
SUMBAWA

MAP 1

ACKNOWLEDGMENTS

The Iris & B. Gerald Cantor Art Gallery at the College of the Holy Cross, Worcester, Massachusetts, is proud to have presented the exhibition *Gold Cloths of Sumatra: Indonesia's Songkets from Ceremony to Commodity* as part of our 2006 - 2007 exhibition season. Over the past decade, Cantor Art Gallery has offered a series of exhibitions dedicated to the study of Southeast Asian textiles, specifically from Indonesia. This current exhibition conceived by Susan Rodgers is the most ambitious to date, drawing on remarkable collections of both historical and contemporary hand-loomed Indonesian heritage cloths and highlighting the continuing vibrancy of contemporary markets.

We are deeply grateful to Professor Susan Rodgers, Department of Sociology and Anthropology at the College of the Holy Cross, and to Southeast Asian textile scholars Dr. Anne Summerfield and Dr. John Summerfield for their dedication and hard work throughout every aspect of this project. This book is designed to bring aspects of Sumatran songket excellence to broad audiences.

To the following individuals we offer our sincere thanks and gratitude for their contributions: Professor Marla Berns, Director, and Sarah Kennington, Registrar, UCLA Fowler Museum of Cultural History; Mary Jane Leland, Los Angeles, Sumatran textile researcher; Susan Schmalz, Textile Conservation, Los Angeles, CA; and Curatorial Assistance, Pasadena, CA. Frank E. Graham, Hudson, MA., took excellent digital photographs of many of the 19th century and contemporary textiles for the exhibition; we draw on those images for this book. Karen A. Jacobson, editor of numerous important museum publications nationwide, pored over the book's text and thereby greatly improved it. Special thanks, too, to the dedicated staff of the Iris & B. Gerald Cantor Art Gallery: to Paula Rosenblum, administrative assistant, and to Timothy A. Johnson, preparator and exhibition designer. Their unwavering talents helped make "Gold Cloths" shine. Among the many departments that contributed exhibition and publication support are the Holy Cross Departments of Audio-Visual Services, Jessie Anderson and John Buckingham; and Graphic Arts, Henry Roy, Tom Parsons, and especially our superb Graphic Designer, Sharon Matys, by now a veteran of several demanding texts on Sumatran arts. Also instrumental to this entire project's success were Professor Timothy R. Austin, Vice President for Academic Affairs and Dean of the College of the Holy Cross; Debbie Neal, Director of Academic Budgets and Operations, Dean's Office; Professor Edward H. Thompson, Jr., chair, Department of Sociology and Anthropology; Professor Thomas R. Gottschang, Holy Cross Asian Studies Director; and Professors Richard Matlak and Susan Cunningham, director and assistant director, Center for Interdisciplinary and Special Studies, Holy Cross. We also gratefully acknowledge the on-going support of Iris Cantor, and Judith Sobol, executive director of the Iris and B. Gerald Cantor Foundation.

Roger Hankins, Director, Iris and B.Gerald Cantor Art Gallery

Primary thanks for an exhibition of this sort and its associated volume of course go to the Indonesian weavers from the 18th, 19th, 20th, and 21st centuries who crafted the magnificent textiles we study and present to broad publics. Heartfelt gratitude also goes to the songket shop entrepreneurs in Bukittinggi, Pandai Sikek, Palembang, Jambi, and Jakarta who generously shared hours of their time with me for interviews during the field research portions of this work, 1995-96, in summers, 2003-2006, and during my sabbatical, 2005-2006. Special thanks to H. Elly Azhar and H. A. Sutan Madjo Indo of Toko Aladdin, Bukittinggi, and to the family of Agus Haji Hussein Rahmat of the Fikri Koleksi, Palembang. Master weaver and songket designer Ibu Sanuar and her son and business partner Bapak Adyan of the Pusako Weaving House, Pandai Sikek, West Sumatra, have expended so many hours over the last twelve years instructing me about songket heritages that it is fully impossible for me to repay the debt. Also due deep thanks are Holy Cross's three tireless student docents for the exhibition, Class of 2007 graduates Melanie Chapman, Colleen Germain, and Sarah Thibeault. Their good cheer in learning about Indonesian textile histories was inspirational. Financial support for the research was provided by the Holy Cross Committee on Research and Publications, the O'Leary faculty fellowship program, and the Dean's Office.

Susan Rodgers, Professor, Anthropology, Department of Sociology and Anthropology
Holy Cross

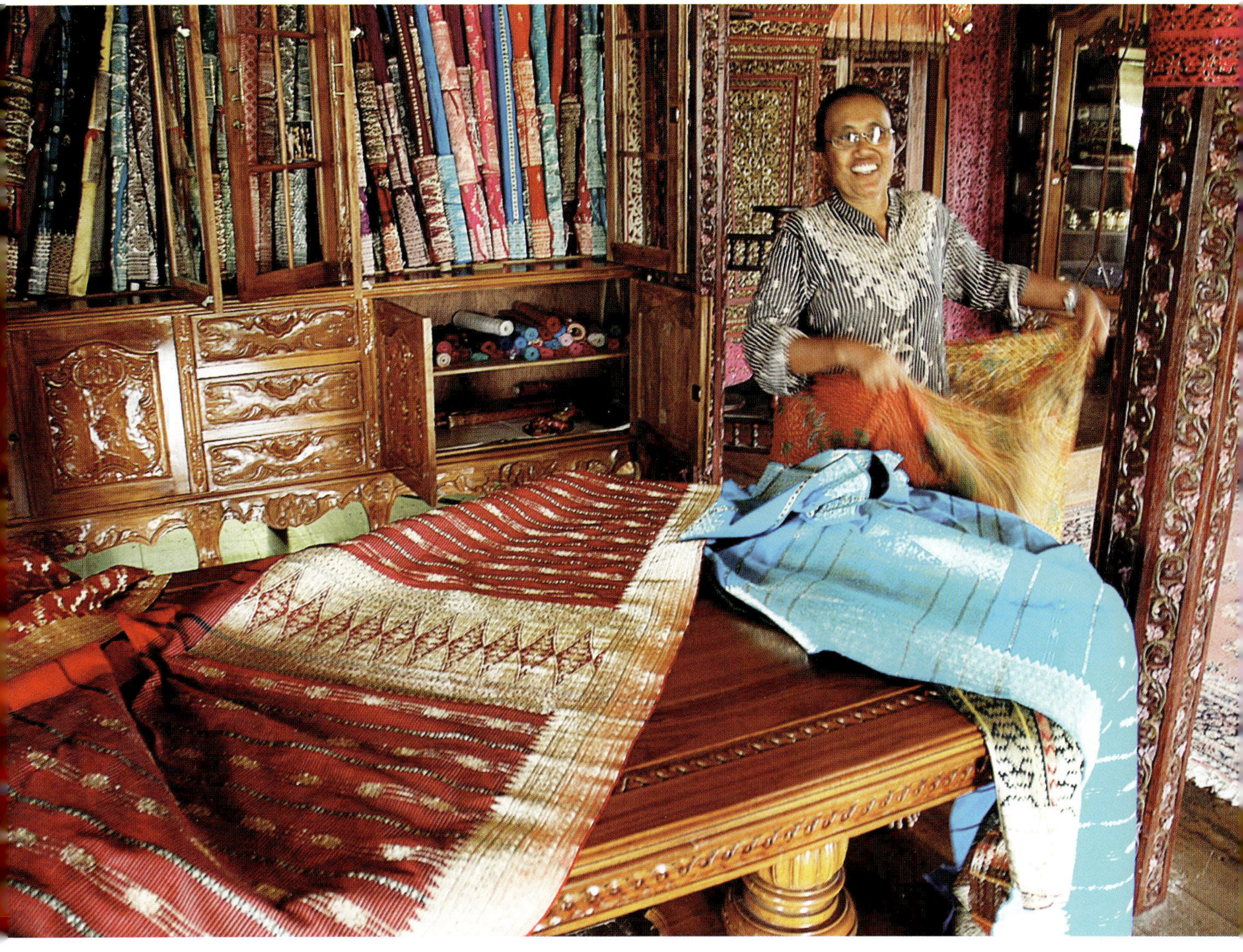

Ibu Tafsinar, inside a famous songket shop in the Minangkabau weaving village of Pandai Sikek, 2006. This gold cloth emporium is the Rumah Tenun Pusako, the Pusako Weaving House.

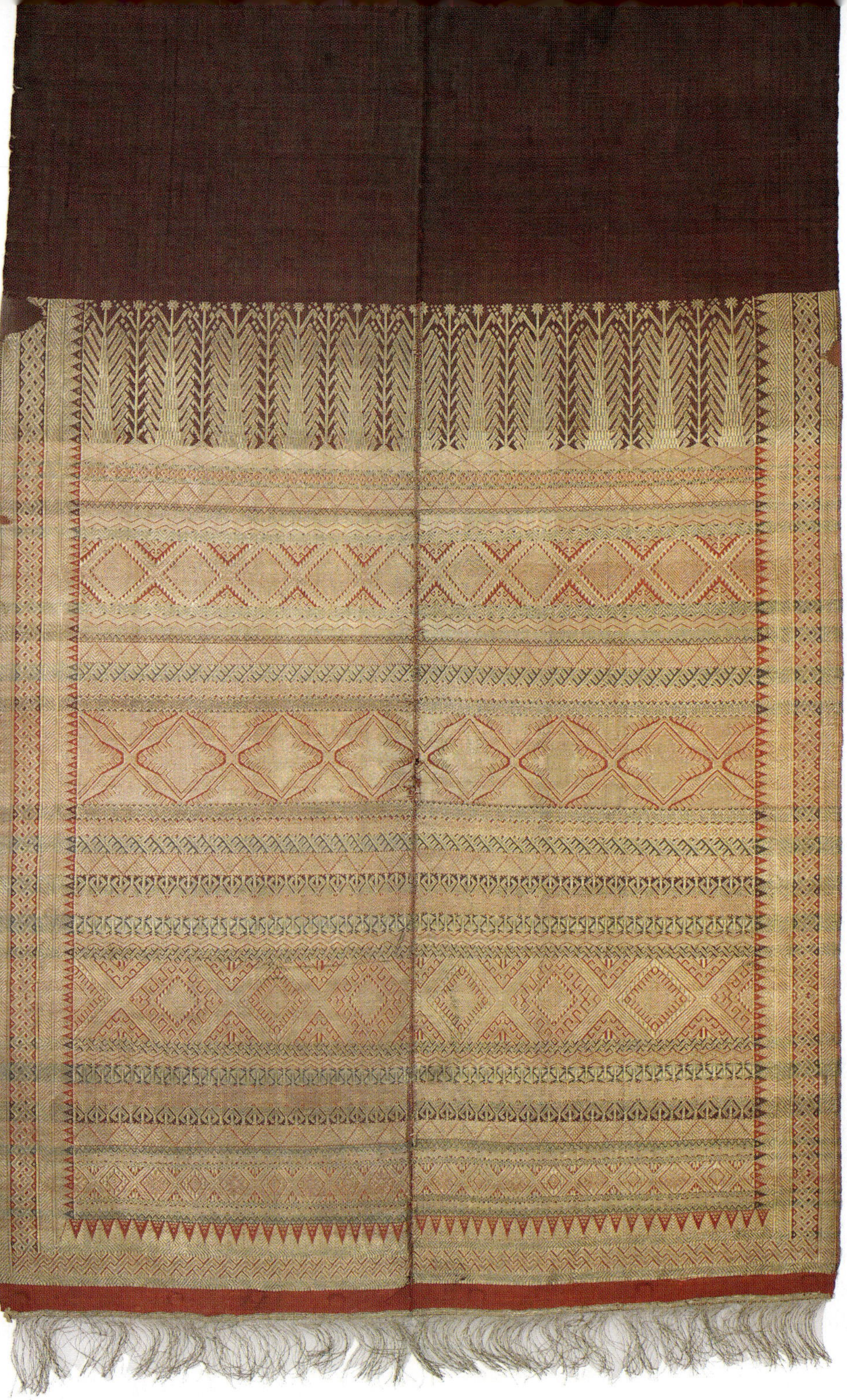

Fig.1.0.
***Tangkuluak**, (headdress), circa 1800*
Minangkabau people

Pitalah, West Sumatra
Silk, gold-wrapped thread, ramin
Plain weave, supplementary weft with gold-wrapped thread

Two panels, 110 x 29-1/2", 279 x 74.9 cm

This rare textile was woven with warps that are all bast fiber. Since the plants that provide the bast seldom grow taller than eighty inches, the fibers must be knotted to provide enough "thread" to warp the loom. There are probably 2500 knots in this weaving. The gold-thread supplementary weft weaving work is also especially fine, a quality associated with old songkets from Pitalah. The village also once produced exquisitely woven ceremonial belts (see fig. 5.34, Summerfield and Summerfield 1999: 91).

Anne and John Summerfield Collection

1. Introduction

Susan Rodgers

Songket is a type of golden cloth made in Indonesia and Malaysia, a ceremonial textile made of metal-wrapped threads that course across a ground of silk or cotton, forming intricate decorative patterns (fig. 1.0). Songket's origins probably lie in the fifteenth or sixteenth century, but some textile researchers see a much earlier date for this type of cloth. Its weaving techniques (fig. 1.1) and use of metal threads are a possible outgrowth of intensive cloth trade from the 1500s to the 1700s between Muslim North India, coastal entrepôts in peninsular Malaysia, and old Sumatran commercial centers such as Palembang. These developments built on an earlier cloth commerce between India and Sumatran societies. Songket home industries and sultan's court production may connect to an even earlier trade in silk and Chinese brocade imports to the Palembang area. This possibly dates to the Buddhist trade kingdom of Srivijaya (late 7th to 12th centuries, C.E.). The motifs used in the extraordinary songkets woven by the Minangkabau people of West Sumatra demonstrate linkages between this textile type and the ceremonial fabric arts of mainland Southeast Asian cultures in Laos, Cambodia, and northern Thailand. These cloth arts can be traced back to times far before the 1500s.

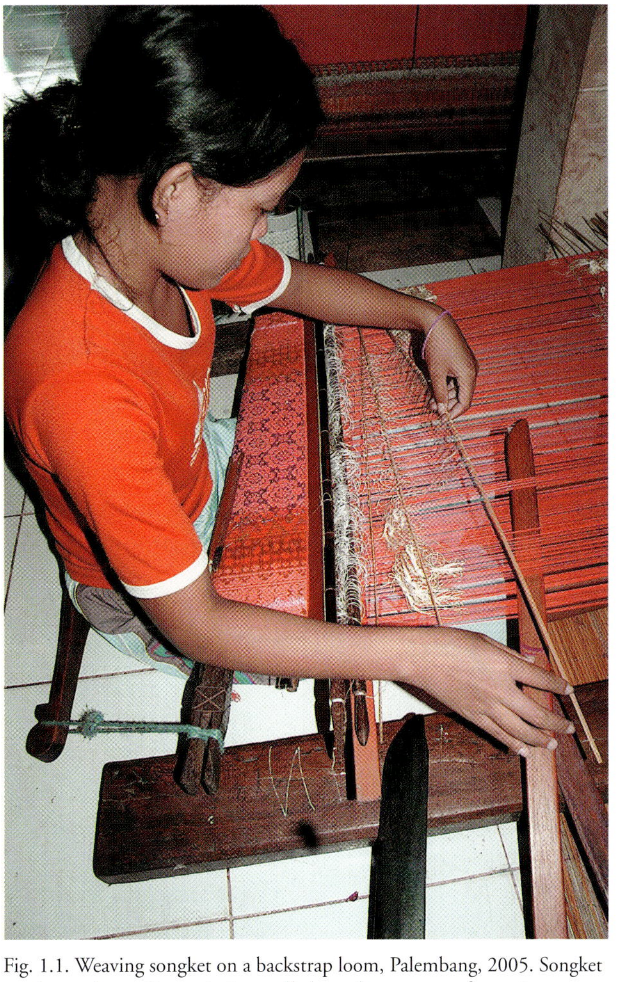

Fig. 1.1. Weaving songket on a backstrap loom, Palembang, 2005. Songket employs a demanding technique called supplementary weft weaving wherein decorative gold-wrapped threads are inserted across the weft, following the path of the pattern sticks.

Since at least the late 1700s songkets have been used in several regions of the Muslim Malay world as shimmering luxury wear. The songket-wrapped body has long denoted economic privilege and high social status in places such as Terengganu, Malaysia, and western, central, and southern Sumatran kingdoms. These Sumatran realms, from Aceh to Minangkabau to Jambi to Palembang, are now part of the nation of Indonesia, a republic since the 1945–49 national revolution. This freed the island chain from more than three hundred years of Dutch colonial control.[1] The European colonial presence in Sumatra strongly shaped songket "heritages" (traditions that are deeply historical, as are ideas of *adat*, or "inherited wisdom").

Beyond status concerns and more immediately in terms of Sumatran worldviews, songket wear and ritual use in these areas have long emblemized beauty. In certain social sectors in Sumatran and Malaysian trade towns and in elite circles of hereditary nobles in places such as Agam, West Sumatra, the young person bedecked in songket and walking along in stately ritual procession is the very image of loveliness. A bridal bed or a royal throne similarly "attired" in golden raiment is also a stunningly pleasurable sight for many onlookers in these

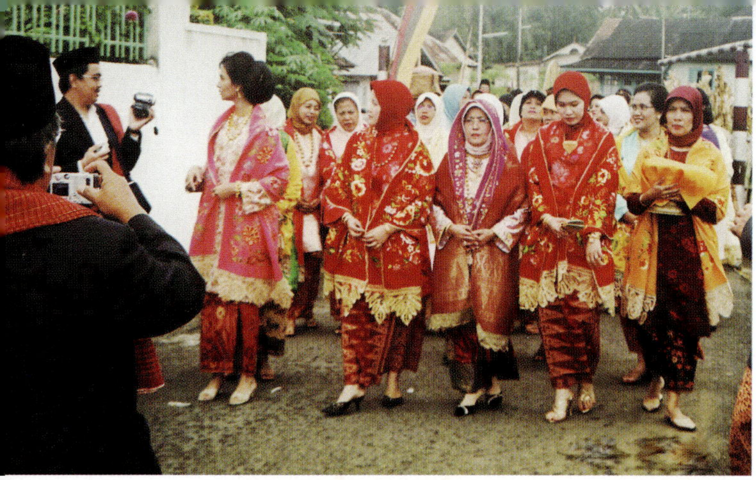

Fig. 1.2a A procession, Kotogadang, West Sumatra, 2005.

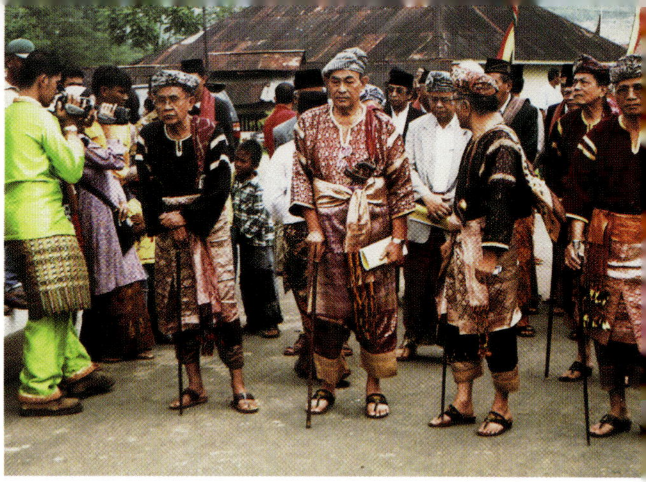

Fig. 1.2b Lineage heads in songket attire in the same ceremony. Photographs courtesy of H. Elly Azhar and H.A. Sutan Madjo Indo.

societies. Gold-thread cloth indexes not just status and glamour but also beauty in a profound artistic sense (fig. 1.2 a,b).

In Sumatra these aesthetic visions reached a height of intensity in late Dutch colonial times, from about the 1830s to about the 1920s. This was the period when the Dutch East Indies government consolidated military and administrative control of many of the huge island's small, fractious independent kingdoms. These polities had historical ties to Sumatra's Indic states of the 700 to 1300s C.E. period; Sumatra's small kingdoms also grew from Malay trade states.[2]

In the 1800s Dutch colonial hegemony pushed the small kingdoms' economies toward the production of tropical crops for sale on international markets. South Sumatran and Acehnese pepper, West Sumatran spices and mountain coffee, and plantation-grown tobacco in east coast Deli (another Malay sultanate and songket-producing center) accelerated the cash economies of these areas of the colonial Indies. By the mid 1800s differences in social status became more marked in villages and towns in many regions, and richer indigenous elites thirsted for more, and more expertly woven, songkets.[3] Women and girls in specialized craft villages produced magnificent cloths at this time, for intensifying luxury markets (fig. 1.3).

By this period, songket waist wraps, head ties, shoulder cloths, and ceremonial belts had also become swept up into Sumatran Muslim imaginaries of the properly attired ceremonial body and the appropriately decorated ritual space for events such as communal circumcisions for groups of village boys. A wealthy Muslim Malay family living in Palembang, for instance, would use small songketted covering cloths for infants during the name-giving ceremony so often considered part of Sumatran Islamic ritual.

By the national period and especially by the 1970s (when a degree of prosperity returned to some Sumatran market towns and cities following the national upheavals of 1965), the linkage of gold fabric, wealth, and a wearer's exalted social position had begun to shift significantly. Now virtually any person of means could purchase songket (if sometimes in down-market versions). The shining textile was emerging as a consumer good, although it definitely retained its connections to storied old Sumatran and Malay kingdoms and to Islam. A vigorous contemporary songket market was developing, one that extended into many non-songket-producing regions of Sumatra (a trend tracing to at least the late 1800s). The metallic cloths were also becoming staples of the "heritage floors" of large department stores in the capital, Jakarta.

Today songket weaving is still widely practiced in Sumatra, at times at a high level of craft expertise. Changes are many, however. Some regions of the island, for instance, have seen a drastic diminution of their number of weaving villages over the last ninety years or so. This is the case in the Minangkabau people's home regions in highland West Sumatra. In the city of Palembang, songket weaving has expanded since the late 1960s as Muslim business families have intensified their marketing of this textile. And, in many present-day weaving communities, production is shifting from home looms to shop floors. Handlooms are still the norm, however, despite the increasing importance of factory looms in some songket-weaving sectors of peninsular Malaysia, such as Terengganu.

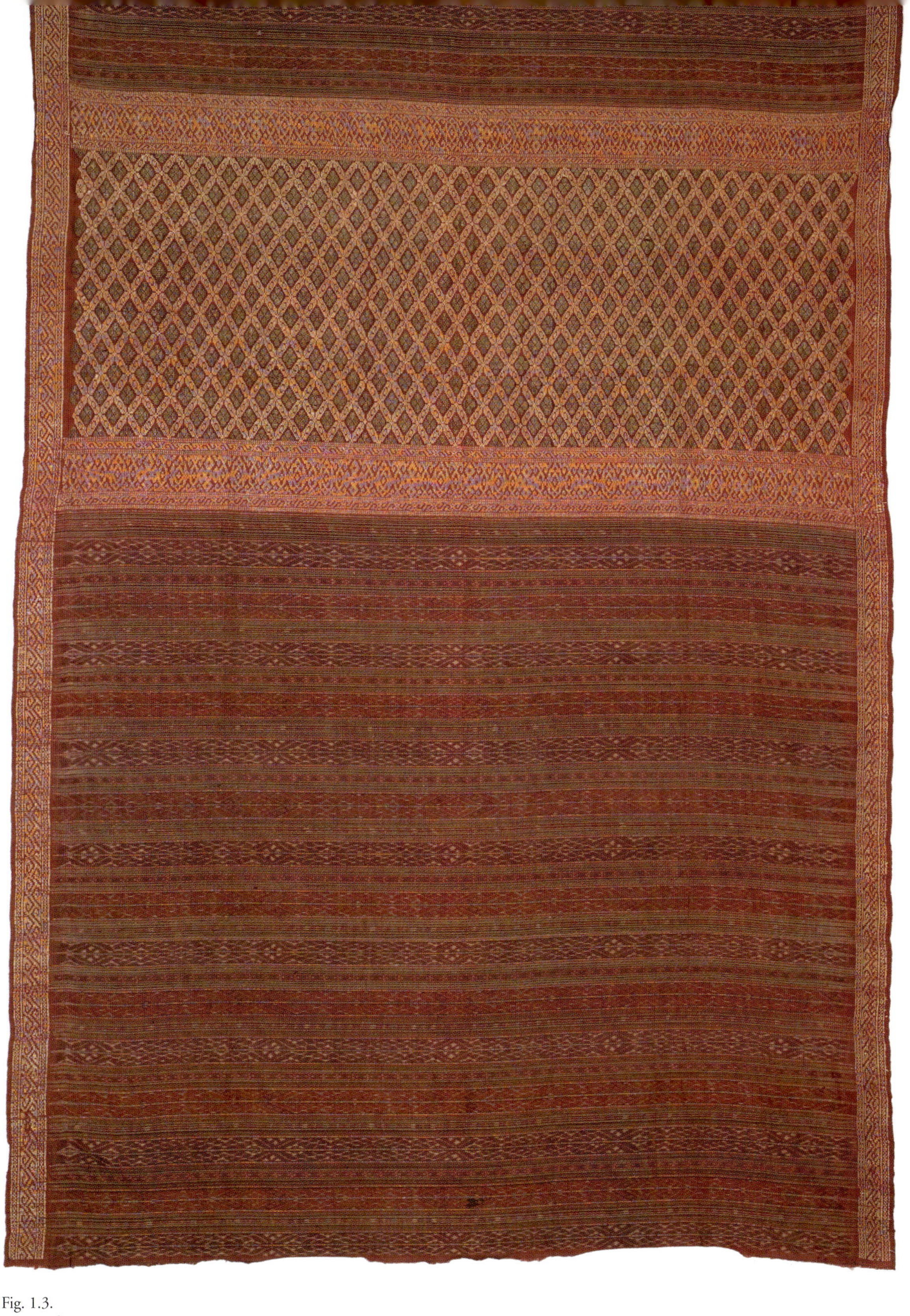

Fig. 1.3.
***Sarong for a woman**, circa 1800*

Terengganu State, Malaysia
Silk, gold-wrapped thread
Single panel, 80 x 40", 218.4 x 101.6 cm
Plain weave, weft ikat, supplementary weft
This elegant Malaysian sarong is woven mostly to the Malaysian convention: supplementary metallic threads "float" over only three, five or seven warps, producing a less fluid design than the typical Sumatran songket. The latter has no such restriction. Dark colors suggest Islamic influence. Subtly woven great songkets like this one were woven for indigenous elites throughout many prosperous Malay World trade towns and cities in the first half of the 19th century.

Anne and John Summerfield Collection

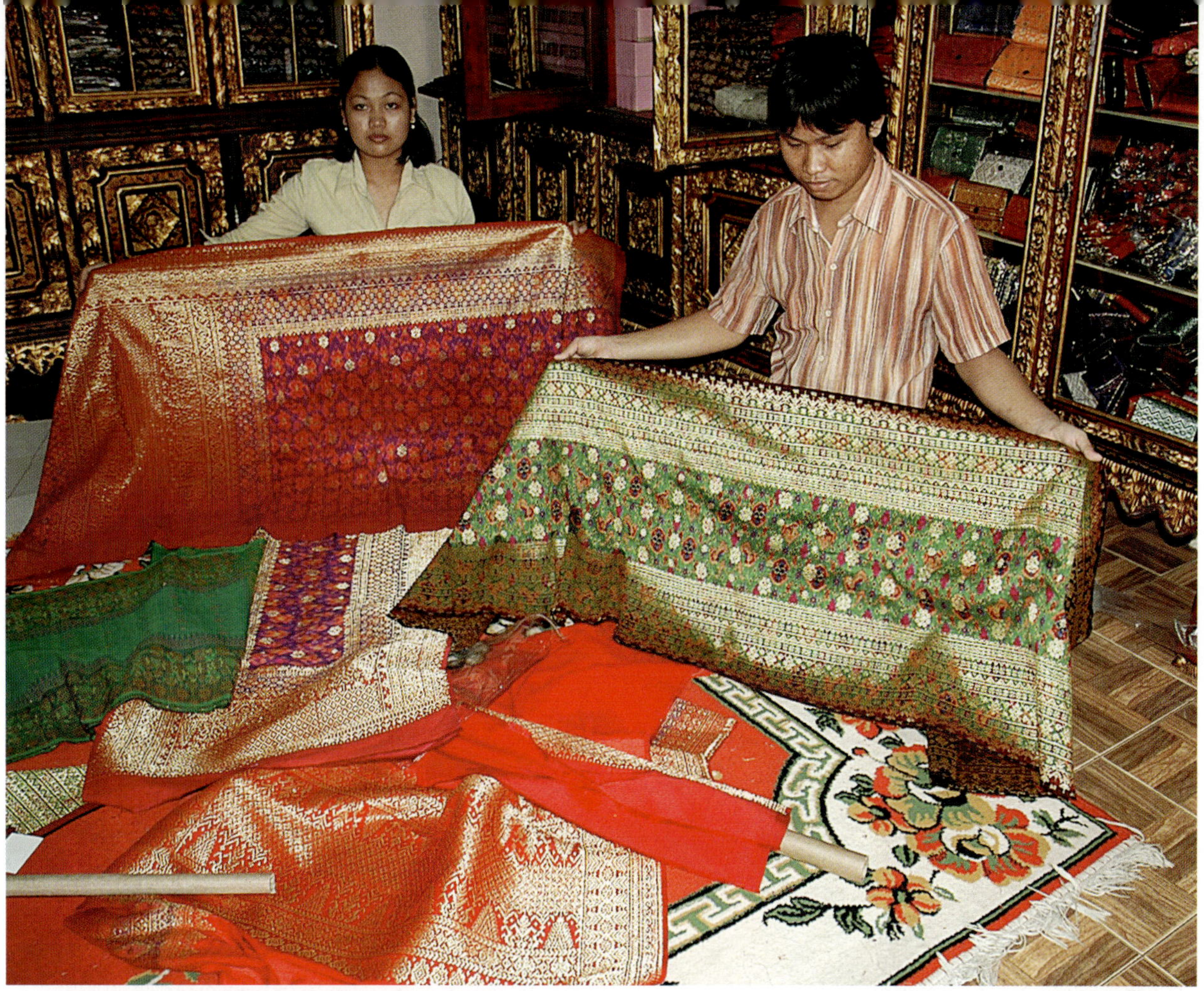

Fig.1.4. Songket is a cloth of the marketplace and a textile imbued with Malay World Muslim business acumen. Palembang families today come to shops such as the Fikri Koleksi, shown here, to purchase songkets for ceremonies. 2005.

Through the 1920s songket artistry in Minangkabau craft villages took place in significant part in family settings, on looms in homes or near the houseposts. Women and girls would weave there in their off hours from farm tasks and childrearing. Since that time, by contrast, songket has become a much more secular business (fig. 1.4), with songket shop entrepreneurs setting up weaving pavilions where they employ young people. This is decidedly the pattern in Palembang, where weaving pavilions were once associated with the sultan's Kraton or palace and sometimes with professional weavers (Uchino 2005: 209-213; B. Andaya 1989). Home-based weaving certainly continues, but it has been reoriented fully toward the market in all these areas; today few weavers produce songket strictly for their own family's use.

Given this, a relatively wide range of songket cloths, from moderately priced ones to expensive silks, are being woven today. These cloths are vigorously marketed by indigenous entrepreneurs. Families of modest means (though not the poor) can sometimes buy a few of these remarkable ritual textiles for their weddings and other happy events. Alternatively, they can rent songket ritual fashions for their nuptials from bridal shops. At Sumatran weddings, brides and grooms are often put on public display as queen and king for a day, seated atop decorated platforms amid banks and banks of pillows, which are themselves encased in special cloths.

These elaborate marriage ceremonies evoke times when actual kingdoms in Sumatra still had political substance. The reality today is otherwise: the bride may be a dentist or accountant, the groom an Internet café proprietor, and their *suku bangsa* (ethnic society) a populace within the multiethnic nation-state of Indonesia. In Sumatra today, such minority societies have *tradisi* (old traditions—a telling usage in anglicized Indonesian). But these societies often have little political coherence or clout vis-à-vis the central state based in Jakarta. The cultural tone and agenda of the national government there is influenced primarily by Java,

Fig.1.5. A coverlet for an infant for Palembang ceremonies welcoming a baby to the family and the larger Muslim community. From the Fikri Koleski Shop, 2005. An affordable cloth for a wide market.

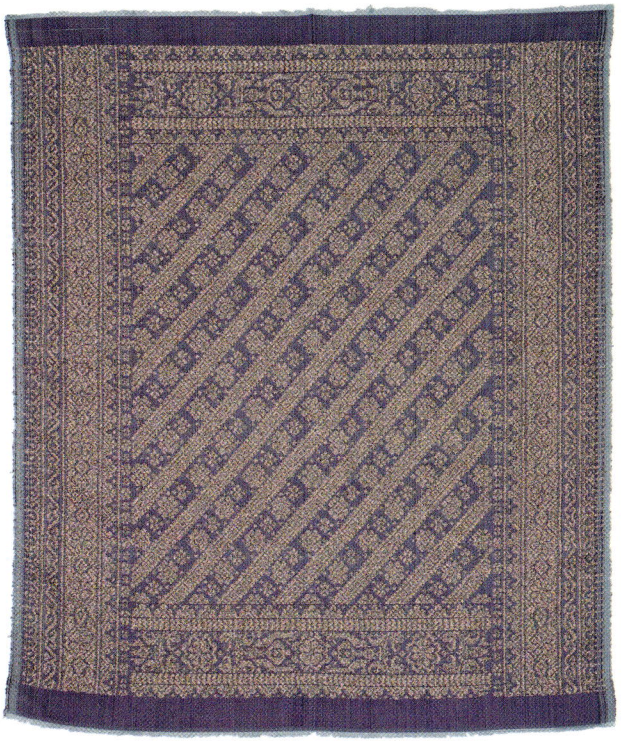

Indonesia's most populous society by far. Songket ritual finery has become emblematic of some Sumatran traditional worlds—of Minangkabau heritage, of Palembang Malay ways—within the Java-centric nation as a whole, but this cloth type's political agency in this regard is muted nevertheless. Indonesia is much better known internationally and even domestically for the palace arts of Java's Yogjakarta and Solo, Java and Bali's wayang shadow puppet plays, and gamelan music than it is for Sumatra's songket textiles.[4]

In this highly charged political and economic setting, in real-world commerce, in the cultural spaces of nostalgia between suku bangsa ethnicity and Indonesian state, songket continues to prosper as a living textile art. In fact, gold-wrapped-thread songket cloths enjoy markedly robust health today in West and South Sumatra. This occurs in several cultural niches, in both economic and aesthetic terms (figs 1.5, 1.6).

First there are the relatively affordable songkets mentioned above. These have emerged since the 1970s as consumer goods denoting "old traditions" for emerging middle classes among peoples like West Sumatra's Minangkabau. This is also true for South Sumatra's Palembang Malays and for Malay Muslim residents of Jambi (a growing commercial city and the site of an old Malay kingdom). Particularly enmeshed in this songket sector's net of memories regarding old ethnic traditions are family members who have migrated far from their ancestral regions to cities throughout Indonesia. Jobs as merchants, businesspeople, and professionals have carried them on these journeys to the *rantau* (the lands beyond the home regions). Songket ritual wear for special events such as traditional-style weddings works as an icon of beauty for these urbanites; the cloths also serve as a way to announce a wearer's continuing adherence to home-society tradition. For these migrants, songket wear occupies a small part of their cosmopolitan, urban lives. It is important to note that this is a portable tradition indexing social memory. Unlike "traditional houses" and other large symbols of Sumatran ethnic traditions, songket textiles are of course readily carried to the rantau. There they can be worn for special events (even for Jakarta's evening *resepsi*, upscale receptions held in business or national government contexts). Songkets can also be displayed on living room walls in rantau cities, in the international style of "museumified" home furnishings.

Fig.1.6. Backstrap looms, Palembang, 2005. Ateliers produce affordable fine songkets.

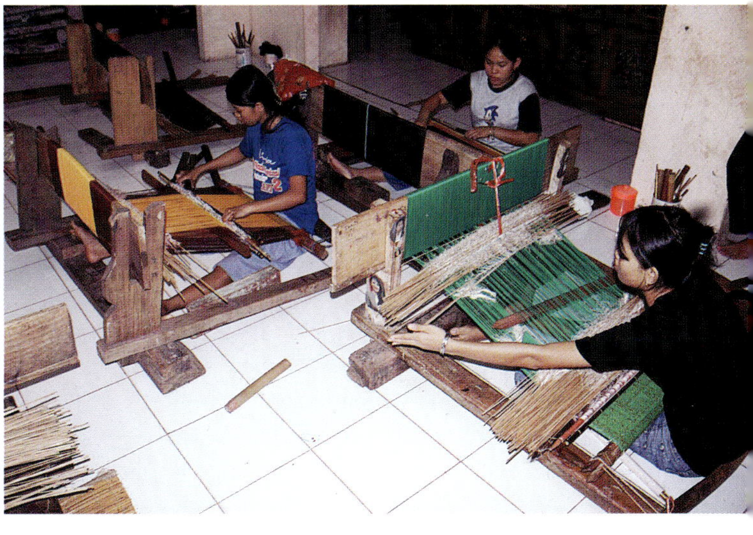

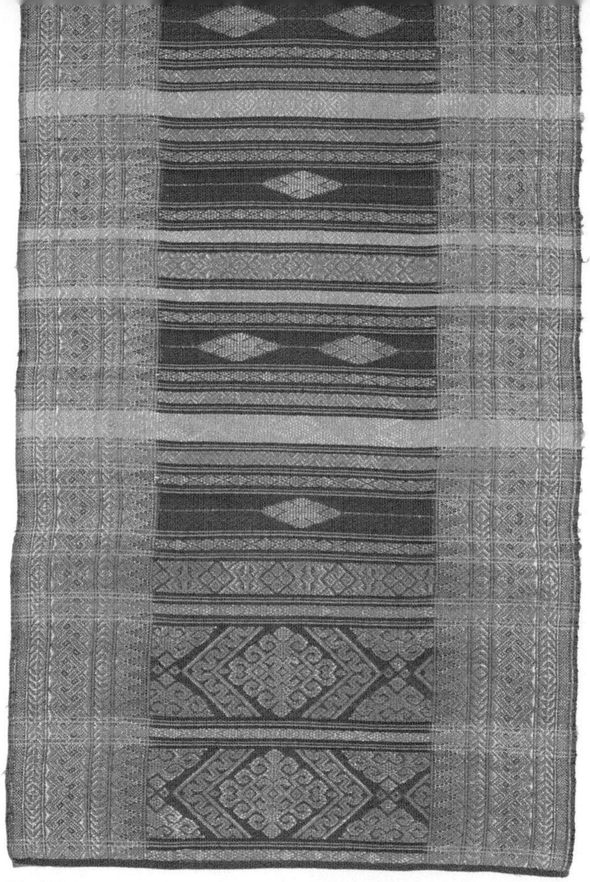

Fig.1.7.
A songket shoulder cloth woven in Pandai Sikek, West Sumatra, 2006. Metal thread weaving thrives in a few weaving centers today and is being successfully marketed to broadening publics.

The much finer all-silk songkets woven by unusually expert weavers in specialized craft villages occupy the other end of the contemporary gold-cloth spectrum in Sumatra. These are spectacular cloths of great opulence and are normally owned and used only by the wealthy. At times, these high-end songkets intersect with indigenous collectors' markets. These in turn articulate with international art collecting connoisseurship and with museum cultures worldwide.

This intensely cosmopolitan market dimension of Sumatran songkets is not totally new by any means. The sociological fluidity of today's songket markets echoes trade histories of the 1800s in these same regions of Southeast Asia. At that time indigenous merchants from places like the central Minangkabau highlands around Batusangkar and Bukittinggi had grown rich in colonial-era pepper and coffee businesses and also in the cloth trade itself. By this period the latter business sector included the buying and selling of Javanese batiks, cheap manufactured yard goods from Europe, Indian cottons, and indigenous luxury cloths such as songkets. With newfound wealth, the Minangkabau elite in West Sumatra expanded and diversified beyond the traditional class system based on (purported) ancient royal lineages. Rich families of many sorts sought luxury wear for their ceremonial occasions. Indigenous elites employed in the colonial bureaucracies of the Dutch also sometimes had the money to buy into songket culture, so to speak.

Songket-producing villages expanded in number to meet this demand, and weavers developed more refined techniques. Then, by the early 1900s, with the rise of formal public schooling for girls, some craft villages found it increasingly hard to staff their home looms. In the weaving village of Kotogadang, for instance, by 1920 getting a diploma from a Dutch-language elementary or secondary school began to have more prestige (both socially and in terms of a woman's marriageability) than did fine weaving skills. Anti-colonial nationalist sentiment also discouraged "over indulgence" in the arts of display in the 1920s and 1930s. By the time of the national revolution of 1945–49, the Minangkabau upland area no longer had the twelve or so major songket-weaving centers that had thrived in the 1800s. By the 1950s there were just a handful of such settlements left. Today there are two: Pandai Sikek and Silungkang, with a few additional weaving neighborhoods in the towns of Payakumbuh and Batusangkar (fig 1.7).

Pandai Sikek songkets have been much caught up in social flux for decades, and these cloths illustrate in miniature the volatility and resilience of the entire island's traditional textile industry. This village's gold cloth production is exceptionally fine, with historical ties to the great weaving center of Pitalah. The national revolution was violent in Pandai Sikek, and in 1947, when Dutch-led forces attempted to storm back into this part of the Indies, many of the villages' great houses were burned to the ground. The population fled to forest huts on Mount Singgalang, and some fine old songkets were saved from fire by being buried in bamboo tubes in the ground (spices were tossed in to deter insect infestation). With national independence the village was reestablished. But Pandai Sikek ritual cloth production was quiescent in the 1950s and 1960s. The late 1950s were a troubled time in the region;

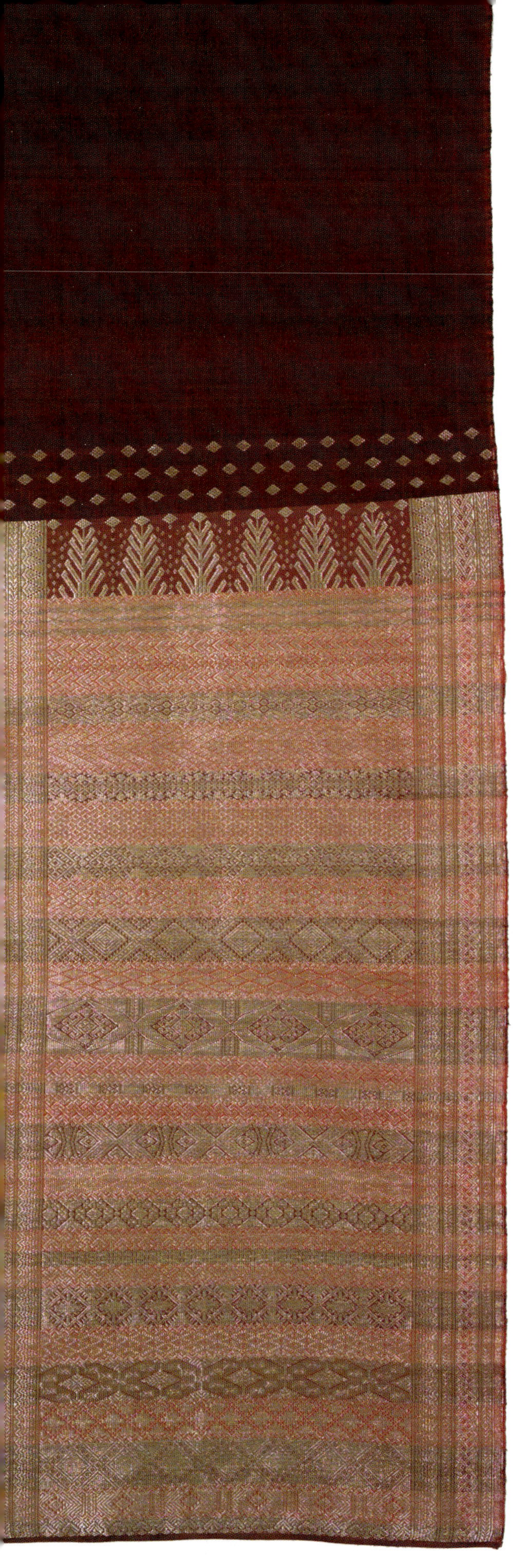

Fig. 1.8.
Selindang, *(woman's shoulder cloth),* 2005
Minangkabau people
Weaver: Ibu Us

Pandai Sikek (Tanjung), West Sumatra
Cotton-polyester blend, gold-wrapped thread, supplementary weft

Superbly woven songkets like this one by 37 year old Ibu Us occupy the high end of the gold cloth weaving continuum.

Iris and B. Gerald Cantor Art Gallery Study Collection

many residents were active in the unsuccessful PRRI (Revolutionary Government of the Indonesian Republic) separatist rebellion against the central state. Pandai Sikek almost suffered the loss of its weaving heritage during these years. Then, in the 1970s, under the leadership of a master weaver named Ibu Sanuar and her artist-entrepreneur husband, A. Ramli Dt. Rangkayo Sati (and with the sponsorship of the then-governor of the province), Pandai Sikek gold-thread weaving came roaring back. The settlement was consciously refashioned into a craft village and tourist attraction for both domestic and international visitors. Today Pandai Sikek girls and women—and now, a few adolescent boys and men—weave some of Asia's finest gold cloths (fig. 1.8).

Songkets, then, were and are cloths of the marketplace, not some unchanging Indonesian or Malaysian "traditional textile" hermetically sealed off from history. If anything, in fact, these metallic cloths *embody* historical change and are enmeshed in the complex social class transitions of the region.

Songket cloths have also developed in counterpoint to the other heritage arts of Indonesia: batik, ikat cloth, ritual jewelry, ceremonial house decorations, and the palace arts derived in part from the display aesthetics of Indic states. Songket cloth has grown further in interaction with overtly Muslim arts: Arabic calligraphy crafts and jewelry and ceramics whose styles emerged from trade encounters with the Ottoman Empire.[5] Songkets have changed too in response to increasingly globalized markets for Indonesian traditional objects, some of which are being turned into fashion wear.

Songket as a cloth type itself is imbued, as noted, with a Muslim identity in many Sumatran and wider Malay world social locales. For many publics there, this "traditional cloth" is one that is seen both as a marker of piety and as an emblem of adat heritage, attuned as that can be to "Minangkabau traditions," "Palembang Malay traditions," and so on. Adat, a word derived from Arabic, refers, as noted, to "inherited custom." This combination of an asserted Muslim piety with a conspicuously luxurious form of gold status wear has not been unproblematic in some of these communities.

Beyond all this—for this particular sector of Southeast Asian weaving is nothing if not complex—late eighteenth-, nineteenth-, and early twentieth-century songket cloths participate today in an active international art collectors' market. Old Sumatran and Malaysian songkets emerge here as sought-after "antiques." Some of these fabrics have also entered museum collections, in Jakarta, Kuala Lumpur, Singapore, Leiden, Canberra, Los Angeles, Washington, D.C., and beyond.

In this volume we seek to trace some of the artistic, social, and economic journeys that this eminently peripatetic form of Asian handloomed cloth has taken over the last 150 years. Our prime focus is on West and South Sumatran songkets *as living art*—as a changing, flexible, evolving heritage cloth that is still very much being woven, worn, and constantly rethought. This takes place in an Indonesia on the move through political and social history. As songket has penetrated further and further into globalizing processes of ethnic, national, and personal representation, this textile type has gained new creative depth. As object and art, songket has by no means disappeared as Indonesia has become a nation on the global stage. Rather, the exquisite golden cloth has prospered in the hands of forceful weavers, enterprising cloth brokers, and discerning, demanding, and knowledgeable buyers.

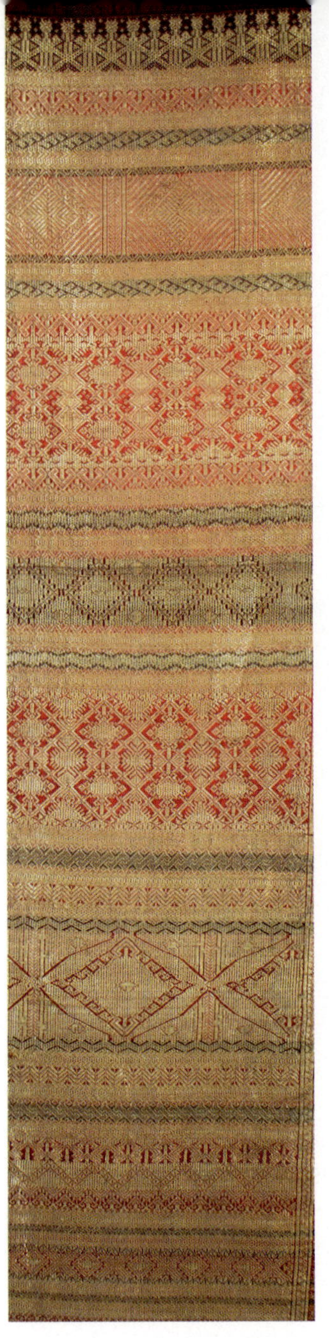

Fig. 1.9.
Selindang, *(shoulder cloth),*
detail1850

Minangkabau people

Koto Baru or Pandai Sikek, West Sumatra

Silk, gold-wrapped thread

Plain weave, gold-wrapped thread, supplementary weft

Detail, single panel 109 x 18", 276 x 45.7 cm

Textiles from this region of West Sumatra are often patterned with repeating weft rows of motifs that are visibly dominant. Nineteenth century weavings from Pandai Sikek like this one have become collectible antiques and continue to go through many contemporary transformations, evidence of vibrancy in this sector of Sumatran weaving.

Anne and John Summerfield Collection

NOTES

1. Sources in English on Indonesian history are readily available. Particularly rewarding is Jean Taylor's *Indonesia: Peoples and histories* (2003). For a thematic history of Southeast Asia, see Anthony Reid's *Southeast Asia in the age of commerce, 1450–1680, vol. 1, The lands below the winds* (1988). A succinct overview is provided in D. R. SarDesai's *Southeast Asia, Past and Present* (2003); see especially chaps. 3 and 4 on Indic kingdoms, viewed regionally. On Sumatran history specifically, see Elizabeth Graves 1981, Anthony Reid, *An Indonesian frontier: Acehnese and other histories of Sumatra* (2005a), Reid 1995 for translations of early travelers' accounts, and the essays on West Sumatra and the Bataks in Anthony Reid and Lance Castles, eds., *Pre-Colonial state systems in Southeast Asia* (1975). A descriptive classic is William Marsden's *History of Sumatra* (1811 [1986]). For excellent case studies of southern kingdoms in the Dutch colonial era, see Barbara Andaya, *To live as brothers: Southeast Sumatra in the seventeenth and eighteenth centuries* (1993) and Elsbeth Locher-Scholten, *Sumatran sultanate and colonial state: Jambi and the rise of Dutch imperialism, 1830–1907* (2004). See particularly Barbara Andaya's "The cloth trade in Jambi and Palembang societies during the Seventeenth and Eighteenth Centuries" (1989). Especially valuable also is Megumi Uchino's "Socio-cultural history of Palembang *songket*" (2005). On Minangkabau a rewarding recent history of early colonial era power relations is Jane Drakard's *A Kingdom of words: Language and power in Sumatra* (1999).
2. On Srivijaya, see O. L. Wolter's classic *Early Indonesian commerce: A study of the origins of Srivijaya* (1967). In 1939 the Palembang museum curator and intrepid Sumatran explorer F. M. Schnitger published his speculative but fascinating account *Forgotten kingdoms of Sumatra*, on Hindu Buddhist temple ruins in Portibi, Muara Jambi, and southern Sumatra (1939 [1989]). For a thought-provoking anthropological history attempting to link the seventh- to thirteenth-century Indic trade kingdoms to upriver peoples and societies throughout the archipelago linked by Muslim trader peoples such as the Bugis, see Thomas Gibson's ambitious *And the sun pursued the moon: Symbolic knowledge and traditional authority among the Makassar* (2005), especially chaps. 3, 6.
3. For economic (and political) histories of colonial West Sumatra, see Christine Dobbin 1974, 1977; Ken Young 1994. Also excellent in this regard, on changing Minangkabau peasant economies, are Joel Kahn 1980, 1992. F. Von Benda-Beckmann 1979 is also a foundational study. See also T. Kato 1982.
4. On the political construction of Minangkabau "traditions," see Kahn 1992; on the political invention of "Java" itself, see Pemberton 1994 and especially Sears 1996. On social class, religion and the invention of Batak identities, see Rita S. Kipp, 1993.
5. On the impact of Ottoman Empire trade on Sumatran societies, see Anthony Reid's "The Turkish connection" (2005b).

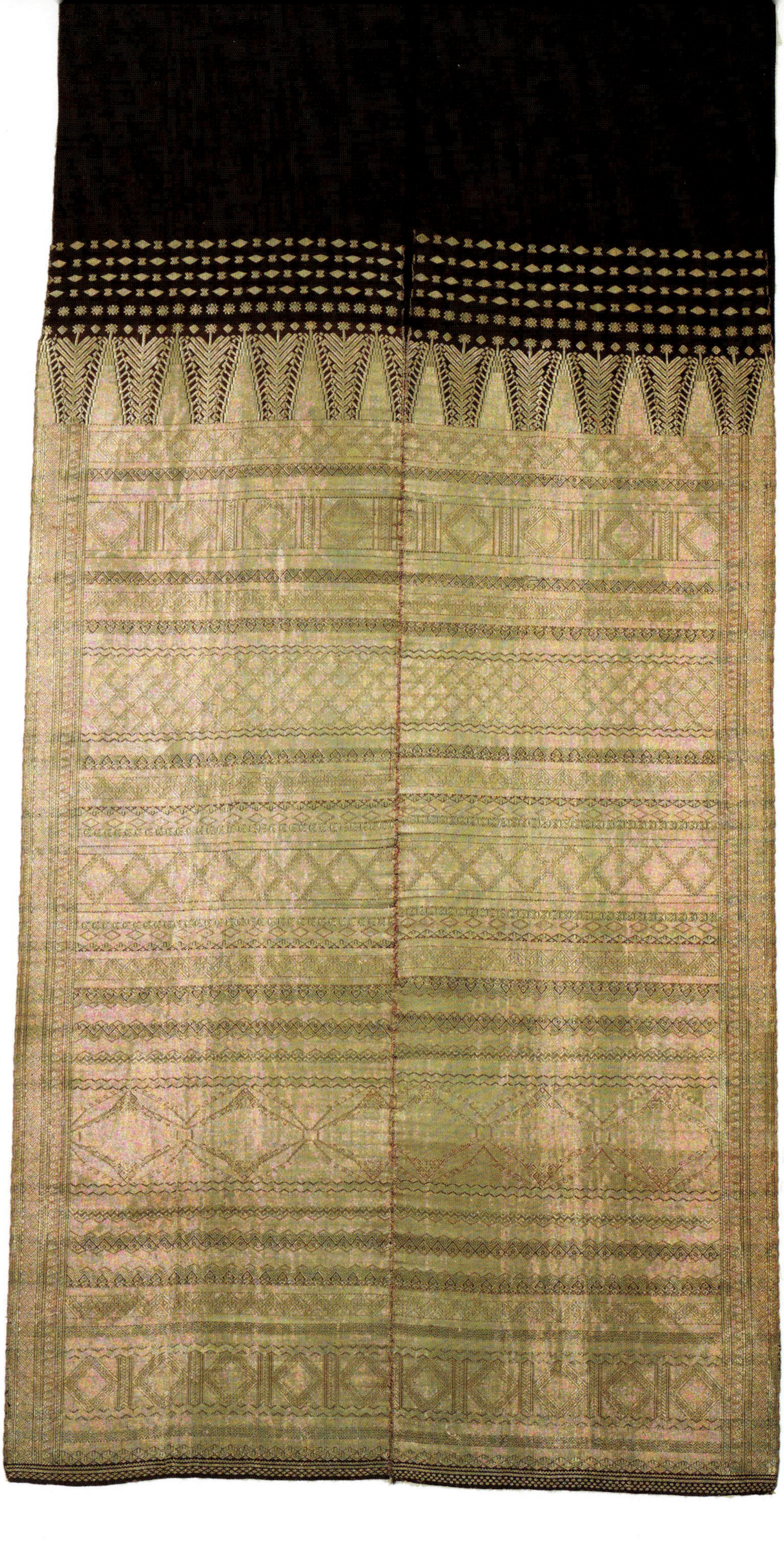

Fig. 2.0. ***Tangkuluak*** (headdress), circa 1800. Minangkabau people

Pitalah, West Sumatra

Silk, silver-wrapped thread. Plain weave, silver-wrapped thread supplementary weft.

Fragments of old songkets of this sort sometimes serve as pattern templates for weavers today.

Anne and John Summerfield Collection.

2. Sumatra's songkets: Not a fragile tradition

Susan Rodgers

The 2007 College of the Holy Cross exhibition *Gold Cloths of Sumatra* came at a specific moment in the history of museum displays of Southeast Asian traditional art. Even the phrase "traditional art" is fraught in the study of a region of the world that is the site and subject of powerful and increasingly globalized discourses about "ethnic traditions" as they exist within and across nations in relation to heritage objects.[1] "Art" itself as a category is also much in play in these charged scholarly (and governmental) conversations about Indonesia, conversations touching on handweaving, wood carving, and stone sculpture, not to mention the performance arts of dance, music, oratory, and processionals. As a point of entry to a discussion of these matters, I would like to begin with a specific cloth: an old Minangkabau songket that has now also emerged in another form, as "replica" art—or, more precisely, as one weaver's way of imagining what replicating an old-style cloth would entail in both a market context and an artistic one (figs. 2.0, 2.1). This weaver's cloth brokers (proprietors of an upscale art and antiques shop in the West Sumatran city of Bukittinggi) are also integral actors in the creation of Minangkabau "replica" songket art. Note immediately that these new cloths are not motif-by-motif replicas of old textiles, by any means.

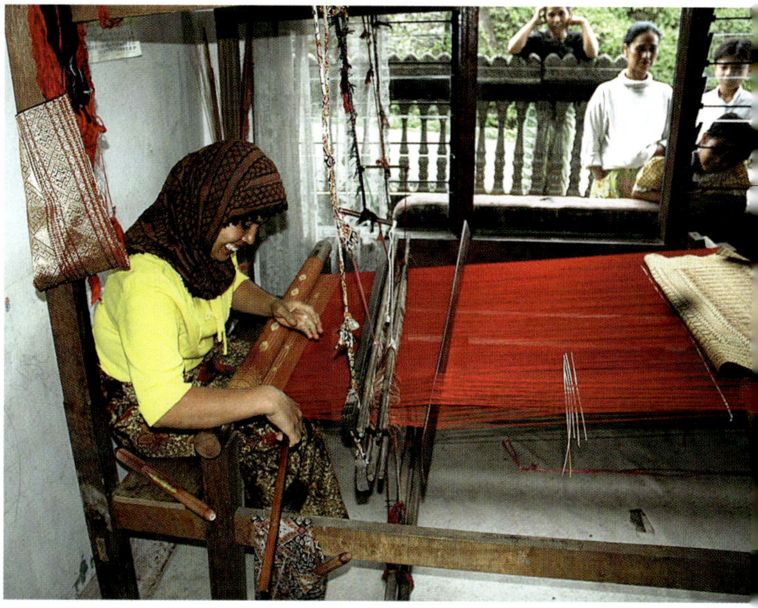

Fig. 2.1. Ibu Us at her loom, Tanjung, Pandai Sikek, 2006. This great weaver models some work on old songkets such as that at left.

The fine old silk songket from Pitalah Village, West Sumatra, illustrated on the opposite page was woven by a Minangkabau craftswoman on a frame loom in the 1800s. Minangkabau songket weaving is distinctive in Indonesia in using this large sort of loom. Several other songket hand industries in the country (in Palembang, Jambi, and also East Bali) employ Indonesia's more ancient loom, the backstrap form, for songket production. Frame looms are also found in parts of mainland Southeast Asia for weaving some types of metal-thread textiles.[2]

This particular cloth (a head wrap) illustrates songket's sumptuous quality and the superb weaving work that this textile form often demands. Pitalah is in the highland heartland region of the Minangkabau home district in Indonesia (as shown in map 2). Minangkabau weavers have produced some of the most breathtaking songkets. It is not too much to claim that West Sumatran women and girls pushed this cloth type to its artistic apogee between the 1790s and the 1920s.[3] Songkets from this era were woven to be used as sarongs, belts, shoulder cloths, and head ties, almost always for ceremonial occasions in adat and Islam. These "metal cloths" were typically paired with ritual weapons and ornate gold and coral jewelry to form arresting tableaux of the decorated body. Both women and men wore songket costumes in the 1800s, as some continue to do today for special occasions.

Some songkets were tied into elaborate headgear arrangements for women. Distinctive ways of tying these gold head wraps denoted a wearer's village or village cluster origins in matrilineal Minangkabau. Clan and lineage descent are passed through the female line in this society, from a grandmother to her daughters and sons and then on to the

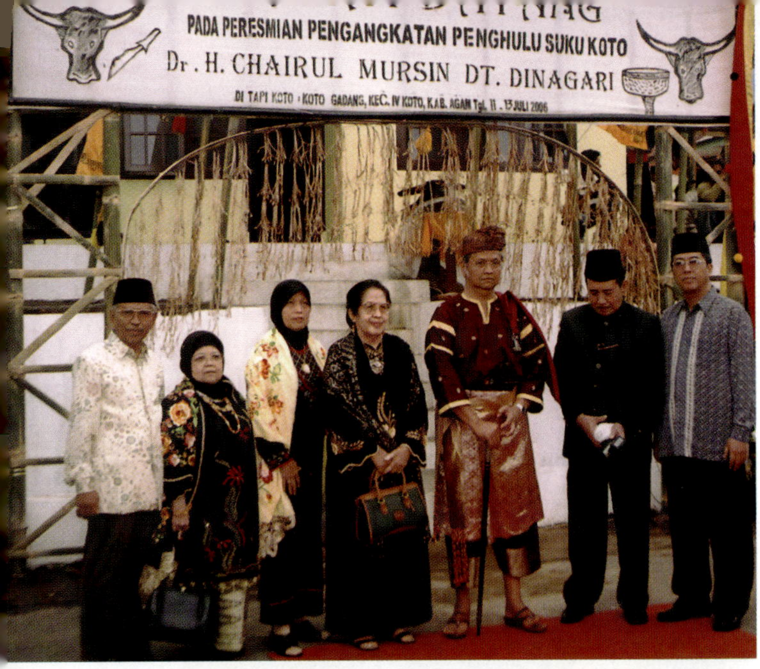

Fig. 2.2. Third from left, to right: village leaders in songket and embroidery wear in Minangkabau village of Kotogadang, 2005. Adat demands precise, elaborate costumes.

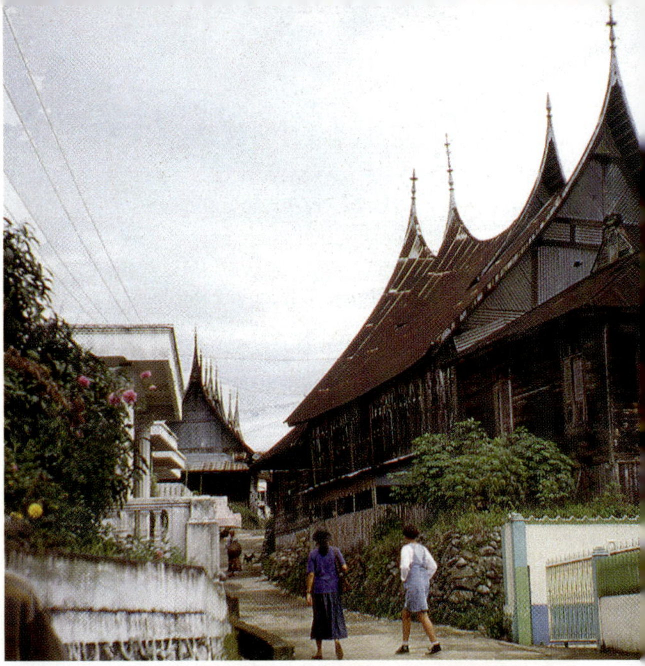

Fig. 2.3. Multiple household Minangkabau great houses, 1996.

daughters' daughters. In Minangkabau adat (fig. 2.2), or inherited custom, the heirlooms of an ancestral house (a lineage's family ornaments, ceremonial weapons, songkets from past generations) are passed down the female line. The ancestral house itself (at least in the official kinship ideology) also passes from generation to generation through female-to-female linkages (fig. 2.3). Lineage chieftains are men, part of the matriline through their mothers.[4]

Matrilineality is rare in Indonesia. Societies that have clans there more commonly practice patrilineal inheritance of names and goods, with smaller portions of land and treasure going to daughters than to sons. Many Indonesian societies do not have clans at all. It is certainly not true that all songket-producing and songket-wearing societies in Indonesia have matrilineal descent. But in the Minangkabau highlands and to an extent among the numerous diasporic Minangkabau in the *rantau* (that is, again, in the lands beyond the home region, in this case typically cities such as Jakarta and Bandung), display aesthetics for garbing the female body and glorifying the power and wealth of the matrilineage and its core houses are intensely connected to songket finery.

At least since the 1890s, songkets such as this Pitalah head wrap have been deployed by Minangkabau as heritage dress—that is, as special costumes of great loveliness and public impact that have been used to evoke a people's past, not just the individual wearer's identity. A Pitalah gold-thread head wrap shouts out Pitalah village origins but also Pitalah character. As well, for some audiences such a songket can also point to a more generalized, pan-Minangkabau identity within an Indonesia-wide field of ethnic societies and so-called local languages (Minangkabau, Balinese, Toba Batak, and so on). These languages number about three hundred.[5] The national language, Bahasa Indonesia, is spoken by most school graduates in addition to such home-region languages as Minangkabau. Bilingualism is the norm in Indonesia, which is an unusually language-conscious country. In late colonial times, knowing Dutch afforded an individual and a family considerable prestige. Speaking Dutch connoted access to the most exclusive range of primary and middle schools. Today there is a sharp and almost equally competitive interest in learning English, the gateway language for high-status jobs in Indonesian cities and an icon as well for "being modern." Indeed, Indonesian citizens are often caught up in personal and community quests to be both modern and traditional. Iconography is correspondingly rich.

West Sumatrans who are knowledgeable about adat can often identify a songket's specific village cluster origins. Other Indonesians (and some visitors to the country) can look at a songket-based ritual costume that includes such a cloth as this and tag it as Minangkabau wear much more generally, versus Javanese traditional wear, or Balinese wear, and so on.

Adult Indonesian citizens are encouraged to wear *Indonesian* national dress for many formal public

Fig. 2.4. Baginda Hasudungan, Ompu Raja Oloan Siregar, Angkola Batak orator, in national Indonesian wear, 2002. The women at left wear everyday clothes.

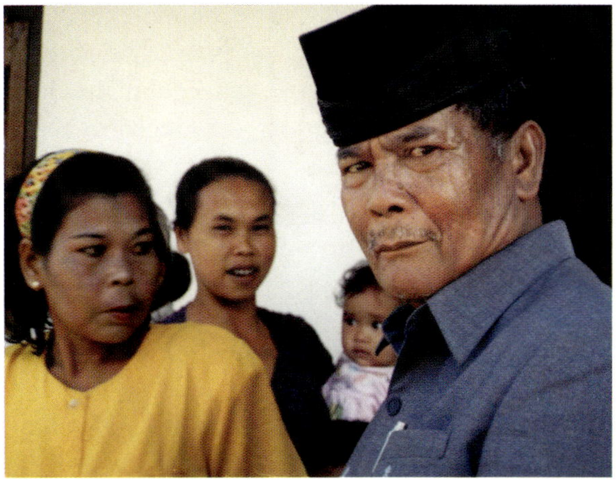

Fig. 2.5. Minangkabau children in t-shirt attire, 1995.

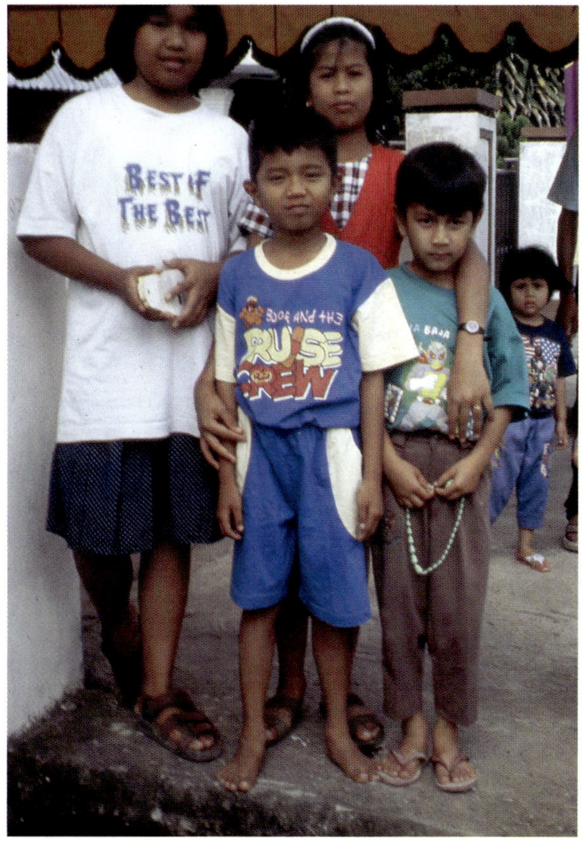

occasions (for instance, for the dedication of a new public school). This ensemble consists of the black *peci* hat and shirt and trousers for men (fig. 2.4) and the lacey *kebaya* jacket, sash, and batik sarong for women. Some Sumatran women from songket-producing regions use songket sarongs in place of batik for such occasions as official receptions and government events. For "Minangkabau events" or "Javanese events" and so on (traditional weddings, for example), full-scale ethnic dress comes to the fore for some. In West and South Sumatra, songket use figures quite heavily.

This textile form is indubitably central to ethnic identity construction on public ritual stages that are marked for *tradisi,* or tradition. But in places such as Palembang or Padang, overtly Muslim events such as circumcisions for groups of boys also employ songket-based "traditional fashion." Such uses of songket textiles combine Islamic references with invocations of adat.

Songket garb is enfolded into even more complex social settings. In contemporary times, everyday fashions in Indonesia have often highlighted globalizing identities or self-consciously Muslim dress. Individuals can wear blue jeans and T-shirts and thereby proclaim a modern identity (fig. 2.5). For women and adolescent girls, donning long-sleeved tunics, long skirts, and the *jilbab* (head and neck covering) invokes Muslim piety and modesty (fig. 2.6).[6] In interviews with mothers of adolescent

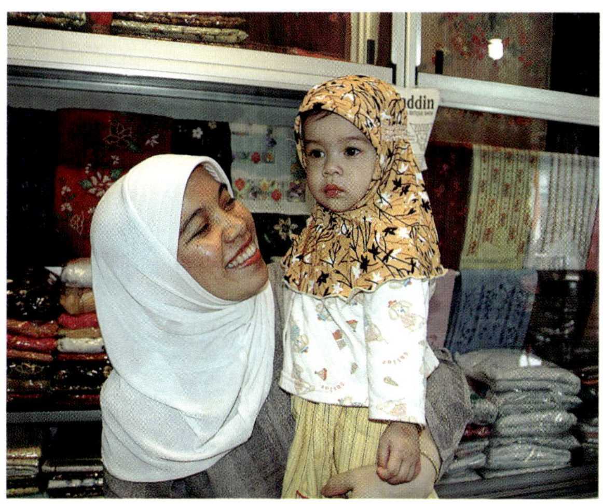

Fig. 2.6. Devi M. Azhar, co-proprietor of a Bukittinggi antiques and embroidery wear and songket shop, with her daughter. Both wear jilbabs, 2006.

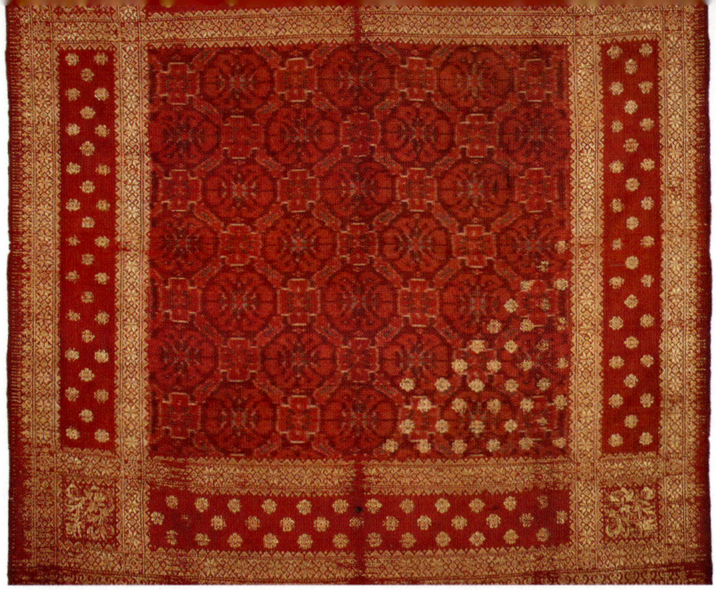

Fig. 2.7. A silk kain limar-style man's headtie, with songket edges. Palembang, circa 1920s. Such textiles are now sold as antiques.

girls in Bukittinggi, these women often cite a need to protect their young daughters from harassment by lascivious men by enveloping their daughters in yards of cloth. Such Muslim fashions allow the girls (these mothers aver) to venture out into the public sector, to school, far from home. Songket wear, by considerable contrast, is more multivocal. Alongside this ritual fabric's somewhat muted Muslim associations, as noted, these cloths can also proclaim ethnic group tradition, accomplishing that within cosmopolitan contexts.

Songkets as clothing thus carry Sumatran historical rhetorics within Indonesian discourses about objects and the past in sometimes anxious ways. Is the songket wearer really sufficiently Muslim? Has he or she allowed local traditions too much sway in defining a personal identity within what should be a universalist religion? Might showy songket attire detract or even contradict the subdued type of human personhood encouraged in some strains of modernist yet conservative Islam? Tensions of these sorts come out in conflicted fashions at times. In some conservative and self-consciously pious villages near Bukittinggi, for instance, brides wear both spangly gold headdresses from the adat (with all the songket clothing accoutrements that that implies), *and* the jilbab.

Songket textiles thus imply questions. These go beyond Islam/tradisi issues. For example, as songket wear has become increasingly accessible to buying publics that include new, emerging Indonesian middle classes, how has this heritage cloth, with its associations with village nobility, been reconfigured? How has this occurred both sociologically but also at the level of the craft object itself? How can this be studied in terms of social context and in relation to songket artistry and weaving technique?

Songkets exist both as art and in history. In this light, other queries occur. How have the commodification processes tied to the popularization of songket as a cloth-for-sale, to anyone, affected the textiles as objects and as art? How have Indonesian ideas related to *kesenian* (art) been implicated in these processes? Has the songket weaver herself perhaps undergone a degree of commodification, of personhood, as her craftwork has emerged as an item of consumption and, for collectors, as art (fig. 2.7)? How does the present-day songket weaver's clear-cut interest in making money from her craftwork enter into all this?

Beyond this, what is the role of "Minangkabau heritage" and "Palembang Malay heritage" (as carried by such textile work) within the multiethnic yet Java-focused Indonesian nation? All Sumatran societies, no matter how populous, are minority peoples in Indonesia, vis-à-vis the Javanese. As noted the latter constitute two-thirds of the nation, and Javanese culture dominates most understandings of national culture, domestically and internationally. Sumatran peoples often chafe against these claims.

Not surprisingly, the conspicuous consumption of glittery luxury goods is sometimes critiqued by reform Islam in Indonesia today. How do songket cloths, associated for some Indonesians with Muslim virtues, fare in that setting? Ironically enough, although the years from the 1970s to the present decade have seen a growth in conservative Islamic fashion in parts of Sumatra, this time period has also been one of considerable artistic growth and intensification of weaving technique within some sectors of contemporary Sumatran songket craft.

To return to the old cloth at hand: by the 1800s, when this particular head wrap probably came off the loom, Dutch colonial control of this part of the Sumatran uplands was in place (if somewhat shakily) in both military and bureaucratic terms.

During this period songket weaving in Pitalah and nearby villages reached extraordinary heights of technical brilliance and artistic accomplishment. It is fair to say that songket had become a great art by this time (if one largely unknown to many outside publics).

Correspondingly, there have been several international museum exhibitions that have celebrated antique songkets from this precise era from the Minangkabau core districts in the uplands. These are Agam, near the mountain city of Bukittinggi; Limo Puluh Koto, around Payakumbuh; and Tanah Datar. The latter includes the home villages of Minangkabau royal families that trace their descent to the fourteenth-century court of King Adityavarman.

Museum exhibitions of antique Minangkabau songkets have been impressive. In 2003 the National Gallery of Australia's *Sari to Sarong: Five Hundred Years of Indian and Indonesian Textile Exchange* presented a large and excellent array of Sumatran songkets from Aceh to the southern tip of the island.[7] A number of fine Minangkabau cloths were included. Pre-1930s Minangkabau songket textiles per se were the focus of a 1990 exhibition at the Textile Museum in Washington, D.C., entitled *Trailing the Tiger to Golden Cloths of Sumatra's Minangkabau.* In 1991 the Santa Barbara Museum of Art presented *Fabled Cloths of Minangkabau*, and in 1999 the Fowler Museum of Cultural History at the University of California, Los Angeles, offered an even more comprehensive show, *Walk in Splendor: Ceremonial Dress of the Minangkabau*, accompanied by an anthology of essays on Minangkabau ritual arts. Textile scholars Anne Summerfield and John Summerfield curated these three Minangkabau cloth exhibitions.[8] These museum presentations of Minangkabau songket cloths from the late 1700s through the 1920s clearly demonstrated the excellence of this sector of Indonesian textiles, itself of course a domain of surpassing accomplishment when seen in worldwide fabric arts perspective.

Our study represents two thematic departures from these museum introductions to this remarkable Asian weaving. The first innovation is geographical, while the second is theoretical and temporal and has called for a different engagement with Indonesian textile histories than those commonly employed in the previous scholarship.

Songkets, Sumatra-wide

We consider Minangkabau gold cloths in *Sumatra-wide* perspective, in relation to the songket arts of such southern Sumatran regions as Bengkulu, Jambi, and Palembang. The cloths of such places as Pitalah, we feel, gain extra layers of interpretability when seen against the fuller palette of songket-weaving work from all these sociologically and artistically diverse but connected parts of this island.

Our undertaking could have been even more geographically ambitious, for metallic-thread weaving of this type has been practiced widely in Southeast Asia from as early as the fifteenth century or perhaps earlier, as noted. In some form, songket-like weaving may have even been present in the fourteenth-century court of King Adityavarman. This was located near the Pagaruyung area of what is now West Sumatra.

Songket weaving in this part of the Indonesian archipelago has multiple historical ties to other parts of Asia. One theory holds that Mughal traders from North India brought a form of decorative gold-thread weaving to the Indonesian islands in the 1400s and 1500s (Kartiwa 1986: 4-5; see also Maxwell 2004). Songket work (doubtless much transformed to conform with indigenous weaving worlds and their standards of beauty) possibly proved attractive to local elites from coastal mercantile Muslim sultanates at this time. It is not too much to claim that the privileged, anywhere in the world, are often glad to clothe themselves in gold costumes.

All these dates, it should be noted, are hotly disputed by some historians and textile researchers.[9] Some aspects of Southeast Asian gold-thread decoration of cloth may date back to Indic kingdoms such as southern Sumatra's great Buddhist

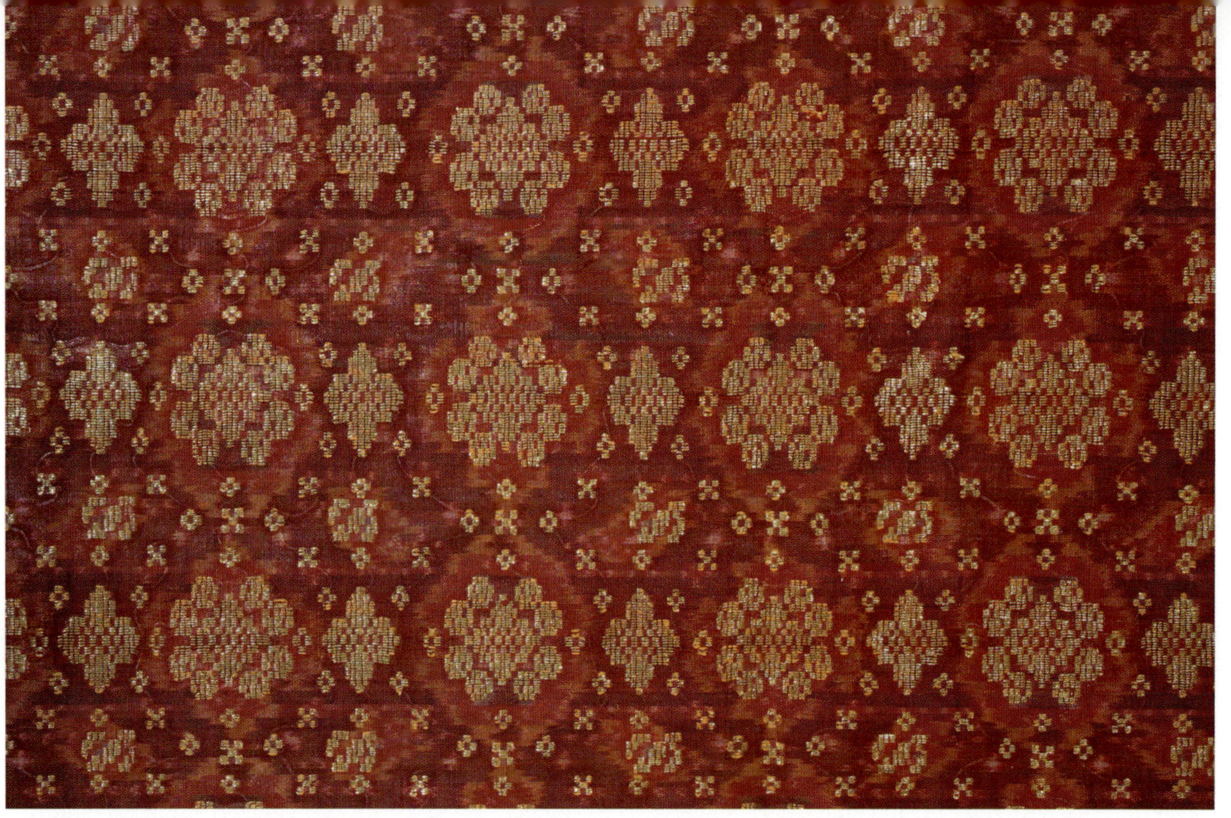

Fig. 2.8. Detail, Palembang songket sarong, circa 1800. The textile's florals and geometrics mesh with Islamic decorative art worldwide.

trade state, Srivijaya (c. late 600s–1100s, C.E.). Srivijayan courts were bound in tribute relationships to Chinese emperors, who used this part of the island chain as their gateway to the Indian Ocean.

Buddhist priests from China stopped off in Srivijaya, sometimes for months. They were awaiting a change in the trade winds so that they could journey onward to South Asia. While in Srivijaya the priests polished their Sanskrit skills, and this Sumatran commercial kingdom became an important inter-Asian center for Buddhist study. Emissaries from the Chinese court visited Srivijaya and exacted tribute for trade protection. As part of this state-to-state relationship, silk thread and, possibly, highly crafted silk costumes came to Srivijaya nobles as gifts from the Chinese emperors. Regal silk garb had also been bestowed on local elites in coastal states in northern Sumatra, along the Straits of Malacca, as early as the sixth century C.E.[10]

Coursing back in the other direction from Srivijaya to China were forest resins and gold ore—and political loyalty. Gold thread may have been imported to Sumatra at this time from China. Silk was almost definitely an import. A local luxury cloth industry could have developed during this era, although there is no concrete documentation of that.

Songket per se, as the textile is known today, has a pronounced reliance on geometric designs and florals. Further, it uses a specific weaving technique: the insertion of decorative threads via supplementary-weft weaving. All this bespeaks connections to Indian weaving and a Muslim aesthetic (fig. 2.8). This probably indicates a more direct origin time for this precise type of textile, as a specific package of weaving techniques, thread types, and design schemes: that is, the late 1400s to the early 1600s, when the India-to-Indonesian islands cloth trade was at its most intense.[11]

Not found to any great extent in Sumatran songket are the hearty animal motifs and spirit figures of outer-island Indonesian cotton ikat weaving. Islamic theology discourages the pictorial portrayal of such beings (and of humans, the prophet Muhammad, and God). Valorized instead in the arts of Muslim Indonesia are geometric patterns such as interlocked zigzags and rhomboids and botanical images such as blossoms and fern tendrils. Such figures as ducks and peacocks do sometimes sneak into some Sumatran songkets, however, in abstract form (fig. 2.9). These are not hidebound fabrics by any means.

Beyond Sumatra, lovely songkets have been produced in peninsular Malaysia in the courts of the Malay sultans since at least the 1600s. These cloths are in fact the classic status textiles of these Muslim rulers and their entourages. Songkets were also woven in profusion in Malay coastal settlements in Kalimantan and in southern Sulawesi, another

Fig. 2.9 Jambi waist cloth, with peacock designs in songket, 2005.

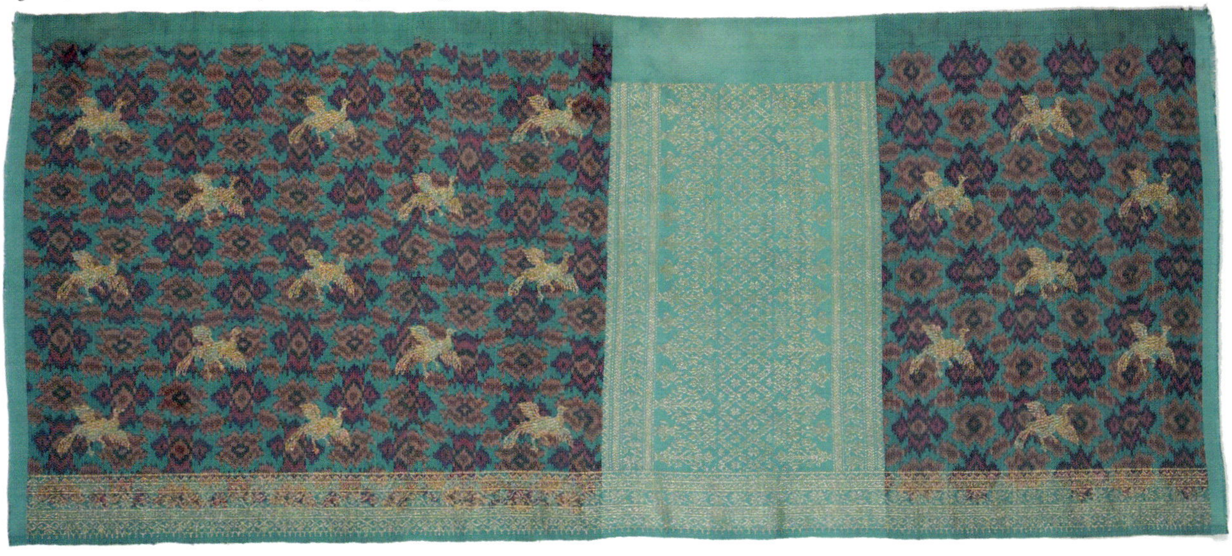

Malay peoples' hub. The Bugis and Makassarese seafarer traders helped spread Malay influence throughout this entire region in the 1600s and 1700s. Songket cloth was a prime currency of this expansive realm. This probably occurred both in terms of favored court arts and through the use of songkets as tribute and trade goods.

These regions also have contemporary songket industries. And the connections between Malay songket weaving in particular and the home looms and, now, shop floor looms of Sumatra are direct and long-standing. For instance, the great songket weavers of the southern Sumatran city of Palembang hail from immigrant Malay communities there. These weavers *are* Malay in terms of ethnic background, self-conscious identity, home language, and immigration history. Palembang's Malay weaving houses have been in that southern Sumatran city for at least seven generations.

In the widest Indonesian and Malaysian historical context, then, songket is a prestige cloth of a wide circuit of Muslim, mercantile, Malay sultanate cultures, wherever these are found. Map 1 indicates the wide sweep of these societies, which were often linked to one another through trade.

Significant offshoots of this basic type of patterned metallic-thread weaving have thrived as well in places such as Klungkung, East Bali (fig. 2.10).[12] Silver- and gold-thread technology had spread to home looms and temple center craftspeople there by at least the 1800s if not earlier. Gold- and especially silver-thread songkets gained a following among East Balinese priests and kingly courts alert to the pleasures and sumptuary wear possibilities of metallic textiles. But East Balinese songkets are tailored to Balinese kingdoms' Hinduism: such figures as heroes and heroines from the Ramayana epic of the Balinese shadow puppet plays appear in songkets there. Songkets similar to those from Bali are also woven in Lombok and Sumbawa. Finally, and quite importantly, fabrics for ritual wear using songket's distinctive

Fig. 2.10 Songket weaver at a backstrap loom, East Bali, 2005.

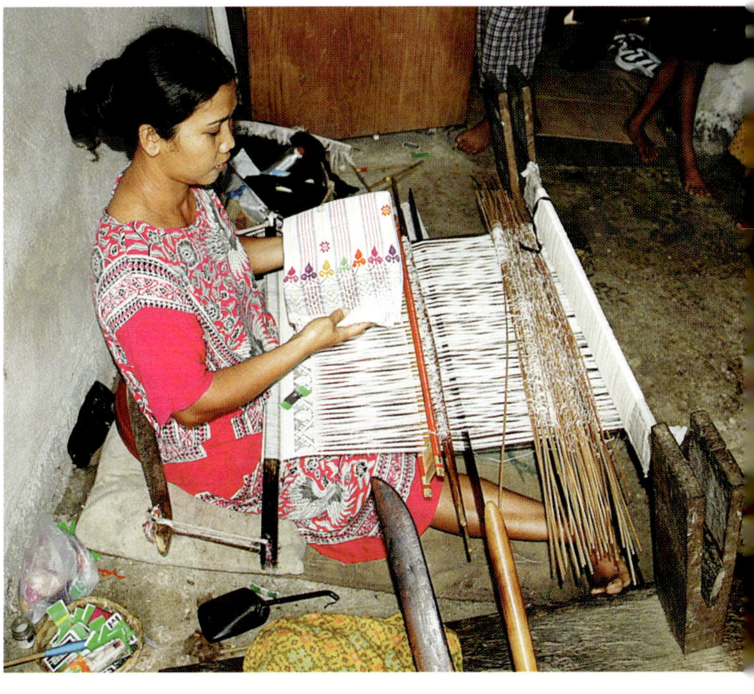

supplementary weft weaving technique and metal-wrapped yarns have also been produced for many years, perhaps for centuries, in Cambodia; in Pattani, in southern Thailand near the border of Kelantan, Malaysia; and in the Lan Na courts of northern Thailand and Laos.[13]

Including many of these regions (especially the Malay peoples' locales) and their songket arts for consideration here would have been attractive. We have taken the more modest route, however, of concentrating on Sumatra's own considerable gold cloth attainments. Sumatran songket-weaving communities have immediate and concrete historical linkages to one another. These can be investigated in a thematically focused endeavor. Furthermore, many Sumatran weaving communities draw on a common well of motifs but then combine them in creative ways, which then go on to become "tradition."

Certain motifs have long been shared among geographically distant weavers in north, east, west, and south Sumatra through trade links. Sometimes the weaver women themselves would move from one village or court art area to another at marriage. Other villages have strict endogamy rules; these can work to keep valuable weaving knowledge planted in place. In other instances a single songket cloth ranged far from its home village, inside or atop a trader's pack. Weavers could use the imported piece as a motif template. Look, study, borrow, weave seems to be the Sumatran weaver woman's fundamental ethos. And, although the island has at least fifteen to twenty ethnic societies, many with distinct languages and dialects, art worlds have long interpenetrated.

In Sumatra as a whole, motifs and motif structures have fractured into a glorious multitude of local cloth pattern traditions, from Aceh to Minangkabau to Jambi, Bengkulu, and Palembang and up the east coast toward Deli, near Medan. These motif repertoires undeniably extend also into Malaysia and far-flung Malay settlements throughout island Southeast Asia—a topic, perhaps, for a later inquiry.

Sumatra's various metal-thread cloth production systems also all had certain common experiences in dealing with Dutch colonial trade policies for the regulation of textiles and thread importation. This also gives the region a certain unity as a field of ethnological and textile art study. For instance, weavers throughout Sumatra's societies had to deal with the Dutch colonial state's efforts in the late 1800s to flood local markets in places such as upland Minangkabau with cheaply produced cottons. In important ways, the intensification of songket artistry in places such as Pitalah in the mid- and late 1800s was a response to these international trade policy decisions. Local Minangkabau elites rejected the rough, mass-produced European- and Indian-brokered goods for their own exacting ritual wear needs. This fed a local market for finely crafted, highly detailed songkets made of imported silk thread. Similar processes in the globalization of traditional cloth were also at work during this period in peninsular Malaysia.[14]

Sumatran songket wear from Aceh to Palembang has also made related adjustments to national-era Indonesian markets and to national Indonesian standards of dress. Following the national revolution of 1945–49, Sumatran peoples emerged as "ethnic groups," all of which have been subsumed into the nation. This subordination of local peoples has taken place within a sometimes markedly assertive nationalist rhetoric. Resentments linger. Sumatran textile traditions as much as ethnic imaginaries have been redefined numerous times within such contexts.

Colonial-era trajectories of ethnic group formation, at the levels of practice and ideology, lie behind these processes of artistic change. As anthropologist Joel S. Kahn has astutely written in *Constituting the Minangkabau; Peasants, culture, and modernity in colonial Indonesia* (1993), "the Batak," "the Minangkabau," and so on were in important part socially constructed notions of peoplehood that can be traced to the contentious dealings of Sumatrans with the colonial state in the mid- to late nineteenth and early twentieth centuries. The ethnic map of the island that both outsiders and many

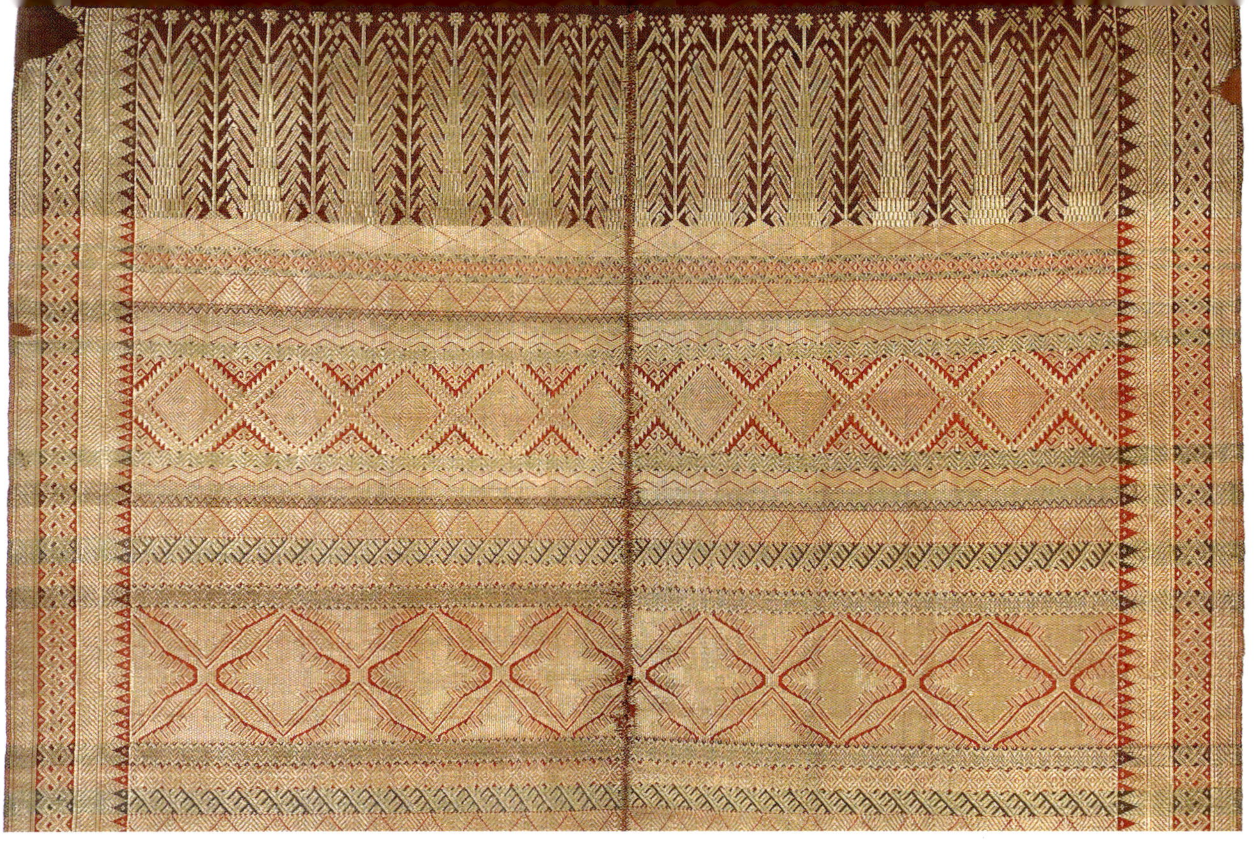

Fig. 2.11. Finely wrought motif bands in a circa 1800s headtie. Pitalah, Minangkabau people, West Sumatra.

Indonesians imagine to be real is in many ways a chimera. Ethnic boundaries are not clear-cut, and neither are songket traditions.

Songket Commodified, as Ethnic Wear and as Collectible

Beyond our primary focus on Sumatra, our second innovation concerns time, commodification, and the associations between the marketing of songkets and their resilience and creativity, which are evident in terms of both the materials and design of these textiles—thread type, motif-band composition, and band juxtaposition—and their ritual use. Although we discuss superb nineteenth-century gold cloths at many junctures in this study (fig. 2.11), we focus thematically on Sumatran songkets as a contemporary status cloth today. Songkets are ethnic heritage objects for peoples such as the Minangkabau and the Palembang Malays, but this is so in a particularly ironic way today. This cloth type is not a relic of the past, although nineteenth-century songkets are still preserved. Songkets are being woven today in great abundance, sometimes at high levels of technique, in some of the Sumatran regions we consider. We pose the question, Why is this so?

Peoples from all these areas who have the means to afford them are avid buyers of the most expensive newly woven songkets. If they are not wealthy enough for that, they can buy less expensive examples, or, as noted, they can rent impressive or at least glittery songket costumes for weddings from the ubiquitous bridal wear shops. Antique songkets, for their part, have a continued existence—not only in Indonesian and international museums and in private collections but also as inherited house treasures in places such as Pitalah, where a few families have held onto their heirlooms and still use them on ceremonial occasions. Such situations make fuller sense when placed within a historical context, and in relation to recent scholarship by anthropologists on Indonesia's heritage arts.

Some old-line aristocratic and merchant Minangkabau families once had rolls and rolls of songkets but have sold them to antique dealers. This was already occurring in the 1920s, when some Western collections of songkets were amassed, and when some Minangkabau peddlers were first transforming themselves into antiquities dealers. But the flood of old songkets out of house treasures occurred mostly in the 1970s and 1980s. This sometimes happened under pressure from imams, who chastened families for displaying inordinate

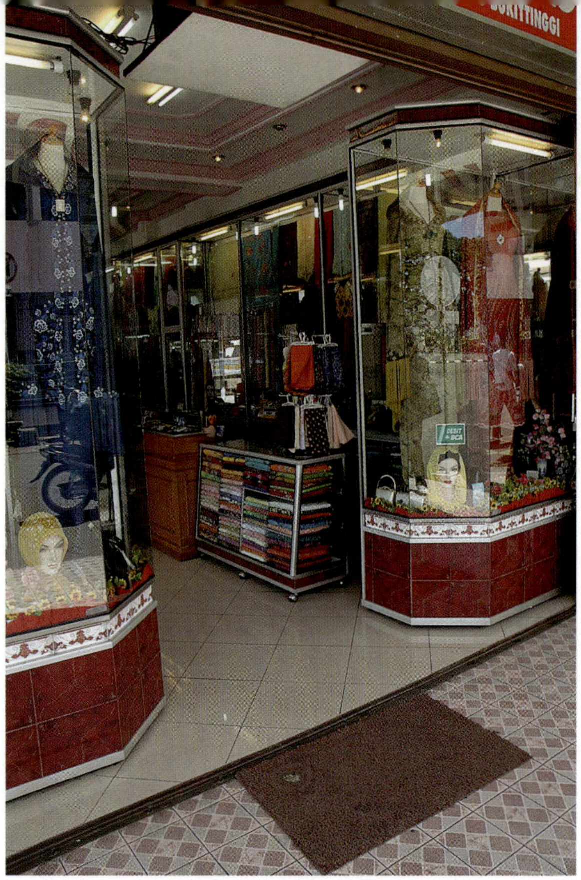

Fig. 2.12. Embroidery wear shop, Bukittinggi, 2006. The middle class invests heavily in finery fashion today, for long-sleeved overblouses and long skirts. This operates in tense interaction with songket marketing.

wealth. Another major motive for selling old songkets to dealers (who were themselves most often Sumatran Muslims) was to raise money for children's university education.

Some of the songket cloths woven today are designed (not to mention merchandised) quite self-consciously by Sumatran textile dealers as "replicas" of songkets from the 1800s—a perfect purchase, they assert in interviews, for families who have sold their treasures to dealers. Cloths of this sort are a special focus for us, as is Sumatran Muslim business acumen in managing such transactions. As we shall see, these new textiles are not by any means exact, motif-by-motif replicas of old songkets.

Thanks to processes like these, involving subtle mimicry of old forms, Sumatra's songket craft is far from being a fragile tradition, to take a phrase from an important anthology that documented the disappearance of some indigenous arts of outer island Indonesia. In the essays in *Fragile traditions; Indonesian art in jeopardy* (1994), anthropologists, art historians, and collectors detail in fittingly alarming tones the decline and sometimes the outright disappearance of indigenous arts such as wooden effigy sculptures in some eastern Indonesian islands, or stone stools in Nias. A rapacious international art collectors' market for outer-island Indonesian tribal antiquities is partly to blame.[15] Massive conversion to Islam and Christianity in all these regions greatly altered local epistemologies of the worth of indigenous ritual objects such as carvings for contacting the dead and securing their blessings.[16]

Village weaving in outer-island Indonesia (that is, beyond Indic Java and Bali) continues today, but sometimes (as the *Fragile traditions* authors assert) at lesser levels of technical expertise than was the case in the past. Commercial dyes have often replaced natural vegetable dyes, resulting at times in harsher tones. Some cotton handspun is produced for home and ritual use, but the tourist art sector is significant and is filled with rough products at times. Cheap collectibles are available for international or metropolitan Indonesian travelers who want tokens of their visits to East Sumba, say, but who are not willing or able to seek out the best weavers or to invest the hundreds of dollars it takes to purchase an old handspun cotton in an antique store.

Sumatra's songket-weaving industries are fundamentally different in kind from these other Indonesian cloth-scapes, so to speak. Far from being on the edge of disappearance, songkets are currently produced in large and profitable quantities, often at estimable levels of weaving and design excellence (figs. 2.12, 2.13). These metallic cloths are also made largely for *internal* Indonesian and Malaysian markets, mostly though not exclusively for Muslim, Malay-related peoples (fig. 2.14). Since songket is bought today for ceremonial wear for weddings

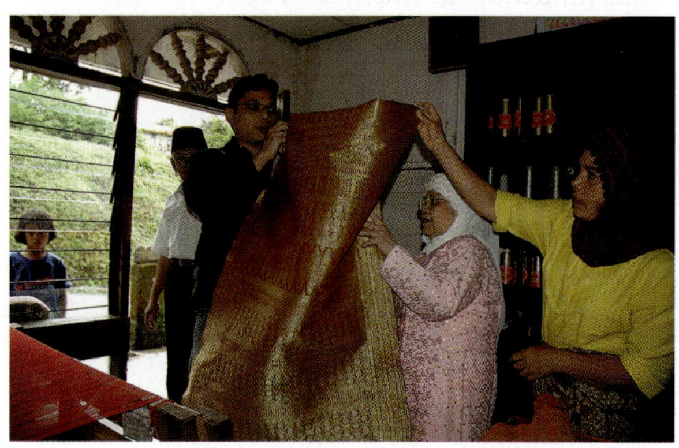

Fig. 2.13. Accomplished weaver Ibu Us, at right, displays one of her songkets replete with antique motifs. 2006, Pandai Sikek, Tanjung.

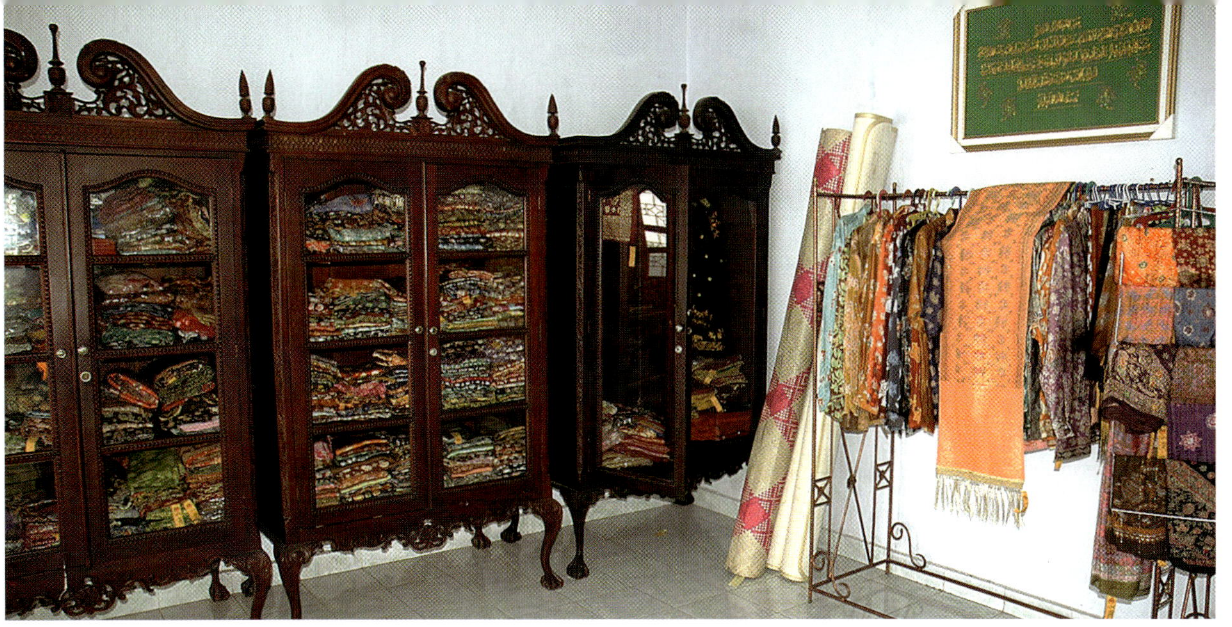

Fig. 2.14. Songket and batik shop, Jambi, 2005.

and similar occasions or adat celebrations such as a baby's first haircut, the installation of a new sultan or lineage leader, or village boys' Muslim circumcision rites, there is a perennial need for such finery. This market is vibrantly local and not dependent to any great extent on international patronage.

Few international travelers of the backpacker or casual tourist sort apparently know much about new songkets and their design repertoires. Books in English on songket are hard to come by in Indonesia, in comparison to numerous publications on batik or even ikat. Price is also a factor. Even a small, sampler-size, ten-by-ten-inch songket from West Sumatra (fig. 2.15) costs about the Indonesian rupiah equivalent of $20—too expensive for many short-term visitors to Sumatra (although this sampler format was developed in the specific hope of exploiting just that market).

There is a small and fervently devoted worldwide group of collectors of old songkets. But this group is less influential in Indonesian art-collecting circles than are the connoisseurs of Javanese, Balinese, and eastern Indonesian antiquities in cloth, stone, or wood. International songket connoisseurship has certainly affected Minangkabau and Palembang Malay cloth production, but it has not overwhelmed it.

Beyond songket's sheer survival skills, especially intriguing is the fact that in some parts of Sumatra this sort of weaving is now experiencing a pronounced boom in artistic creativity and variability of form. We explore this by looking at new cloths and interrogating their weaving artistry.

Color is an important issue here. Though West and South Sumatran songkets traditionally tend toward deep, rich reds, buyers today can find songkets in aqua, lime green, creamy white, and even "baby pink" (a Palembang dealer's exact term for a cloth on sale in January 2006).

As travelers to Indonesia would expect, songkets are also being made as table runners, purses, pencil holders, and lipstick cases (fig. 2.16). This is a nationwide merchandising ploy for hawking traditional cloth. Reflecting a much higher level of weaving accomplishment, some songkets these days also come decorated with Arabic letters. They present words or short phrases from the holy Koran, suitable for framing and wall display. Making the Arabic letters in songket is a significant technical challenge, given the calligraphy's curvilinear shapes.

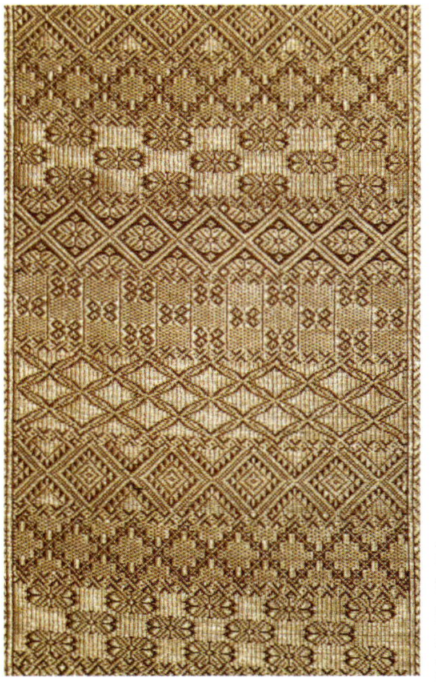

Fig. 2.15. Detail, sampler-type songket for tourists. Pandai Sikek, West Sumatra, 2006.

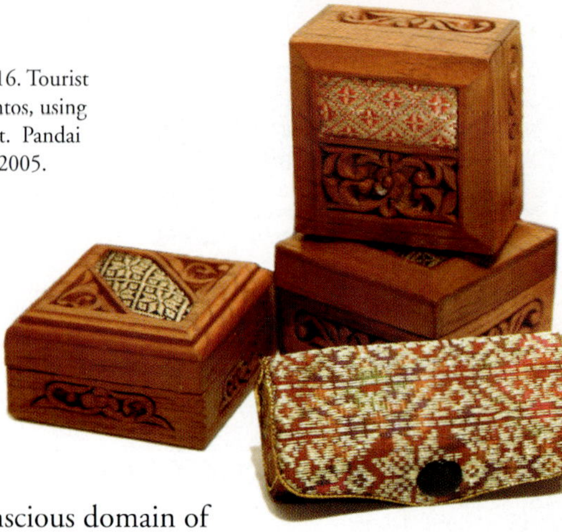

Fig. 2.16. Tourist mementos, using songket. Pandai Sikek, 2005.

There is also the high-end, high-weaving-quality, would-be replica market. This is a particularly self-conscious domain of craftwork, one in which weavers purposely try to recapture the past and sell it to members of their own society and in a few instances to collectors (both domestic and international ones). A customer can buy a fine new songket woven in the style of, for example, a nineteenth-century Pitalah cloth.

That is exactly the case with a well-woven songket created in linen and polyester yarns and gold-wrapped thread in 2005 by Ibu Us. She is a thirty-seven-year-old weaver from the Tanjung neighborhood of Pandai Sikek Village in the Minangkabau highlands. Pandai Sikek is West Sumatra's great remaining weaving village; the best songkets come from there. Local weavers estimate that about 90 percent of the village's homes have looms; Pandai Sikek songket weaving is famous as far away as Kuala Lumpur and the province of Negeri Sembilan in Malaysia. The latter is an area of significant Minangkabau migration starting in the late nineteenth century. Today Negeri Sembilan Minangkabau families of means sometimes travel to the Bukittinggi area on songket shopping expeditions to acquire especially beautiful trousseaux. Malaysian national law restricts the importation of foreign-made songkets, so these shopper-tourists are perhaps trying to circumvent that situation to buy better-quality (but at the same time cheaper) songket sarongs and shoulder wraps than they can get at home, from looms in Terengganu, for instance.

In this cloth, Ibu Us has created not a replica of an old textile but a kind of Pitalah songket fantasy—an intriguing cultural site of inquiry (shown in ch. 6., fig. 6.6, p. 93; see also fig. 2.17). The business concerns that provided the impetus for this textile are key. Sutan Madjo Indo and his wife, Ibu Elly, are prominent, knowledgeable antique dealers in Bukittinggi. They appreciate fine weaving and hoped that good replicas (their understanding of the matter) of antique West Sumatran songkets would sell well. At their behest Ibu Us used a fragment of an old Pitalah songket as a pattern template in creating this new textile. She has carefully replicated some of the old motif structures but has also added her own creative touches. She takes pride in this: these added effects (for instance, a mixture of motifs associated not just with Pitalah weaving but also with that of several other villages and a spatial reversal and simplification of some motifs), joined to her good weaving technique, joined to the exactness with which she has copied some motifs, make this cloth a beautiful one. This is Ibu Us's view and also the opinion of her art shop collaborators, Sutan Madjo Indo and Ibu Elly.

Ibu Us wove this cloth on commission, hoping that the Madjo Indos could sell it to one of two clienteles. The first would be a wealthy Pitalah family now living in the rantau, perhaps one that had sold off all of their inherited songkets and

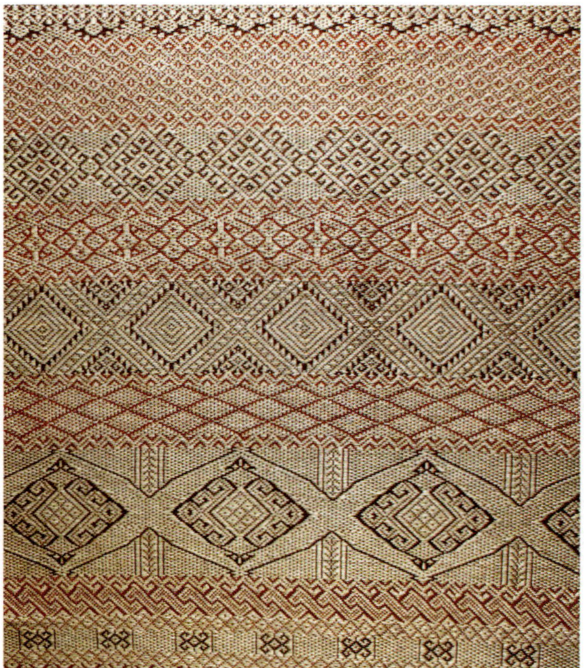

Fig. 2.17. Detail of Ibu Us' songket.

needed new ones for a forthcoming wedding. The second potential sort of buyer would be a collector: a foreign connoisseur or an urban Minangkabau man or woman who fancied the old Minangkabau arts and wanted to patronize the high end of Pandai Sikek weaving to foster its growth. The Madjo Indos' shop, Toko Aladdin, sells such textiles. There are several additional arts shops in Kuta and Sanur, Bali, that specialize in marketing their goods to buyers of this sort from Sumatra. Or, rather, there used to be: Indonesia's economic downturn following the Southeast Asia currency crisis of 1997 depressed this Bali art shop market seriously. The terrorist bombings in Kuta in October 2002 harmed these businesses further, as there was a disastrous drop-off in the number of moneyed international travelers to Bali. In any event, however, I purchased Ibu Us's estimable cloth for this study and the exhibition it accompanies, *Gold Cloths of Sumatra*.

Our project forefronts this sort of economic and artistic transaction, highlighting recently woven Sumatran songkets such as Ibu Us's ambitious yet artistically ambiguous shoulder cloth. To give a wider perspective on the variety of new songkets (and on the question of why there is such a variety), we also discuss examples from the middle range of weaving expertise: sarongs, shoulder cloths, and head wraps that would typically be bought and used not by collectors or extremely well-off Sumatran families but by the middle class (schoolteachers, government clerks, news shop owners, for instance). We also study pieces such as the Arabic-letter wall hangings, the household goods, and the lipstick containers. We do this precisely to begin documenting a precise moment in Sumatra's cloth history—that is, the present time, as songket-weaving worlds are much in transition and serve too as a topic of public debate, in places such as Bukittinggi shops, Pandai Sikek, Jambi craft neighborhoods, and the old Malay kampongs (in-city villages) in Palembang.

In this respect our project is similar to that of anthropologists Jill Forshee and Andrew Causey in their respective books *Between the Folds; Stories of Cloths, Lives, and Travels from Sumba* (2001) and *Hard Bargaining in Sumatra; Western Travelers and Toba Bataks in the Marketplace of Souvenirs* (2003). Both researchers use ethnographic fieldwork and archival research to investigate contemporary versions of "old arts": old-style and new-style brightly colored ikats in Sumba, and souvenirs and replica-market wooden sculpture in Toba. Forshee and Causey do this in the setting of these objects' travels to new market spaces today: to Kuta art shops and Jakarta salons for the cotton cloths from Sumba, and into sometimes hilarious touristic encounters with "primitive art" and "primitives" on Samosir Island for the Toba carvings.

Forshee and Causey take care to listen carefully to the indigenous shapes of narrative as East Sumbanese weavers and cloth dealers and Toba wood carvers tell tales about their works and about craft, and also about Sumba and Toba in Indonesia and the wider world. In the present volume I draw on my training as an anthropologist to collaborate with two textile researchers, Anne Summerfield and John Summerfield, to listen to the stories of weavers such as Ibu Us and dealers such as Sutan Madjo Indo and Ibu Elly. We attempt a similar account of songket weaving on the move. In our several chapters, we also propose what we hope will be a useful, newly holistic way of seeing and studying Indonesia-area "traditional" handwoven cloths.

It is evident by now that *tradition* is a slippery word in relation to Sumatra's cloth arts, much as definition of *art* itself is often much in contention in contemporary Indonesian cloth-scapes. To capture nuances, we have designed our approach to go beyond the current purviews of our two fields when they operate independently, as, unfortunately, they sometimes do in the study of Indonesian textiles. There is a need for dialogic studies of Southeast Asian cloth, an approach that combines close attention to the social settings and political and economic origins of heritage textiles (a strength of anthropological approaches) with an engagement with these special fabrics in their lives as works of art (characteristic of research by textile scholars). In our separate chapters, and in our jointly authored entries about specific songket cloths (chapter 6, "Biographied textiles"), we seek to join a study of the aesthetics of Indonesian textiles, alert to their formal qualities, to a forthrightly social scientific engagement with these remarkable fabrics as cultural productions, seen in the context of Indonesian and larger Southeast Asian and world history. Needless to say, the present volume does not purport to offer "the final say" on any of these topics. Ours is an exploratory and methodological investigation, intended throughout to spur more research. We have also used what we hope are accessible writing styles, to bring our work to broad publics.[17]

The following chapter addresses Sumatran songkets' place within the larger range of Indonesian traditional textiles. We then look at ways to evaluate the excellence of songkets and songket-weaving technique using textile research perspectives. Following this is an ethnographic chapter on the contemporary relationships between songket weavers' creativity and the cloth's concrete business settings. We look at this as it occurs in two classic songket-weaving locales: Palembang and Pandai Sikek. A subsequent chapter presents what might be called biographies of individual cloths, an approach we essay with a tip of the hat to anthropologist Janet Hoskins's illuminating essays on Kodi material culture from west Sumba in her *Biographical Objects; How Things Tell the Stories of People's Lives* (1998).

Our research methodology has involved ethnographic fieldwork I conducted in 1995–96 in Bukittinggi, West Sumatra, on the heritage arts businesses there. I supplemented this with numerous visits to Pandai Sikek and Palembang weaving establishments since 1995. Textile scholars Anne Summerfield and John Summerfield have spent thirty years conducting research on the textiles of eastern Indonesia, upland Sulawesi, southern Sumatra, and especially West Sumatra. In Minangkabau, their special focus area, they have worked intensively since the 1970s with weavers, art scholars, and historians.

NOTES

1. For an illuminating discussion of this topic in relation to Toraja art and heritage, coming to be seen as such, see anthropologist Kathleen Adams's *Art as politics; Re-crafting identities, tourism, and power in Indonesia* (2006).
2. On the comparative history of different sorts of looms in Southeast Asia, see Fraser-Lu 1990: 31–41, 42–59. Robyn Maxwell's *Textiles of Southeast Asia* (2003, revised edition) also has good entries on the backstrap tension loom, frame looms, braid and comb looms, and the four-heddle loom.

3. For excellent color illustrations of superb late eighteenth-, nineteenth-, and early twentieth-century Minangkabau songkets, see Anne and John Summerfield, editors, *Walk in splendor; Ceremonial dress and the Minangkabau* (1999).
4. Much of the newer anthropological scholarship on Minangkabau village societies focuses on issues of gender and power. Especially insightful is Evelyn Blackwood's *Webs of power; Women, kin, and community in a Sumatran village* (1999); see also Blackwood 1995 on gender contradictions. Also enlightening is Krier 1995; see Krier 1994 for rewardingly dense ethnographic detail. Peggy Reeves Sanday's *Women at the center; Life in a modern matriarchy* is also useful (2004). Specifically on women's powers and weaving, see Cynthia Ng's dissertation, "The weaving of prestige; Village women's representations of the social categories of Minangkabau society" (1987). Of much use are Anne Summerfield 1999, Anne Summerfield and H.A. Sutan Madjo Indo 1999, and John Summerfield 1999a, b.
5. See Mary M. Steedly's "The importance of proper names; Language and 'national' identity in colonial Karoland" (1996) for an astute account of the political backdrop to the elaboration of the notion of "local languages" in Indonesia.
6. For comparative material on such Muslim wear issues see Suzanne Brenner, "Reconstructing self and society; Japanese Muslim women and 'the veil'" (1996).
7. Maxwell 2004 provides excellent descriptive background.
8. Summerfield and Summerfield 1990, 1991a, 1999.
9. For discussions of songket's history in the Malay World, see Maxwell 2003, under the different songket-producing regions of Sumatra. Useful too is Fraser-Lu 1990: 51–54. Also valuable are Kartiwa 1979, 1986, Othman 1994: 110-121, Heringa 1993 and especially Selvanagam 1990. Masnah Mohamad's *Malay handloom weavers; A study of the rise and decline of traditional manufacture* (1996) is excellent as an economic history. Barbara Leigh's *Changing face of Malaysian crafts* (2000: 44-49) also provides valuable comparative information. Leigh's *Hands of time, the crafts of Aceh* (1989) is also an excellent source (see ch. 5, Silk weaving, pp. 76-92).
10. Kartiwa 1986: 4. Kartiwa provides a detailed summary of the competing theories.
11. Robyn Maxwell's *Sari to sarong; Five hundred years of Indian and Indonesian textile exchange* (2004) deals directly with this issue, as did the Australian National Gallery exhibition of the same title. As background to this see Helen Jessup, 1990.
12. See Hauser-Schäublin 1991: 33–50 on Balinese songket weaving. Contemporary Balinese songket weavers seem to have little awareness of Sumatran weaving traditions, at least as indicated by brief 2005 interviews.
13. Conway 2002 provides fascinating discussion of these metal-thread weaving centers, in the past and today.
14. M. Mohamad 1996 provides a detailed historical discussion of this. See especially her points about the capital intensification of shop floor weaving.
15. Taylor, ed., 1994. See also the essays in Reimar Schefold and Han F. Vermeulen, eds., *Treasure hunting? Collectors and collections of Indonesian artefacts* (2002) for case studies of these processes.
16. There is a large anthropological literature on conversion to Christianity in Indonesian societies. See, for instance, Kipp 1990 and Keane 2007. Again, see Kathleen Adams 2006: 5-7, 60-61, 92-93, 102, 199-202.
17. There is some controversy in the textile literature regarding use of the terms wefts and warps. Some scholars assert that "warp" must refer to the *set* of lenghtwise threads, and "weft" to the *set* of crosswise threads. In this view a writer must use "warp threads" or "warp yarns" in a sentence such as, "This textile's warp threads are blue. Our usage differs from this; we occasionally write phrases such as "the warps are blue in this section of the cloth."

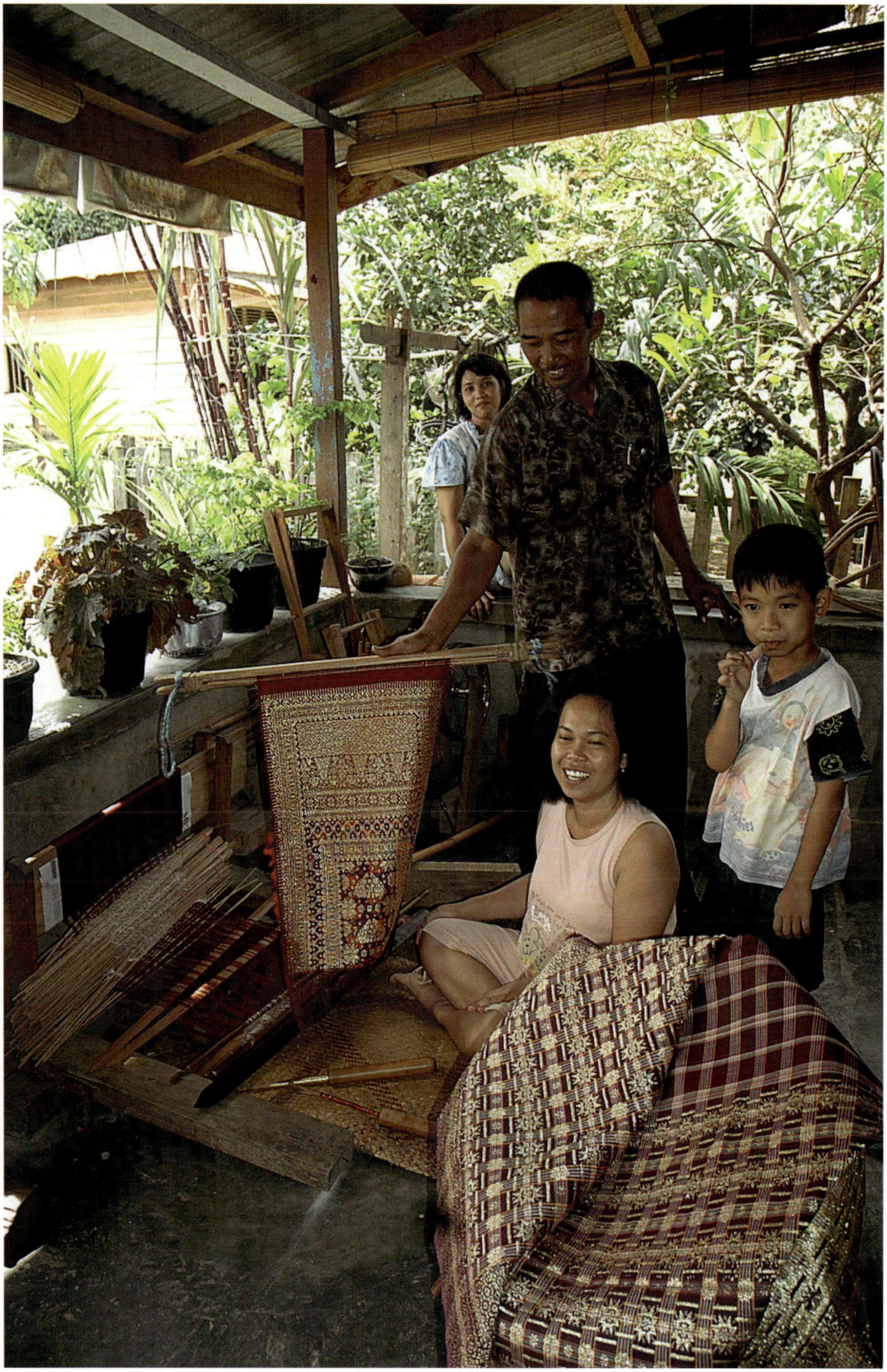

Fig. 3.0. Ibu Mania Ali at her front porch loom, Jambi, 2005.

3. Songkets within Indonesian textile worlds

Susan Rodgers

The decorated cloth in Indonesia

The weaving of handspun cotton cloth on backstrap looms with continuous warps dates to the Bronze Age in mainland and island Southeast Asia.[1] Bronze technology appeared in Vietnam by 1000 B.C.E. and may have been present in Thailand up to 2500 years before that. Core Southeast Asian technologies traceable to this era also include rice cultivation and the production of bronze socketed axes, spearheads, and ornaments (Bellwood 1979).

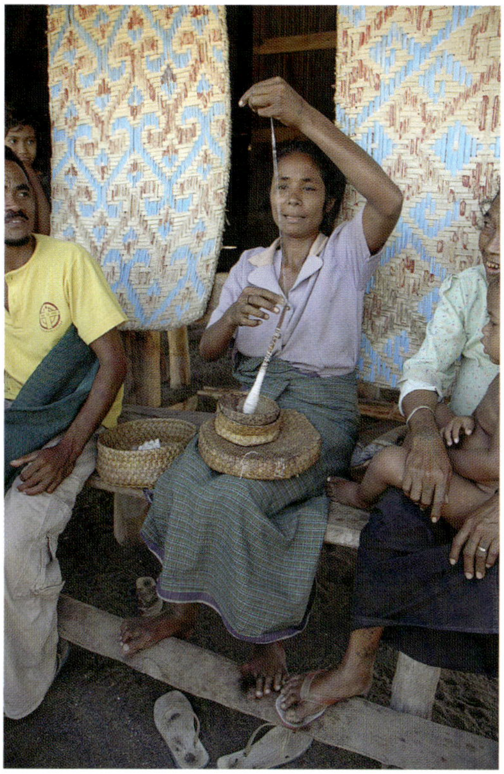

Fig. 3.1. Spinning cotton, Suai, East Timor, 2005.

The production of cotton thread on hand spindles is also historically old in Southeast Asia. Remarkably, like the backstrap loom itself, such spindles continued to be used by girls and women in some eastern Indonesian societies as recently as the 1980s. In fact, in some regions—such as Suai, along the southern coast of East Timor—hand spinning of cotton occurs today (fig. 3.1). Throughout much of the twentieth century, however, commercially spun cotton thread produced internationally has been for sale and readily available to weavers in larger urban centers throughout the Indonesian islands. This was the case in much of Bali, Java, and Sumatra by the late nineteenth century. Sumatran songket-weaving centers have long been cosmopolitan places in ways such as this. Skeins of imported silk yarn can be purchased today in the thread markets of Silungkang, Jambi, and Palembang.

In the most general sense, Indonesian island societies have produced their abundance of special textiles in reaction to and in interaction with four main political and trade complexes. The first of these were the island chain's Indianized court states of the 700–1300 C.E. period. These were extensive polities in Java and southern Sumatra—political systems similar to other powerful, ambitious Indic states in mainland Southeast Asia. In these states, rulers claimed divine status and posited concordances between the kingdom and the structure of the cosmos itself. Unusually productive rice cultivation systems and, at times, linkages to regional trade networks undergirded these prosperous states.

In the Indic dynastic states such as the ones that built Borobudur in Central Java (circa 778-850 C.E.) and the Angkor temples in Cambodia (circa 800 to late 1200s C.E.), aristocrats were heavily invested in glorifying their power through sacred arts (fig. 3.2). These included the building of temples to gods, with the king's power connected directly to that. Borobudur was a temple mountain

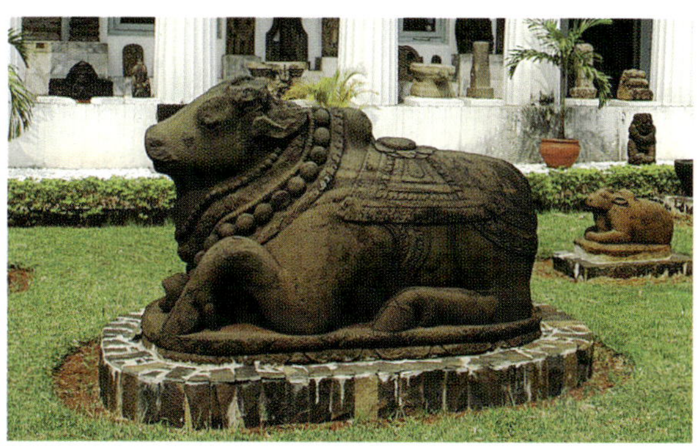

Fig. 3.2. The bull Nandi, Shiva's mount, a sculpture at Indonesia's National Museum. Court arts glorified the powers of deities and kings.

where Buddhist pilgrims could retrace the faith's larger spiritual journey by ascending terraces lined with relief sculptures. Royal families also staged lavish court dances and mighty processions in temples such as Angkor Wat. Decorated boats of state coursing along rivers at ceremonies also represented kingly powers, as did what must have been elaborate, gleaming costume arts for the nobles and their extensive retinues (fig. 3.3). These states tended to be located in lowland rice plains areas or along key interregional trade routes. Court art technologies and motifs could spread outward from the palace centers to other similar states or to smaller kingdoms and chiefdoms along the realm's periphery.

The second cultural complex that shaped the Indonesian textile arts was the long-distance cloth trade with India, from at least the thirteenth and fourteenth centuries. Indian merchants, many of them Muslim, plied this trade in entrepôt settlements along the coasts of major Indonesian islands and along the Straits of Malacca. Islam came to Indonesian kingdoms along such cloth trade paths. Imported cloths from India provided treasure chests of cloth manufacture ideas and motif templates for upland and lowland societies throughout the Indonesian archipelago (Maxwell 2004).The integration of Indian motifs into indigenous textile arts reflects both the aesthetic panache and the political savvy of local artisans. They copied Indian trade cloth conventions for status-hungry localities; in the process, these Indonesian weavers made international styles their own.

The third salient social complex shaping Indonesia's cloth arts was the colonial contact

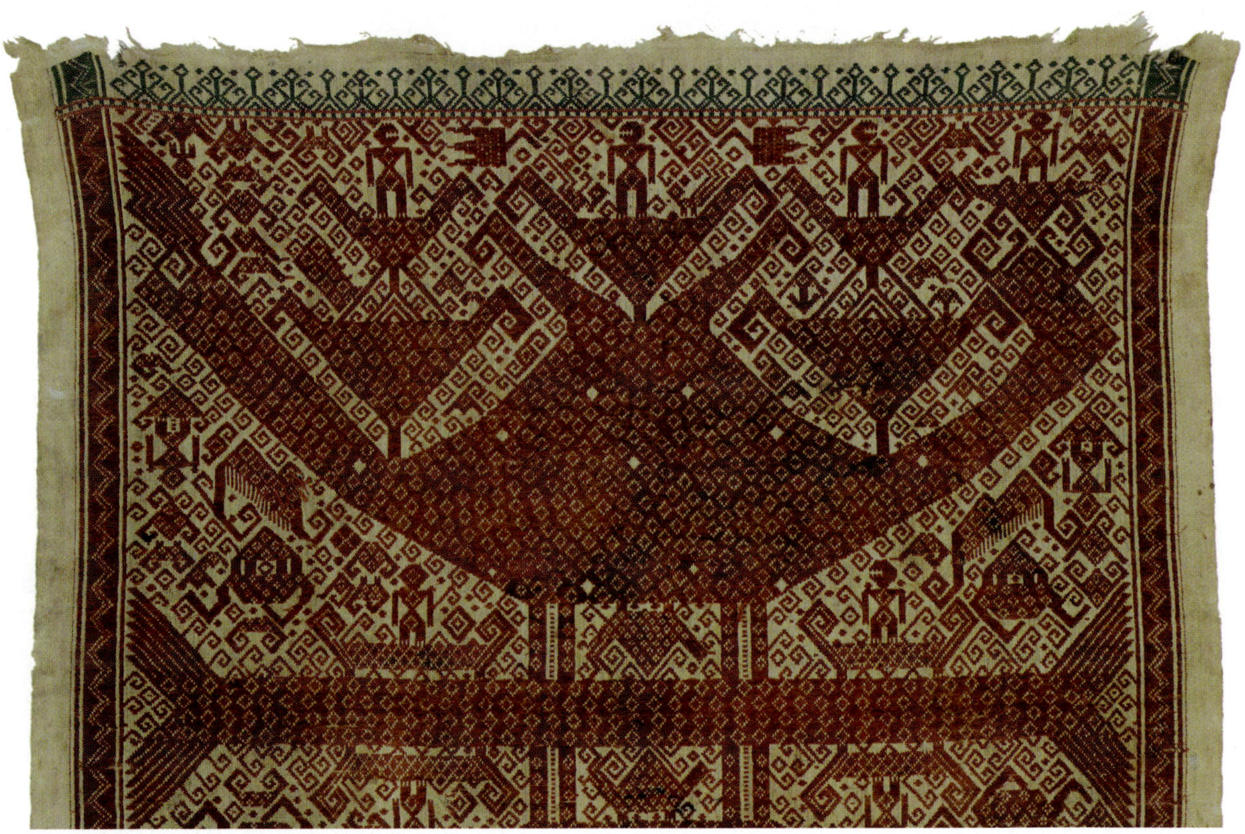

Fig. 3.3. A tampan cloth showing a ship, Lampung. Circa 1900. Ship motifs in southern Sumatra may trace back to Indic Kingdoms.

between Europe and the archipelago's many kingdoms and smaller states and chiefdoms. This occurred starting in the 1500s, initially via intermittent contact between island societies and European traders in search of spices. The Dutch East India Company (Vereenigde Oostindische Compagnie, or VOC) was formally established in 1602 to regularize this trade and make it more profitable for business concerns in the Netherlands. Soon afterward a formal colonial government was established in Batavia, now Jakarta. This state remained in power until the sudden Japanese invasion of February 1942. The Indonesian national revolution followed the world war. Dutch merchants' interventions in the India-Indies textile trade in the colonial period were of great importance to the development of Indonesian textile traditions. So too was the mass importation of cotton thread and cotton yard goods from Europe and South Asia in the nineteenth century.

The fourth cultural complex to affect the Indonesian traditional textile arts has been the post–World War II international fashion and fabric manufacture and marketing scenes. Thanks to this influence, Indonesia's indigenous cloth-producing worlds have been introduced to new styles of dress and, in some instances, have been reshaped by new production technologies that extend to the factory floor. The core, foundational types of Indonesian textiles discussed below have all been shaped by these four institutional, historical complexes.

Possibly the earliest textile patterning form in the Indonesian islands, one that long predates the intensive Indian trade interaction, involved the use of stripes. This is an indigenous, ancient format that today is preserved in *lurik* cloth (Yogi 1980, Wahyono 1981). The latter is used for some everyday garments in rural areas of Central and East Java. But lurik and similar textiles have maintained some apparently very old associations with ritual. One conventional belief about stripes in Indonesian traditional fabrics holds that they help confine spirit forces in the center of a cloth field when used as borders. Another connection concerns striped cloth and the powers of human reproduction. Simple stripes in graduated patterns were once associated in these parts of Java with *kain gendong*, the archipelago's classic baby-carrier cloth (fig. 3.4). A kain gendong allows an adult or older child to strap an infant snugly to the back or side and to safely (not to mention practically) tote the baby around. This yields one of Indonesia's most familiar human body imageries: the tiny child wrapped in a protective cloth. The idea of encircling a vulnerable infant in a shielding, enfolding textile runs deep in many Indonesian cultures. Amulets for a baby are also part of these systems of care. Magical ornaments suspended around the neck or, in the past, in front of the genitals are said to repel supernatural attacks and dire illnesses.[2] Village

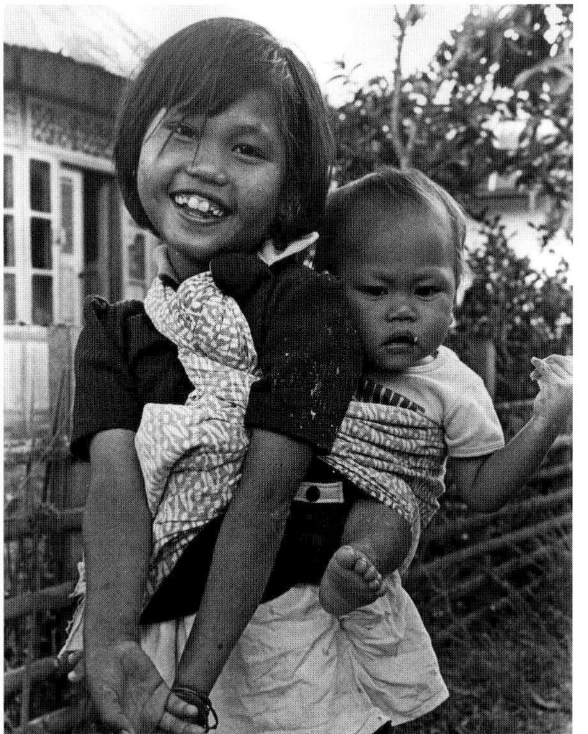

Fig. 3.4. A small child toting a baby sibling in a cheap batik kain gendong, 1976, South Tapanuli, Angkola Batak people.

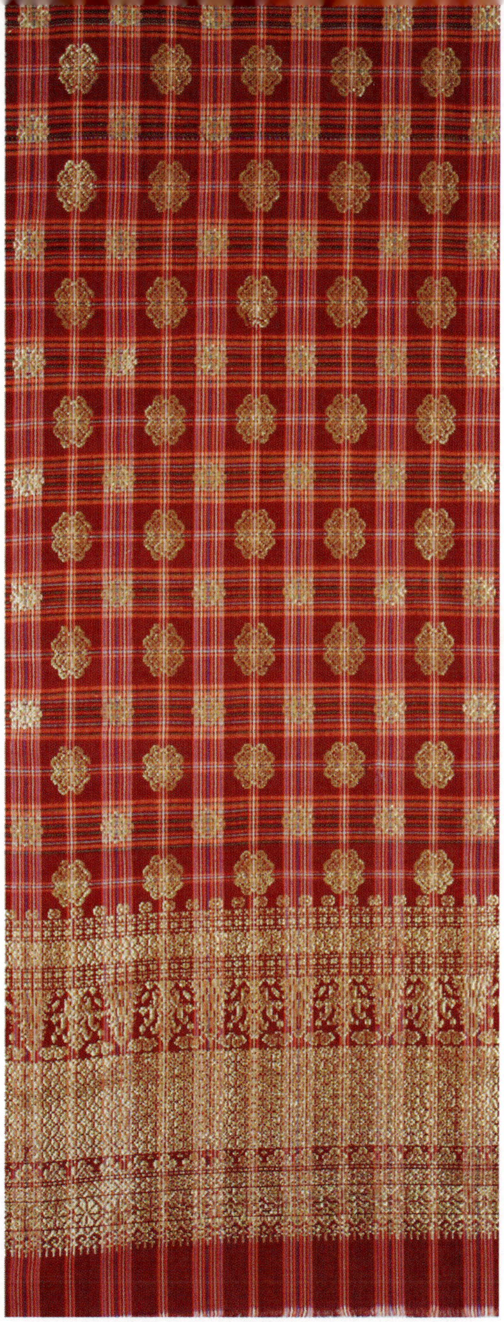

Fig. 3.5. Plaids are often used in Palembang and Jambi songkets. Here, a Palembang weaving from the Fikri Koleksi shop, 2006.

houses too would sometimes "wear" protective objects at entryways in order to repel dangers.

Plaids are also ancient in the archipelago, although the pattern also appears in many imported goods (fig. 3.5). Checks in black and white, which sometimes have sacred connotations, are very old Indonesian cloth decoration patterns too. In Bali today, cloth with large, alternating black and white checks is used to purify temple structures. The opposed black and white spaces (in *poleng*) invoke a dualism of paired, complementary opposites (sky and earth, male and female, human and wild). This scheme of thought is crucial to many Southeast Asian ways of imagining world order. Crafts (textiles such as these dualistic sorts) and certain ceremonial assemblages (a sword bound in a textile, say) are said to temporarily unite opposites. They thus embody generative powers and produce bounty, order, and prosperity in the world.[3]

Songket weavers rely on much more recent cloth design repertoires than simple stripes or checks, but they do also enthusiastically adopt such old conventions in their weavings. In fact, the songket weaver's basic aesthetic seems to be one of creative, self-confident borrowing—from other textile traditions and also from other art forms, such as imported porcelain.

Also many centuries old in Indonesian and wider Southeast Asian textile craft is *ikat*. The ikat patterning of indigo-dyed cotton dates to the first millennium B.C.E. in parts of highland Southeast Asia along the southern border of China. Ikat cloth can also be done in silk, an innovation resulting from later trade contact with China and India. As we shall discover, silk ikat is particularly important in southern Sumatran textiles, in combination with gold-thread technology.

Basic ikat is produced by a dyeing technique in which small bundles of unwoven threads are first bound together under a tie, an ikat (fig. 3.6). The

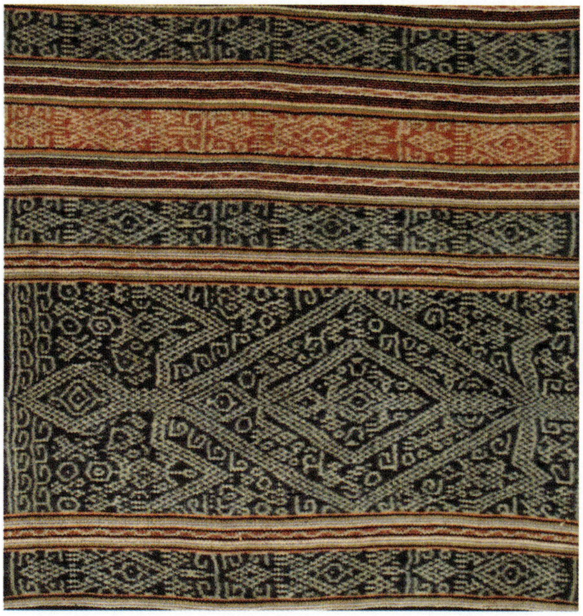

Fig. 3.6. Warp ikat from either West Timor or Timor Leste (East Timor). First half of 20th century.

verb form of this Indonesian word, *mengikat*, means "to bind" or "to tie." The tie (a string, or a short length of palm fiber) creates a resist, which protects the yarn sections underneath when the threads are dipped into a dye bath. Once the unbound parts of the yarns soak up the designated color, the ikatted parts are untied, producing a pattern. The ikat resist process can be repeated numerous times to add successive colors and to yield patterns. An ikat frame can be warped in preparation for ikat tying and dyeing. This produces warp ikat. Weft ikat is also possible. Chapter 4 offers more detailed discussion.

An especially expert dyer can grapple with two special challenges. The first is making double ikat, and the second is producing a cloth in deep, rich tones, which are the result of many carefully calibrated dye baths. Southeast Asian forest and house gardens once had profuse natural dyestuffs and mordants. These included mud, different sorts of indigo plants for producing the blue-black spectrum, and roots and barks (*Morinda citrifolia*, *Caesal pina sappan*, and *soga*) for attaining a great favorite, red-brown. Aniline dyes, with their predictability of color tone and their bright hues, started to come into Indonesian use by the 1890s.

In double ikat both the warps and the wefts are ikatted so that a carefully thought-out picture or design emerges when the dyed threads are put on the loom and the textile is woven. A silk *patola* cloth from Gujarat, North India (fig. 3.7), exemplifies the region's most famous double-ikat type (Bühler and Fischer 1979). Dramatic, figure-filled patolas began to be imported to the Indonesian islands by the late 1400s and 1500s. These eye-catching cloths were typically brought in by merchants from India, who traded them for spices and forest goods. Some imported textiles were bordered by rows of *tumpal* (triangles) at the ends and bold stripes along the selvedges. This way of laying out a textile proved to be an inspiration for weavers in Bali, throughout Eastern Indonesia, and in parts of Java and Sumatra as well.

Fig. 3.7. Detail, silk patola trade cloth from India. Late 1700s - early 1800s.

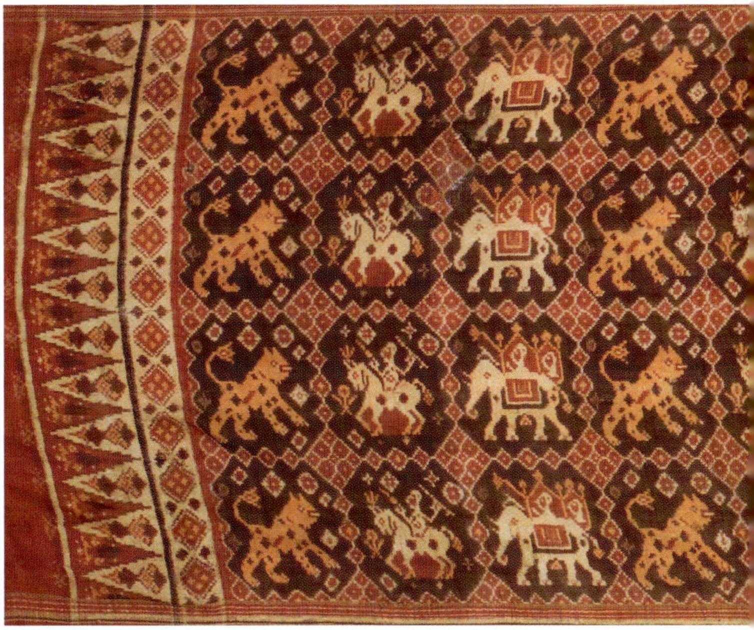

By the late 1500s and 1600s Dutch traders had also discovered the sharp desire that Indonesian elites had to acquire these stunning figured silk cloths. So still more patolas poured into the archipelago, this time brought by European business concerns eager to secure the islands' pepper, nutmeg, and mace as preservatives and flavorings back home. Indian silks in huge dimensions, in sari lengths, were aflame with red-toned figuration. These cloths catalyzed the imaginations of textile workers in many Indonesian island societies.

Some patolas became sacred house treasures for apparently awestruck royal families in places such as Sulawesi. There, prior to the trade influx of Indian silks, many upland weavers had probably known mostly hand-dyed cotton fabrics and bark cloth. The filmy, gleaming patolas—with their luxurious size and their busy, flowing central pattern fields of horses, lions, elephants, warriors, and exotic nobles—would have entranced. Patolas kept as heirlooms in aristocratic households took on magical, protective, even curative qualities. Some of these ideas persist today. Small fragments of old patolas that have fallen into tatters are not thrown away but are used as healing amulets.

Fig. 3.8. Cotton cloak, Lio people, 1900-1950. Flores.

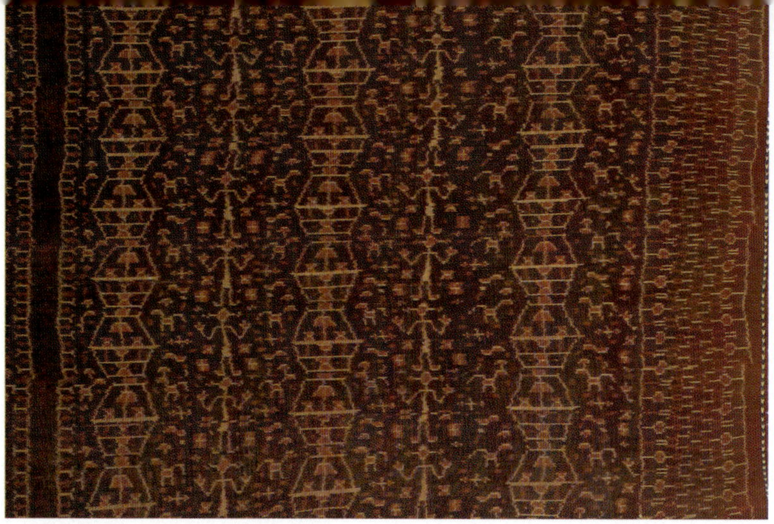

The weavers of Tengangan, East Bali, produce Indonesia's only double ikats today. These cloths are called *geringsing* and have a kind of double life, serving both as collectibles for moneyed visitors (even a recently woven geringsing runs about US $100) and as sacred cloths. For instance, geringsing are used as breast cloths and waist-wrappers in teeth-filing ceremonies for Balinese young people. Filing down the tips of the incisors (often just in a symbolic way) is said to aid in the ritual transformation of children from "wildness" to full human personhood. Geringsing help protect the vulnerable neophytes as they transition away from their animal nature. The hand manufacture of geringsing also entails purification, for the weavers and the weaving materials.

Patola cloths from the 1600s and 1700s are rarely seen today in Indonesian house treasuries, but they continue to cast long shadows in cloth aesthetics, serving as pattern templates for weavers. This practice probably started when these trade silks first came into the archipelago. Weaver women in many islands were apparently charmed by the striking design format of these shimmering silks and went on to create "patola's" of their own. Balinese versions of patolas mediated the spread of this cloth layout format into many Eastern Indonesian societies. A Lio version of a patola dating from the first half of the twentieth century was done in single ikat in warm brown and red tones. The Central Flores weaver who made this piece clearly had a sense of translating an image of a silk picture cloth framed in triangles and stripes, yet this sturdy cotton creation is entirely her own (fig. 3.8). What emerges is a Lio work, one of complete integrity. In southern Sumatra, the basic patola format has also structured significant sectors of cloth craft, as can be seen in numerous examples throughout this volume.

The second great challenge for an ikat dyer is the production of lush, intense hues. Dark, rusty red-brown; maroon; and blue-black are unusually hard to attain through vegetable dyeing of natural cotton, since the dyer must get the yarns to soak up hue with both intensity and color precision. A sarong from Lembata, east of Flores, illustrates a pinnacle of the dyer's art (fig. 3.9).

Indigo dyeing in some parts of the archipelago invokes hidden planes of religious meaning vis-à-vis gender and the special powers and secrets of women. Anthropologist Janet Hoskins discusses how this works in a society in West Sumba in

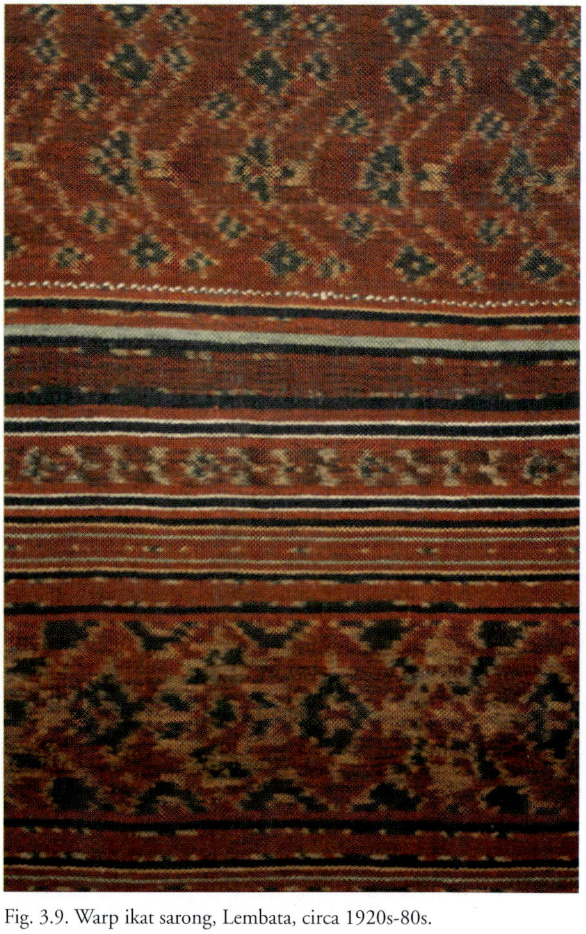

Fig. 3.9. Warp ikat sarong, Lembata, circa 1920s-80s.

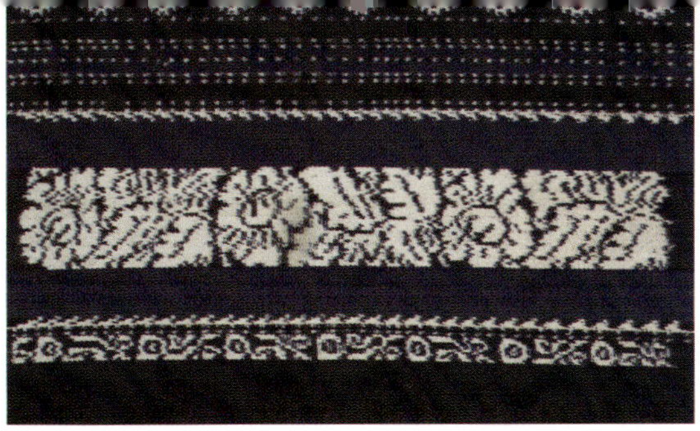

Fig. 3.10. Indigo-dyed ikat, from Savu.

"Why Do Ladies Sing the Blues? Indigo Dyeing, Cloth, Production, and Gender Symbolism in Kodi" (1989). Hoskins's study helps explain the frequent association found in Indonesian systems of thought among dyeing, weaving, and the cycles of reproduction and death (fig. 3.10). The putrid stink of the indigo leaves as they ferment in their round earthen dye pot is like the smell of death, Kodinese say. Only spiritually powerful people can come near a corpse or a smelly dye pot. Women past menopause possess these special powers and thus are the appropriate master dyers in Kodi.

The cotton threads soaking up the inky blue in the dye pot are also likened to the fetus in the womb in this society. The female body/fetal growth/cloth-in-process imageries overlap in many ways. For instance, if a young wife experiences an early miscarriage, older women may console her by saying that the baby was not to be, that the threads were not taking up the dyes anyway. Kodinese women past menopause, once again, are the chosen persons who can come close to the explosive powers of fetal growth (ones so close to death). Thus these women serve as expert midwives. Moreover, if a wife wishes to use an abortifacient, she consults the same women, the dyer-healers. The latter control various substances for transforming life into death and vice versa.

If a young wife has a baby who dies in its first days of life, Kodi adat (custom) says that the extremely young newborn is not a full person. No funeral need occur; the family buries the body without ceremony in the house yard. But if the mother secretly mourns the child, the midwife/dyer can again be consulted. She may counsel the woman to plant herbs atop the spot where the baby was buried. When the plants come up, the mother should clandestinely come out of the house at night and eat the green shoots. Some months later, when she is pregnant again, the lost child has come back to her in a way. But the mother keeps this a secret from the men in her family. They assume that it is they who control reproduction and the continuation of the lineage. Gender ideologies throughout Indonesia are in fact often full of contradiction, competitiveness, hidden conflict, and inconsistencies. The sexes sometimes have contrastive views of their status and spirituality.

In many parts of Indonesia the weaving of an ikat cloth on a loom is indeed women's craft, allied to her childbearing powers. When a new cloth is finished on the loom and the woman cuts it off with a knife, the terms used suggest cutting a baby's umbilical cord in many Indonesian languages. The motions of weaving cloth on a loom are also associated with women's beauty and allure and possibly also with the physical motions of sexual intercourse. The weaver's craft and her life as a woman generate the soft parts of existence: cloth, babies. These inevitably fall into tatters or die. Men's metalsmithing yields durables: hard, dense objects like swords, linked not to pregnancy, but to violence and war. Durable house treasures pass down through the generations; ikat textiles circulate among houses more in the present time. Cloth-metal songkets, as we shall see, occupy an interesting middle ground here.[4]

Beyond ikatting, traditional cloth has also been decorated in other ways in the Indonesian islands. *Pelangi* (or *plangi*, "rainbow" in Indonesian) involves gathering up little bunches of cloth and tying them off with string or a small palm fiber cord (fig. 3.11). This forms a resist when the textile is then dipped into a dye bath. A rainbow-colored array of striking circular patterns can be produced across a

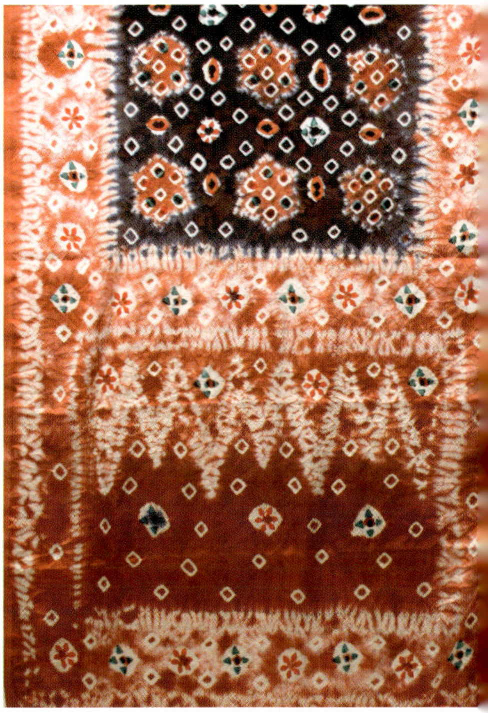

Fig. 3.11. Contempoary silk pelangi cloth, from the Fikri Koleksi, Palembang. 2006.

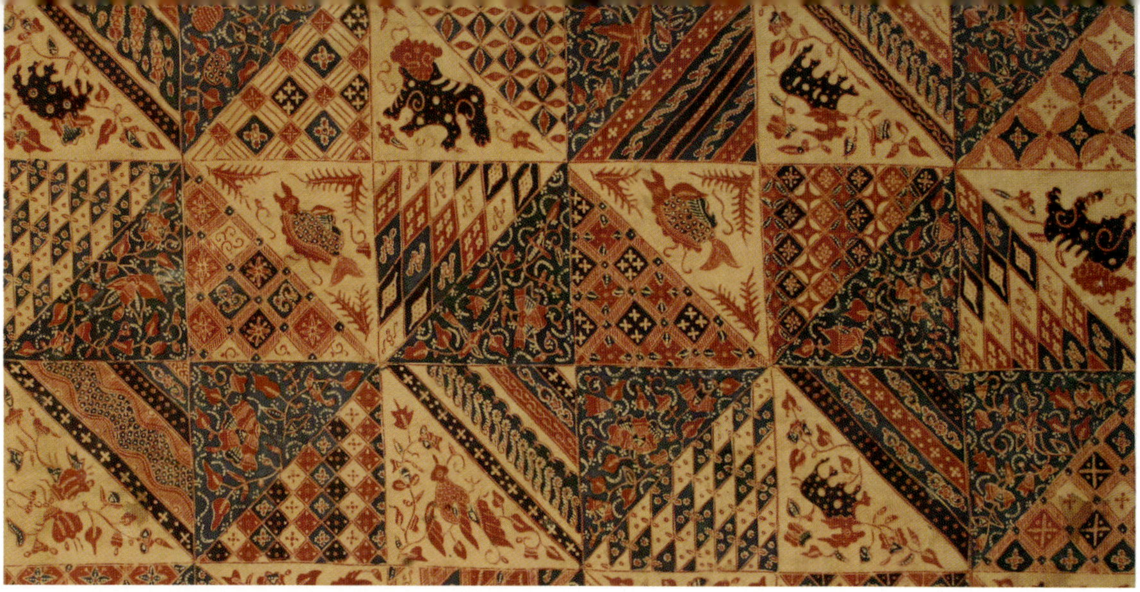

Fig. 3.12. North coast Java batik, from Lasem. Late 1800s to 1910. Note the fine detail on the animals.

cloth field in this way. Pelangi cloth is used today for upscale fashion wear in Jakarta ateliers but is also employed in ritual assemblages. In southern Sumatra it is sometimes combined with dark red songket in ceremonial displays and wedding costumes (bridal attendants wear pelangi silks in Palembang, for instance). In Bali pelangi is a crucial component of ritual dance costumes.

As is well known, wax-resist *batik* dispenses with the string or cord ties of ikat and pelangi entirely to build up designs (geometrics, pictures of flora and fauna, or a combination of both) through the application of melted wax to a plain cotton fabric stretched onto a frame (fig. 3.12). The batik craftsperson in Java is typically a woman, although men often do the dye-bath work. The batik artist first draws her intended design on the cotton in hot wax (a mixture of beeswax, paraffin, and resins). She applies this with a stylus, called a *canting*. This yields *batik tulis*, hand-"written" batik (Jasper and Pirngadie 1916). The wax dries and forms a resist; the cloth is immersed in a dye bath, and the parts under the hardened wax do not take up that particular color. The cloth is then boiled in a water bath to remove the wax (a part of the procedure often done by men). Many successive applications of hot wax to different sections of the cloth and many successive dye baths and boilings can yield intricate pictorial fields.

An intensification of the Central Javanese and north coast Javanese batikking industries in the period from the 1890s to the 1920s was directly linked to the increased availability of good-quality cotton cloth, which could be used as a batik base. Such cloth was often produced in Europe and imported to the Indies, an indication of the globalized associations between the industrialization of thread and cloth production in Europe and the elaboration of the so-called traditional arts in the Dutch East Indies.

There are many batikking subtraditions in Java and also in the Jambi and Bengkulu areas of southern Sumatra (fig. 3.13). And the ikat home industries in eastern Indonesia are almost too numerous to count. Both types of cloth are often used to represent and reinforce social difference. For example, until national times, Javanese batiks were particularly inflected for social status regarding a wearer's closeness to or distance from the traditional courts of Solo and Yogyakarta. Certain colors

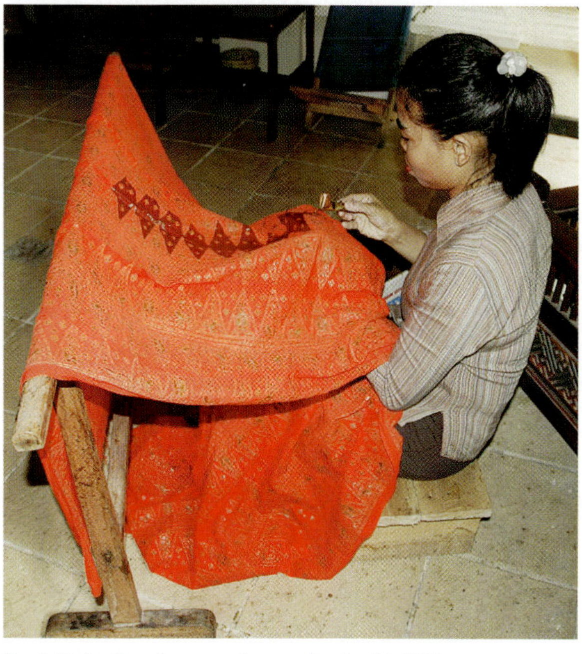

Fig. 3.13. Batik craftswoman in an atelier, Jambi, 2005.

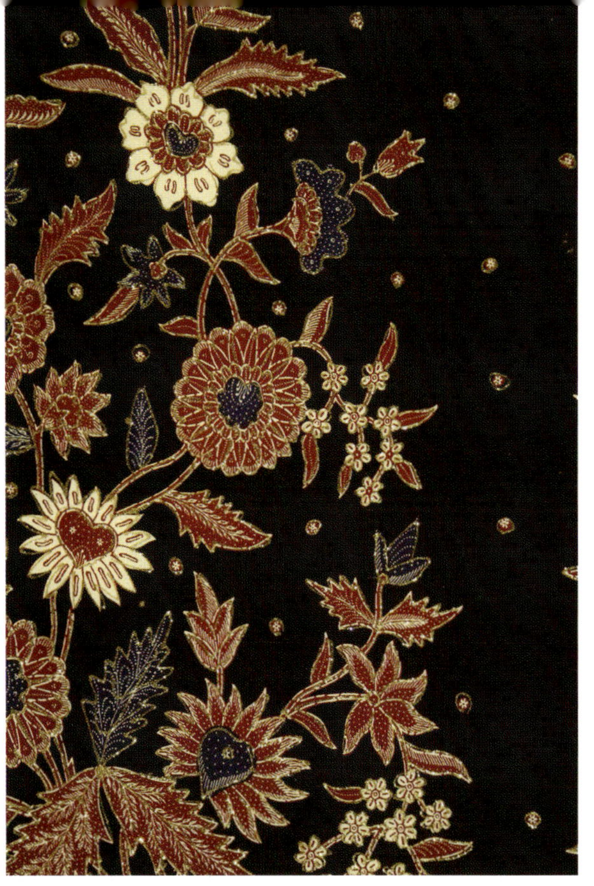

Fig. 3.14. Prada gold leaf, on a North coast Java batik. 2005.

and patterns were reserved for high aristocrats. In a system of indirect rule, the Dutch colonial state favored certain cooperative (or co-optable) aristocrats. The Dutch authorities fostered the development of "traditional Javanese court arts" such as gamelan orchestras and shadow puppetry as part of that process. This general approach, which also valorized batik as a traditional art of Java, led to an artificial intensification of some sectors of Javanese batik production, as traditional court wear.

Other domains of batik manufacture and use, however, also grew exuberantly between the 1870s and the 1920s. For instance, the fashion tastes and buying power of *peranakan* Chinese women (the Indonesian Chinese) in the Indies supported highly creative specialist batik ateliers in Cirebon and Pekalongan, along Java's north coast. Batik designs here included bright colors and clouds, flowers, and birds and other fauna.[5] The Indies' large Eurasian population based in the sugar and tea plantations and growing business cities such as Surabaya and Semarang also provided another market for these vibrant north coast batiks. These cloths prospered far from the old court centers.

Through the end of Dutch colonial times, Eastern Indonesian ikats were associated with smaller-scale states than these grand Javanese courts. Handspun cotton ikats in Sumba, Flores, Roti, and Timor were linked to the circulation of ritual goods between craft-producing villages and settlements where no weaving was done. A frequently encountered pattern in these small kingship societies also involved a noble lineage that would exact tribute in practical goods and ritual items from an array of leaders in subsidiary villages. The high nobles at the center would also work to secure the political loyalties (and warfare services) of petty aristocrats at the periphery of their realms by bestowing gifts on their followers. Ritual cloth exchange was part of these circuits.

Cotton ikats from societies in Sumba, Flores, Tanimbar, West Timor, and East Timor (a nation since 1999) also acted as integral parts of marriage exchange. They still do today, to an extent. In a typical pattern, a bride-giving household would bestow their daughter and certain fertility-enhancing gifts (handloomed textiles, woven by women) on the bridegroom's family. Completing the gift exchange and circulating in the other direction would be a flow of masculine gifts: weighty metal objects such as swords, knives, and gold ornaments, given as bridewealth. The pairing of these two opposed but complementary flows of crafted goods was said to empower the marriage and make it fertile. The exchange of practical goods such as cooked food and livestock on the hoof was also part of these traditional economies.

Outside Indic Java and Bali, exchange circuits involving cloth and metal dramatized political position with some precision. But the glint of gold, when it could be added to textiles, proved irresistible in many Indonesian court centers. Not surprisingly, the Indic kingdoms' status wear needs yielded other types of textiles beyond batik. *Prada* is an especially impressive textile of this sort (fig. 3.14). In prada, gold leaf or gold dust is affixed to the finished fabric, hugging the lines of a floral or geometric design, for instance. A batik can be enhanced by prada work if ritual wear calls for more sumptuousness. In the Indonesian fashion sector today, batik for ready-to-wear is also sometimes decorated using the prada technique, as are

Fig. 3.16. Manipulating the pattern sticks in songket weaving. Palembang, 2005.

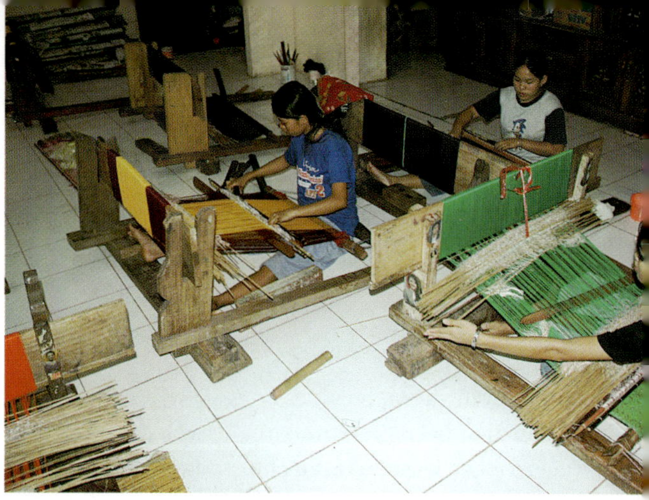

household decorative goods such as pillows.

Some of the ritual display textiles of southern Sumatran peoples such as the Kauer and the Paminggir take this basic idea of embellishing a cloth with gold to what can only be termed extremes, as can be seen in a *tapis* cloth by Paminggir weavers from Lampung. Tapis combines gold thread, mica chips, silk, appliqué work, and embroidery to yield a positively glowing body when the fabric is used by a girl or woman as a sarong.[6]

Songkets made into ceremonial wear or into fabrics to embellish ritual spaces, or used as tribute gifts to be exchanged among hierarchically ranked partners, were and are, if anything, even more shot through with social power than were the textile forms just described. Songkets glowed with power.

Sumatran songkets at the intersections of Asian textile arts

In the most basic sense, songkets are prestige cloths that are lavishly decorated with shining metallic threads added in as extra yarns across the weft. The threads form conventionalized patterns. Thus, songket is not simply cotton or silk that has been decorated with metal-wrapped threads. It uses a distinctive weaving technique called supplementary-weft weaving. In other words, a songket cloth's decorative threads are *extra*, or supplementary, design elements, added to the basic structure of the cloth, which could exist on its own as a stable fabric without the additional gold-thread elements (fig. 3.15).

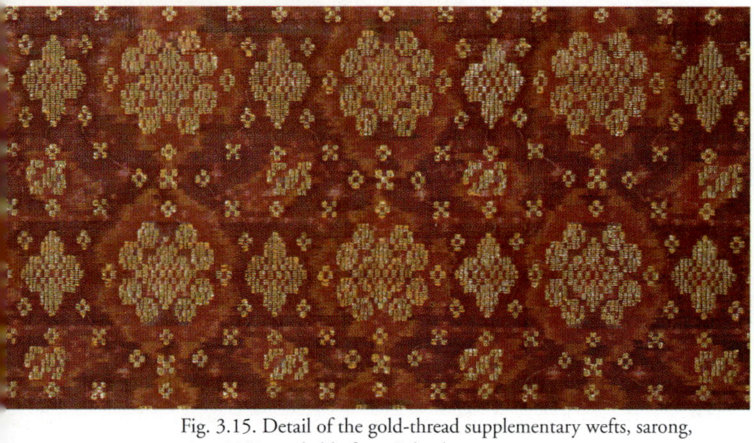

Fig. 3.15. Detail of the gold-thread supplementary wefts, sarong, circa 1850, probably from Palembang.

To insert the supplementary wefts and create the desired design across the developing cloth, a weaver must open up little sheds of space on the warped loom through which to throw the decorative thread. First, she inserts small pattern sticks (*lidi*, which are often made of bamboo) into the warps. The lidi hold down some of the threads and push others up a bit (fig. 3.16). The weaver then pushes in a thin wooden sword, following the pattern stick. She then turns this sword upward to create a tiny empty space, or shed. She shoots her metal-wrapped supplementary weft into this shed, horizontally across the cloth. She follows this with one or more additional decorative wefts before returning to one or several plain silk or cotton yarns. She then can go on to employ another pattern stick path for more metallic threads. She builds up the motifs on her growing songket by moving on to alternate pattern stick arrangements as she weaves over the next hours and days. Chapter 4 provides more details.

In especially fine eighteenth- and nineteenth-century songket weaving, a craftswoman would sometimes have to change pattern sticks every three, or even every two, threads. Literally dozens of pattern sticks would be inserted across the warps. Songket today tends to range from three threads per pattern stick to seven or even eight. This helps determine the fineness or roughness of the textile, according to weavers and Sumatran cloth dealers.

Historically most weavers of songkets in Sumatra have been women. This holds true to a degree today. Palembang and Jambi songket weaving is centered now mostly in shop floor arrangements superintended by entrepreneurial families. In this setting songkets are woven by women ranging in age from fifteen or so to the mid-forties. Keen eyesight is a factor here, so that age is a hindrance.

Until about the last ten years, songket weaving in Pandai Sikek, West Sumatra, was also almost exclusively a woman's craft, but today a gender shift is occurring. Some men, such as Ibu Us's husband, Bapak Herman, are taking up the craft. They are often tutored by their wives, and they weave to earn money to supplement the family income—the exact main reason why Pandai Sikek women weave today. Some male weavers living in Pandai Sikek are quite expert. Many take pride in the arm strength a man can bring to the task of forcefully pushing down the newly added wefts.

Another group of men who are now joining the ranks of Pandai Sikek weavers are young male university students. Typically they have learned to weave by watching and working with older female relatives. The youths weave in the village on holidays from school, and some even take their looms to their rented rooms in Padang near their universities. A good midrange songket *stel* (that is, a pair of cloths, including a sarong and a shoulder cloth) today costs between 1,300,000 and 1,500,000 rupiah when it is purchased in a weaving co-op or a luxury goods shop in Bukittinggi. In early 2006 this was the equivalent of US $145 to $167. Even after subtracting the broker's fee, songket weaving by university students of both sexes makes economic sense.

For an enterprising college student to move a Minangkabau songket loom to the city of Padang is no small undertaking. These are bulky frame looms at which the weaver sits on a narrow wooden bench (see Summerfield and Summerfield 1999: 215, fig. 8.46, for an archival photograph showing two women from Kotogadang Village working together at a frame loom in about 1920). This type of loom has the benefit of allowing the craftsperson to keep her threads tightly and evenly spaced (fig. 3.17).

Frame looms for any sort of weaving are rare in outer-island Indonesia. The songkets of Jambi, Palembang, and East Bali, in fact, are woven on backstrap looms. As we have seen, this is the classic, historically much older outer-island technology for producing handloomed cotton cloths (fig 3.18). Some textile researchers, in fact, assert that the persistence of backstrap loom technology in an imported form such as songket weaving is evidence that Indonesian weaving is exceedingly conservative (Gittinger 1979: 13-14). When metallic-thread supplementary weft techniques came to places like East Bali, it was apparently simply adapted to the core, favorite backstrap loom, which had long been used for producing tie-resist cottons.

West Sumatra's distinctiveness in relying on frame looms suggests historical connections between Minangkabau weaving and that of parts of mainland Southeast Asia such as Cambodia and Laos, where frame looms sometimes predominate in court-based cloth technologies. In one view of the textile's history, songket weaving entered Kelantan and Terengganu Malay courts as early as 1500, due in part to the arrival of royal brides from Pattani, in what is today southern Thailand. These aristocratic women may have brought along retinues of weaver-servants who knew how to make metallic-thread cloth of this general type, probably for court wear and court dances. The circulation of high-status women among Malay kingdoms as brides in strategically arranged marriages may well have

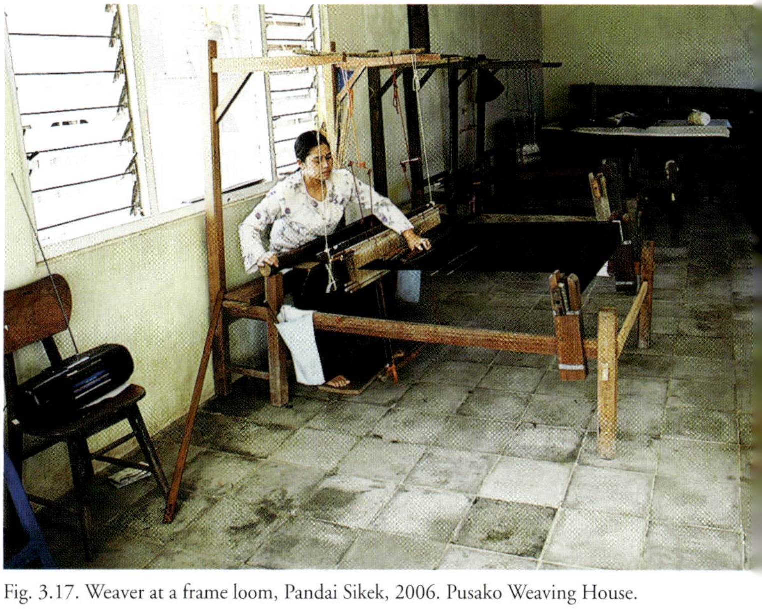

Fig. 3.17. Weaver at a frame loom, Pandai Sikek, 2006. Pusako Weaving House.

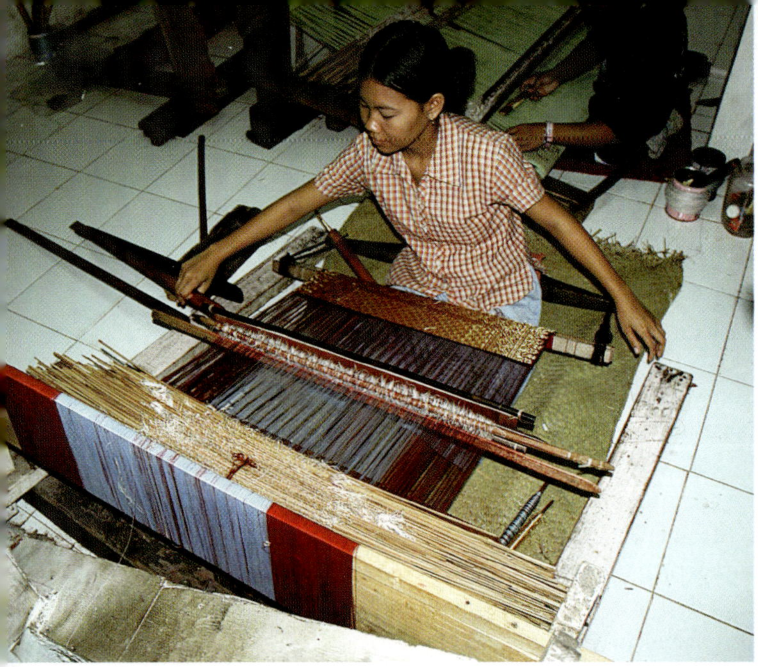

Fig. 3.18. Weaver at a backstrap loom, Palembang, 2005. Fikri Koleksi.

been an important carrier of songket technology throughout the region.

Sumatran songket handweaving industries also have pronounced connections to the court arts of the economically ambitious Malay sultanates of the eighteenth and nineteenth centuries. These small states included ones in Pattani and in Kelantan and Terengganu, in what is today Malaysia. These polities were connected by commerce, Islam, and artistic exchange to successive Malay world kingdoms stretching from Aceh to the pepper-trading states along the coasts of the Straits of Malacca. Also part of this artistically intense Malay court world was the eighteenth-century Malay kingdom in the Riau Archipelago. Merchants and aristocrats in these Muslim sultanates grew rich by trading cloth, gold, pepper, spices, and aromatic resins with other parts of Asia and with Europe. Malay court literature also flourished in these Muslim kingdoms along the waterways and seacoasts of the Malay Peninsula and Sumatra.

In the 1800s songket weaving prospered to an unusual degree amid this bustling commercial universe lining the shores of the straits and pushing inland up into the Minangkabau highlands, via the east coast's great muddy-colored navigable rivers. These nineteenth-century developments built on much earlier trade ties with India, as noted.

Kain Macau: Colonial-era Songkets and the Allure of Distance

European colonialism brought wrenching changes to small Sumatran traditional states in Jambi, Palembang, Deli, the Riau Islands, and the Minangkabau highlands. The latter was of great interest to the Dutch as a promising coffee-growing area and as a potential market for European goods. Palembang and Jambi were pepper-growing powerhouses and trade hubs for wide riverine regions. Deli's economic history was linked to infusions of international capital used to build great tobacco and tea plantations in the hills outside Medan.

In the nineteenth century some of Sumatran songket's gold-wrapped threads came from Macau, near Hong Kong, giving rise to this textile type's once-common sobriquet among Minangkabau weaver women: *kain Macau* (Macau cloth). Textile scholar Mattiebelle Gittinger has noted with insight that one of the defining features of this type of rich fabric is its allure of foreignness and exoticism for Sumatran publics (Gittinger 1979: 79, 102-113). Songket's very materials—silk, for many of these cloths, and gold-wrapped yarn—had to be imported into these societies from afar, from "beyond the seas."

The colonial-era songket took on associations with foreign travel and the social cachet that implies in many Sumatran societies. Owning and wearing a songket thus denoted an air of sophistication beyond the village norm, a palpable connection to other lands—often a way of burnishing status in Sumatra, where migrating to distant cities for trade or going on the hajj pilgrimage to Mecca greatly adds to a person's social standing. A prime Sumatran way to claim a level of experience beyond that of one's neighbor is to travel for trade to Java, the Riau Archipelago, or the Malay Peninsula—that is, in the Indonesian phrase, to *merantau*, to go to the *rantau*, or to travel beyond the home region. Such migrants come home for occasions such as the Idul Fitri celebration closing Ramadan, the fasting month. The stories they tell about distant lands add luster to their standing in their home communities. Songket cloths implicitly do the same, as they are woven of the stuff of overseas travel.

Once woven, songket textiles themselves have tendencies to travel, to merantau. For instance,

Palembang songkets are found in some house treasuries in Minangkabau. Some Palembang cloths have traveled even farther afield. For instance, far to the north, in Tapanuli, in the southern Batak rural regions around the town of Sipirok, Angkola Batak brides are adorned in red sarongs. These are considered part of Angkola adat, but the oldest cloths come from Minangkabau and Palembang.

In the mid- and late 1800s in many parts of the Malay world, income from colonial-era commerce was pumped back into the arts of ostentation by elite Malay and Sumatran families. This often resulted in magnificent textiles. Large imports of silk yarns from China and plied cotton threads from Britain during this period allowed weavers in places such as Terengganu and to produce increasingly intricate songket textiles for thriving local and interregional sumptuary markets. When Dutch colonial state trade policies resulted in a flood of cheap European manufactured cloth into Sumatra in the mid-1800s, local production of exquisite songkets for ritual wear experienced a boom. As noted, the rough imported European goods did not satisfy exacting Sumatran needs for ceremonial wear. Sumatran weavers benefited from this attempt to manipulate the cloth economy to sell more imported goods to Indies publics. As mentioned, a similar upswing in traditional textile production using gold thread occurred in British Malaya in the 1800s for similar reasons (M. Mohamad 1996). British state trade policy led to an inundation of the Malay market with low-quality imported manufactured cloth, which was rejected for ritual wear by upwardly striving, status-conscious Malay elite families (and ones that wanted to become elite). An intensification of Malay songket artistry ensued.

The postcolonial experience in Indonesia and Malaysia has transformed songkets and songket weaving yet again. This time the craft trajectories (which have been quite various) have been toward a constriction of sheer numbers of weaving villages but also toward an increase in the shop production of these cloths, as opposed to strictly home-based weaving. And songket weaving has fractured into an array of creative new forms. This process has again followed the contours of Southeast Asian commerce and weaver women's (and men's) genius.

Songket and success: from emblem of status to token of "tradition"

As gold textiles, Sumatran songkets have always been bound up with the representation of riches and social position. This is so despite the fact that Islamic doctrine in places such as Bukittinggi celebrates the modest, alms-giving social person, not the social grandee.

In the actual family lives of many West and South Sumatran Muslims, songket wear valorizes social presence and clout and announces that the household has disposable income. When wealth levels increased considerably in late Dutch colonial times among some favored aristocrats and successful pepper, spice, coffee, and cloth merchants, Sumatran luxury wear involving songkets expanded in sheer numbers of textiles, and it also intensified in quality in some regions. Weaving villages produced extraordinary specialty products: the ceremonial belts of Pitalah and Pariangan, for instance, and the allover gold-thread *balapak* textiles of Kotogadang, to mention just two examples.

In West Sumatra, the area that is in many ways the heartland of songket weaving, the gold-draped body became if anything even more splendiferous during late colonialism. This upswing in songket weaving and ritual wear intensity was powered by Sumatrans' commercial success. This occurred in acknowledged or unacknowledged collaboration with the Dutch colonial project in the Indies—with the establishment of a forced cultivation system for coffee and sugar, with the capital intensification of some sectors of tropical agriculture and the establishment of plantations, and with the monetization of several sectors of indigenous economies.

By the mid-1800s songket textiles, valued for their loveliness and weaving quality, had become

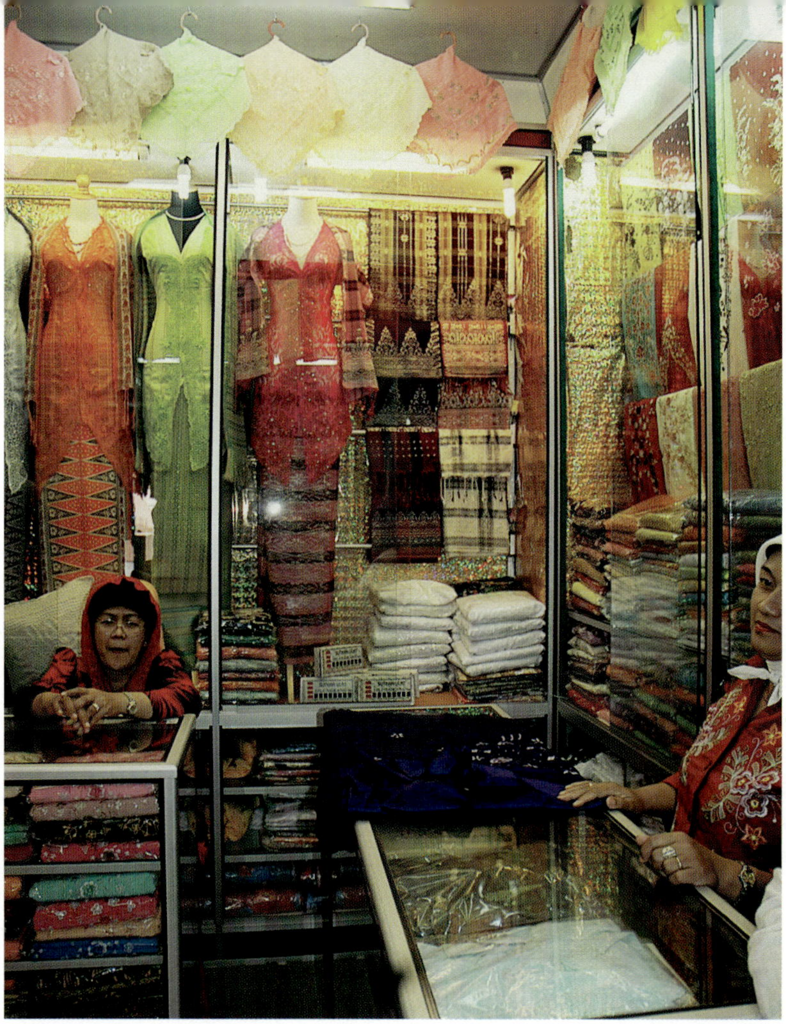

Fig. 3.19. Bukittinggi market scene, 2005. A profusion of glimmering goods for sale characterizes the town's shopping cultures.

central to (in fact, constitutive of) the arts of wealth of the Minangkabau people. This system of display was also one of competition among privileged families and among craftswomen. All this fostered superb weaving at the level of home-based craft. By the mid- to late 1800s the gold-thread cloths of such West Sumatran specialty textile-producing villages as Pitalah, Pariangan, Batipuah, Muaralabuah, Kotogadang, Tanjung Sungayang, and Pandai Sikek had attained astounding levels of weaving excellence. A few villages specialized even further, weaving songkets with valuable, highly breakable ramin fiber, made from the stringy interior surface of bark from a shrub.

It is a telling fact of West Sumatran textile history, however, that today only one of these craft centers still has looms and produces songkets. This is Pandai Sikek, Ibu Us's home village. The town of Silungkang, in south central West Sumatra, is also a songket-weaving community today. Silungkang songkets are well woven but rarely attain the stunning qualities of Pandai Sikek cloths; more mechanization of weaving is also present in Silungkang than in the smaller village. In the small city of Payakumbuh, songket weaving is being regenerated today to a degree. Songket artistry is clearly a dynamic historical phenomenon.

With independence from the Netherlands after the 1945–49 national revolution, the Indies became the Republic of Indonesia. There are upsetting songket stories from West Sumatra from *revolusi* times—the period when ancestral houses in the village of Pandai Sikek were burned and many old songkets were lost. Other songkets were hidden in bamboo tubes in the ground when families fled to the slopes of Mount Singgalang to escape the Dutch and Dutch-backed military forces. Some of these songkets survived.

A subtle shift in the Indonesian interpretation of songket cloth took place during the New Order regime of President Suharto, the former military general who remained in power from 1965 to 1998. That is, some songkets emerged in the 1970s, 1980s, and 1990s as tokens of rather broadly defined ethnic traditions within the nation's ethnic imaginary, under the national motto "Unity from Diversity." This shift was connected directly to changes in the weaving character of songket.

As all observers know, weaving a single songket that includes a great deal of exacting gold-thread supplementary-weft placement demands months of labor time. In home-based handlooming in Pandai Sikek, mothers and daughters generally work on a songket only a few hours a day, if that, although shop-based weaving today has shifted toward a fuller workday. A finished songket, whatever the case, advertises a large investment of time that the buyer has been able to purchase for what are clearly nonpractical display uses.

Beyond this, songkets woven as men's or women's sarongs, ceremonial belts, shoulder cloths, or head wraps gleam and glitter (fig. 3.19), since the metal foils used to wrap the supplementary-weft yarns are shiny if relatively low-grade gold and (more rarely) silver. With its sparkly appearance—and its weighty elegance when wrapped as a sarong and worn by walkers in slow, majestic processions—this specific type of ritual fabric virtually shouts out social privilege (fig. 3.20). This was true in anxious ways for some Sumatran populations in New Order times, with that regime's overblown nationalist rhetoric about Indonesia's peoples all moving swiftly and amicably toward *pembangunan*, economic development. But the monetary proceeds of pembangunan were tipped unfairly toward Javanese elites, many Sumatrans felt. Some Sumatran government officials and their friends *did* enjoy an upswing in personal wealth during the Suharto era, however, and when such favored ones invested in songket finery, other Sumatrans grew resentful.

New Order nationalism posited an archipelagic ethnic diversity that the state conceptualized in cultural terms, not in political ones. Societies like Minangkabau were reconceptualized from the state center as quaint, folkloric, and touristic—not as political entities that might object to state control of their own fortunes. Within this rhetoric, both newly woven and antique songkets from the Minangkabau highlands and from the old Malay sultanates along Sumatra's east coast were often understood, and extolled, by both their weaving communities and by outsiders as "traditional" heritage cloths. Songkets such as the old one illustrated in figure 2.0, page 10, came to be celebrated as extraordinary textiles of "ancient" origins, cloths handed down through the generations and designated for use by moderns for special occasions tied to old customs. Yet different groups manifestly had different access to fine newly woven songkets, due to structural inequities of the Suharto regime. Pleasure in looking at excellent songkets acquired new complexity.

Such gleaming heritage cloths were often seen during this time as "carrying customs," so to speak, and also as marking wearers' particular ethnic identity within multiethnic modern Indonesia. Only certain peoples wear songket, this logic went: the Minangkabau, the Acehnese, the Malays of Palembang, the Deli sultanate people of east coast Sumatra near Medan. These and a few others are the ones who "own" songket wear. In Malaysia there is a similar discourse about cloth, time, and identity (and cultural authenticities). In Malaysia specific songket types and modes of tying headgear are said to denote a wearer's precise sultanate origins. Since songket cloth is still woven today in some of these regions—including Kelantan, Terengganu, and Johor—newly produced gold textiles of the same general sort can and do share in this patina of tradition. Thus, for instance, promotional materials for Malaysia Airlines feature photographs of comely young women attired in Malaysian songket sarongs and shoulder cloths. Apparently these women are put forth to represent the Malay portion of the national population but also, in a more general sense, to denote "Malay traditions" for potential buyers of Malaysia Airlines tickets. It is interesting in this context that Indonesia's national airline, Garuda Indonesia, outfits its cabin staff in batik costumes and in Western-style business suits set off with batik scarves.

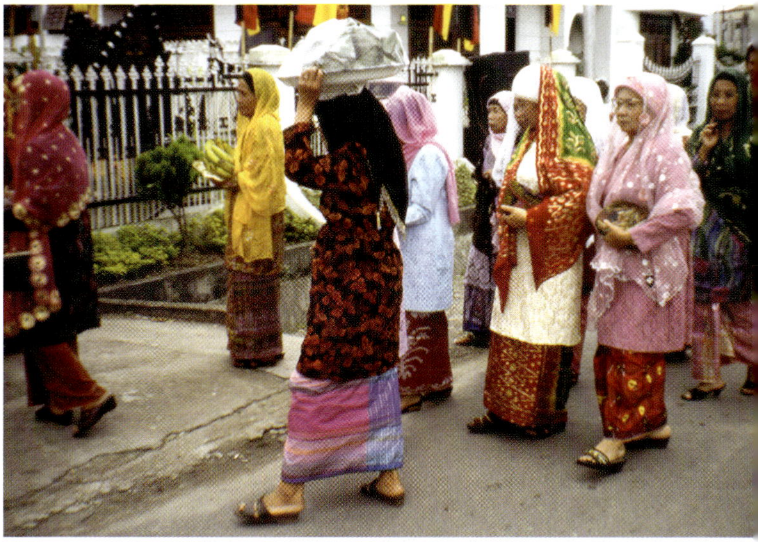

Fig. 3.20. Wedding procession in ornate finery, 1995. Bukittinggi, West Sumatra.

Beyond New Order culturalist propaganda, there was truth to some of these claims about songket and "customs." For instance, Minangkabau women in the New Order years often did wear distinctively designed, dyed, and tied songket headdresses that announced their particular village identities or their regional backgrounds. A woman from the Batu Sangkar area, for example, would sometimes don a songket textile tied in a particular manner. Knowledgeable onlookers interpreted that ritual fashion as a clear sign that she or her ancestors are from that town. Moreover, late eighteenth- and early nineteenth-century songkets from superb weaving villages such as Kotogadang and Tanjung Sungayang in West Sumatra do employ certain motifs that have centuries-old pedigrees. Accepting a songket cloth, or songket weaving in more general terms, as "traditional" in any straightforward way can, however, be problematic when one is looking at songket in the last several decades.

In New Order and also post-Suharto Indonesia, as in the colonial Indies, ideas about ancient origins of regalia, "customary ways," and even such blunt ethnic tags as "Minangkabau" are historically complex claims. This is so as well in international art-collecting circles and in the antique textile trade in Southeast Asia and worldwide. Ideas about a specific textile's traditional nature are social constructions enmeshed in the claimant's political, economic, and biographical circumstances. In these ways, a "traditional" songket can be thoroughly imbued with social ideology—as an emblem of traditions but also as a sign that self-conscious Southeast Asian moderns are "being traditional" when they wear such special garb. Two examples will show some of songket's inherently social character in Indonesia today.

The Batu Sangkar head wrap mentioned above is not as stable an illustration of material object and social identity as one might surmise. In the mid-1990s, in weddings in the West Sumatran subprovincial capital and business city of Bukittinggi, some Minangkabau families had the money to stage large, multiday nuptials for their sons and daughters. This was so particularly for daughters. Since Minangkabau kinship revolves around ideas of matrilineal descent, in which family ancestral houses and house treasuries pass (ideally, at least) from mothers to daughters and on to those daughters' own daughters, it is crucial that young women of prominent houses marry, and marry appropriately. Men are visitors, in a sense, in their homes of marriage; a man's own core house is that of his mother, aunts, and sisters. This residential system has been undergoing sweeping changes since at least the mid-1800s, and the typical city and town household today is structured around a married couple.

The size and sumptuary ambition of the 1990s Minangkabau weddings in the Bukittinggi area were fueled economically by a growth in the Indonesian middle class in Sumatran cities such as Padang and also in Java. In the 1990s socially ascendant Minangkabau households had gained their wealth through various means: through family members' jobs in the professions, through selling things (*berdagang*), and through business acumen in fields such as construction. Famously in Indonesia, selling things is a prime career for Minangkabau men. They are urged by kin to go to the lands beyond the home regions to seek their fortunes before marriage. As we shall see, Minangkabau women are also intensively engaged in business activities. Some money also came into family coffers through government positions in the provincial administration and through those jobs' attendant opportunities for accepting bribes from petitioners for government favors or aid. Money also arrived in Minangkabau households during this time through the sale, by some, of ancestral songkets to art dealers, who would then broker the old cloths to collectors from Jakarta, Singapore, or beyond.

New wealth from all these sources infused a Bukittinggi small boom in "traditional Minangkabau" ceremonies in the 1990s. Ironically, the modern Indonesian circumstance of the rise of a new middle class intensified local interest in "being Minangkabau" in West Sumatra. There were several public stages for this, but perhaps most prominent among them were two: the weddings of favored daughters and a newly passionate interest in songket ritual wear itself, for some.

In the 1990s brides from wealthy families were often women in their twenties or early thirties who had garnered prestigious academic degrees, including undergraduate and advanced degrees in such fields as accounting, medicine, and dentistry. When a lineage segment of a matrilineal clan hosted the marriage festivities for a young woman of such accomplishment, her immediate family would sometimes not stop at simply dressing the bride and relevant members of the wedding party in the matrilineage's traditional songket headdresses, with their distinctive regional modes of wrapping the cloth on the women's heads. Instead, they would launch into an almost giddy parade of traditional Minangkabau headdresses during the reception part of the ceremony, dubbed the "resepsi." They would do this by hiring troupes of "traditional Minangkabau" folkloric dancers. These young women, who were usually employed putting on "authentic" Minangkabau dances for tourists (the tourist economy in Bukittinggi had not yet collapsed), would come to the wedding to help serve food during the reception. They would also help the hosts receive the fancily wrapped wedding gifts by logging them into satin notebooks. The dancers would often number a dozen or so, and each would be carefully costumed in the distinctive ceremonial songket clothing and head tie of a particular region of the Minangkabau highlands (fig. 3.21) or coastal Padang. So there would be a young woman dressed as a Batu Sangkar bride, another attired as a Payakumbuh newlywed, and so on. The multiple bridal bodies thus served as public carriers for the "inherited customs" or adat ways of the various Minangkabau *luak*, or home domains or lands.

In such weddings, the bride/wedding attendant wearing a Batu Sangkar headdress could be seen as an actress playing the role of someone from an entirely different region of West Sumatra. The social lability of Minangkabau cloth, clothing, and customs in these weddings was sometimes more unstable (and inventive) still. In the wedding shown here, for instance, the dancer-actresses had been hired by the bridegroom's family, not the bride's (fig. 3.21). This family was one particularly invested in celebrating Minangkabau customs, for the young man's father and mother were preeminent Minangkabau art dealers in old songkets for national and international clienteles, including museums. The parents, in fact, were Sutan Madjo Indo and his wife, Ibu Elly, the prominent Bukittinggi art dealers mentioned several times above. They are also serious collectors of Sumatran art.

The second example of the exquisitely modern Indonesian (and Indonesian middle-class) character of some Sumatran songket textiles comes from

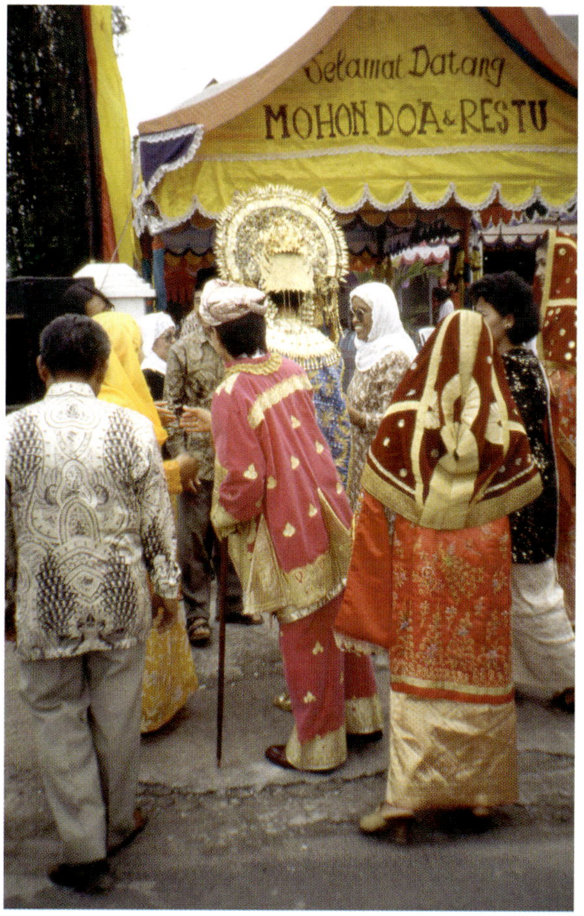

Fig. 3.21. Bridal party, Bukittinggi, 1996.

Pandai Sikek Village itself. Weavers there often consign their finished cloths to weaving co-ops, which are generally run by Minangkabau women based either in the village itself or in shops along the main road leading into Bukittinggi. Pandai Sikek songkets today vary in quality and level of weaving ambition. There are the small, square sampler-type songkets made for the domestic and international tourist market, which cost the rupiah equivalent of about $20. Next are midpriced songket sarongs and shoulder cloths for the domestic Indonesian Minangkabau-style wedding and ceremonial occasion market. These sets range in price between the equivalent of $80 and $250. Far beyond this in price and weaving quality are the $500 to $1,500 silk songket sarong/shoulder cloth sets. These extraordinary high-end gold cloths are bought by wealthy West Sumatran or *rantau* Minangkabau living in cities such as Jakarta or Bandung. A few prosperous tourists from overseas sometimes also buy midlevel and top-quality songkets. As we have already seen from Ibu Us's trade, some of the most expensive and very best Pandai Sikek songkets in silk use "antique motifs" (*motif antik*) taken from the 1820s and 1830s. Weavers work from fragments of the actual old cloths.

One prominent weaving cooperative is run by an especially market-savvy retired weaver in her eighties, Ibu Sanuar. Her equally accomplished businessman son Bapak Adyan is her associate. Their most favored, expert weavers are given old fragments or pattern templates on graph paper of the desired motifs, which are more than one hundred years old, to follow at their looms. At the high end of Ibu Sanuar's songkets for sale are specially commissioned ones in 100 percent silk for upper-middle-class older women living in Jakarta. Some of these women come from the extremely tradition-conscious village of Kotogadang (fig. 3.22).

This large and manifestly rich settlement is located across the Ngarai Canyon from Bukittinggi. Set amid wide paddy lands, Kotogadang is nationally famous as the home of many early nationalist leaders, such as Sutan Sjahrir. The village is equally famous locally as a prideful craft village where men produce silver filigree jewelry and women and girls hook lace and sew embroidered satin bridal scarves. Until about the 1920s Kotogadang was also a great songket-weaving village and a gold-working center. But no looms are active today, and no gold jewelry is made in Kotogadang. Formal schooling and the salaried jobs that can flow from that have gained precedence over older forms of craftwork. The many Kotogadang people living in the rantau, in places such as Jakarta,

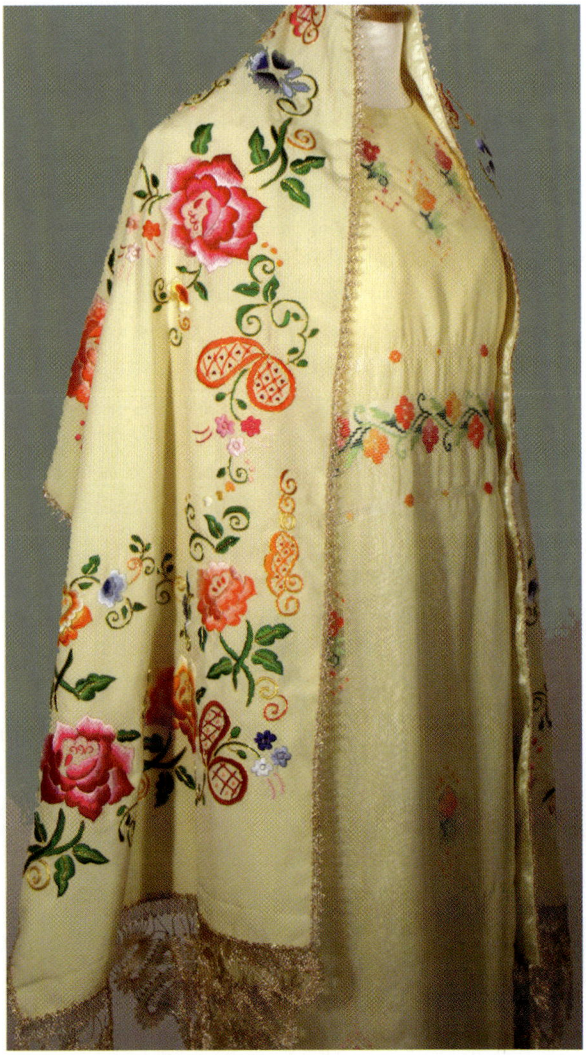

Fig. 3.22. A woman's ceremonial ensemble, specific to the village of Kotogadang, West Sumatra. 2006.

are a social world away from village looms. Some of these families have sold their old songkets. But Kotogadang high-society people in the diaspora still need copious numbers of Kotogadang-style songkets for weddings. So where do they get them? Some borrow them from others who still have some of the great old gold textiles, while others commission new Kotogadang-style songkets from Pandai Sikek weavers. These customers buy their cloths from weaving-cooperative entrepreneurs such as Ibu Sanuar and Bapak Adyan in Pandai Sikek.

Village tradition is thus being manufactured today through these microprocesses of so-called "replica" cloth commissions, special-order weaving, and subtle marketing strategies. Indonesia's huge print culture is also crucial here: Kotogadang antiquarian writers have recently published excellent guides to their village's traditional costumes. Some among their Jakarta contingent also publish a glossy magazine, a monthly called *Canang*. Its focus? What else? Old ways and present-day success stories, of villagers both at home and abroad.

NOTES

1. There are a large number of rewarding, accessible studies of the remarkable textiles of Southeast Asia and of Indonesian societies within that. Notable among the major studies are Gittinger 1990, 2005; Gittinger ed. 1980, 1989; Gittinger and Lefferts 1992; Kahlenberg 1977; and the aforementioned Fraser-Lu 1990 and Maxwell 2003, 2004. Maxwell 2003: 33-138 offers a rewarding discussion of insular Southeast Asian textile history; see also Peter Bellwood's classic *Man's conquest of the Pacific; The prehistory of Southeast Asia and Oceania* (1979). For textile traditions of mainland Southeast Asia, see especially Gillian Green's *Traditional textiles of Cambodia; Cultural threads and material heritage* (2003) and Susan Conway, *Silken threads, lacquer thrones; Lan Na court textiles* (2001).
2. For background information on Indonesian ritual ornaments, see Susan Rodgers, *Power and gold; Jewelry from Indonesia, Malaysia, and the Philippines* (1985).
3. Numerous monographs explore this type of thought scheme in Indonesian cultures. Excellent examples are Adams 1969, on East Sumba, and Feldman 1979, on South Nias. See also the essays in James Fox, ed. 1980, *The flow of life; Essays on Eastern Indonesia*.
4. A 2003 exhibition at the Iris and B. Gerald Cantor Art Gallery at the College of the Holy Cross, Worcester, Massachusetts, explored this metal/cloth interaction. See Rodgers 2003. See also an earlier Cantor Art Gallery catalogue, Rodgers 1995b.
5. See Harper 2000 for color illustrations of such cloths and good archival photographs.
6. See Maxwell 2003:112 (two lovely tapis cloths from Lapang) for illustrations of such southern Sumatran cloths. Maxwell 2004 also has excellent illustrations and descriptions of such ornate sarongs. See also Paul Taylor and Lorraine Aragon 1991:145.

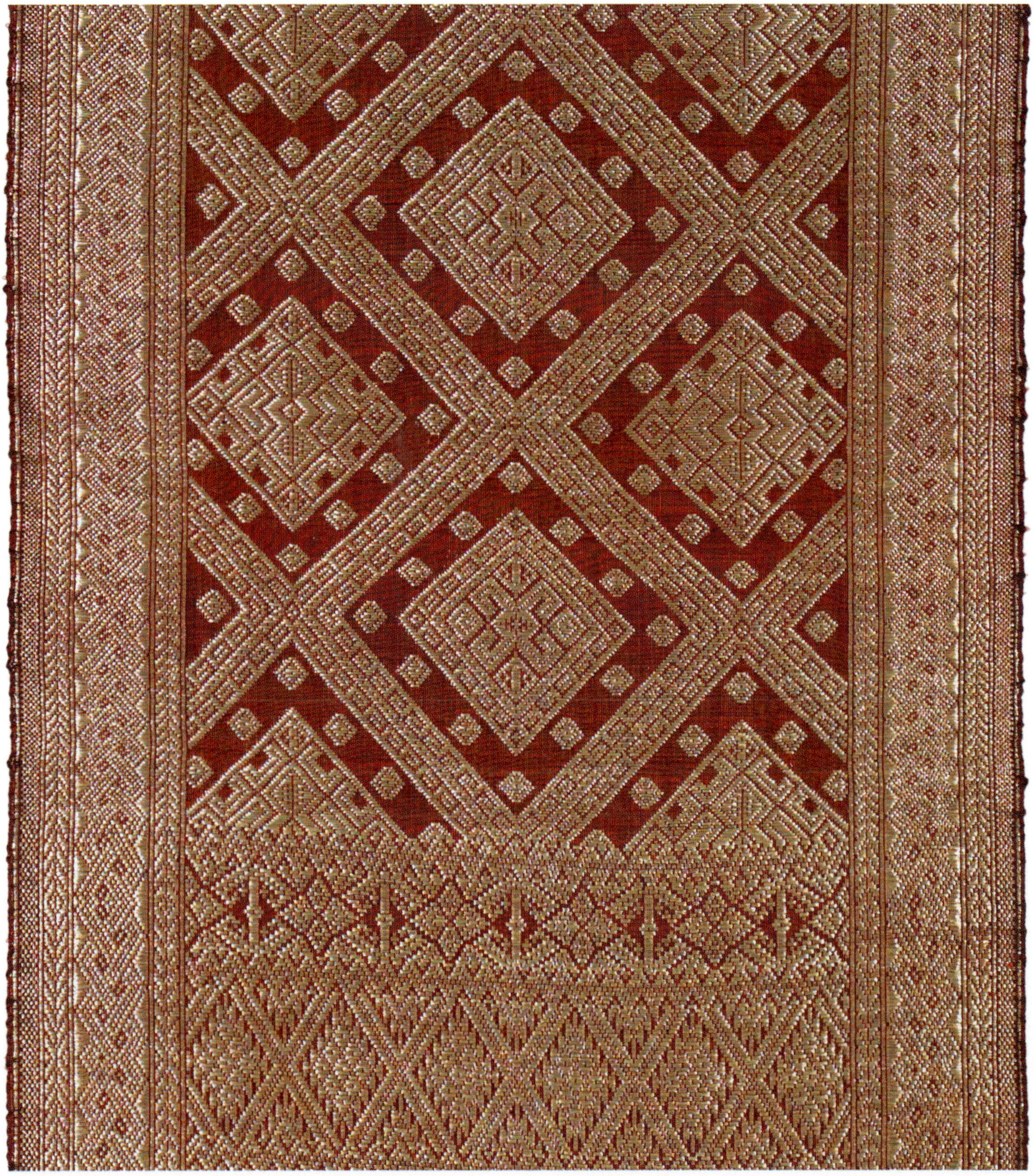

Fig. 4.0. Detail, newly woven shoulder cloth in which the weaver has purposely invoked old motifs, upon the instructions of her broker. Pusako Weaving House, Pandai Sikek, 2006. Iris and B. Gerald Cantor Art Gallery Study Collection.

4. What lies behind a songket textile?

Anne Summerfield and John Summerfield

How do skills and materials that are compounded during weaving affect the quality of a finished textile? What makes a textile superior or even great? In whose eyes? How does cultural tradition influence a beholder's judgment of beauty? Of quality? This chapter explores some answers to these questions, albeit narrowly, limiting consideration to songket weavings of Sumatra and Malaysia. There is near-universal agreement, as might be expected, that regardless of the weaver's geographic location, fine materials and skilled weaving are essential if a finished textile is to be judged excellent. The artistry, the visual and tactile impact of how the materials and skills are used, may, however, be judged differently in different cultures.

The discussion that follows examines types of thread or yarn typically woven into songkets and the skills and techniques required to dye and weave those yarns. Some suggestions are also made regarding how use of materials, techniques, and traditional or social expectations might affect judgment of the quality of a weaving. Finally we appraise the quality of a contemporary songket in terms of objective and subjective measures of excellence developed as a result of the discussion.

Materials used to weave songkets

Seven different types of thread or yarn were or are used to weave songkets in Sumatra and Malaysia: metallic-wrapped (gold or silver) thread, bast (a type of plant-based fiber), silk, cotton, polyester, rayon, and Mylar plastic.

Metallic-Wrapped Threads

A defining characteristic of songket textiles is supplementary weft patterning executed with metallic-wrapped threads. The supplementary weaving process forms those threads into motifs as the textile is woven. The overall patterning of a textile, the totality of motifs formed by weaving techniques and any images created by dyeing, is called the pattern format.

The use of gold thread in textiles has a long history. The King James Version of the Bible, Exodus 39, states:

> And of the blue, and purple, and scarlet, they made cloths of service to do service in the holy *place*, and made holy garments for Aaron; as the LORD commanded Moses.
>
> And he made the ephod *of* gold, blue, and scarlet, and fine twined linen.
>
> And they did beat the gold into thin plates, and cut it *into* wires to work *it* in the blue, and in the purple, and in the scarlet, and in the fine linen, *with* cunning work.

The historical record of use of gold thread in Indonesia and Malaysia is somewhat sketchy. Grace Selvanayagam writes (1990: xviii) that songket was introduced to Malaysia from India through Sumatra's Palembang and Jambi, probably originating during the time of Srivijaya (seventh to eleventh centuries). Suwati Kartiwa reports that Muslim traders brought gold and silver thread into Indonesia after the fall of the Majapahit kingdom in the sixteenth century (Kartiwa 1986: 5). Ruurdje Laarhoven states that the Dutch East India Company (VOC) traded Chinese gold thread to Indonesia "at least as early as the early seventeenth century" (personal correspondence, 1992).

Sumatran weavers call some kinds of gold thread *makau*, a reference to the island of Macao, a Portuguese settlement off the east coast of China. Macao was a flourishing center of trade with Japan that eventually shipped great quantities of Chinese raw white silk, gold thread, and other Asian and Indian commodities to Europe, the Spice Islands, and other Asian destinations.

Of the various forms of gold and silver thread woven into songket, two basic types predominate in textiles woven before the mid-twentieth century.[1]

Type 1

Gold or silver leaf is applied to paper by first floating the leaf on the surface of water and then lifting it from underneath onto a sheet of paper.

When dry, the metallic-coated sheet is cut into narrow strips 0.6 to 1.0 millimeters wide and wrapped around a core (fig. 4.1). The resulting gold- or silver-wrapped thread is 0.4 to 0.6 millimeters in diameter. This gold leaf on paper is not pure gold, but is an alloy with about 20 percent silver and traces of copper.

Type 2

Gold- or silver-colored wire is drawn to a very small diameter and then flattened to make a strip of metal 0.2 to 0.4 millimeters wide that is wrapped around a core (fig.4.2). The resulting thread is about 0.2 to 0.3 millimeters in diameter. The amount of gold in this type of thread varied from 4 to 11 percent in a number of samples taken from a private collection. The remaining material was silver and copper in widely varying ratios. Selvanayagam writes that the gold in antique Malaysian songkets was made of round filament wire wrapped around a heavy core (1990: xviii).

Threads made of metallic leaf on paper (type 1), when woven as supplementary weft into a silk textile, result in a soft, flexible, free-flowing garment that drapes gracefully on a wearer. One deficiency of such a garment is the fragility of the metallic leaf. Frequent folds and friction caused by rubbing result in abrasion. Eventually the thin layer of leaf wears off, leaving only the paper backing and/or core on which the lamella is wound (fig. 4.3). After extensive use, the cloth loses the original luster of the metallic thread.

Thread constructed with a thin metallic strip (type 2), when woven as supplementary weft, usually produces cloth with a stiffer hand than that woven with paper-backed metallic thread. But the garment retains the original brilliance of the thread, even after years of wear. These cloths may not drape as gracefully as cloths woven with paper-backed thread unless the thread diameter is very small or the metal strip has been loosely wound around the core. The latter type of thread detracts from the appearance of the textile. In Palembang as late as the 1980s it was customary in some weaving

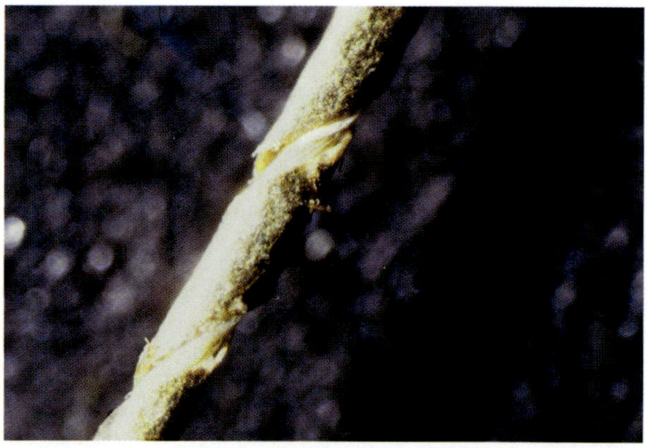

Fig. 4.1. Photomicrograph of gold thread wrapped with strips of gold leaf on paper.

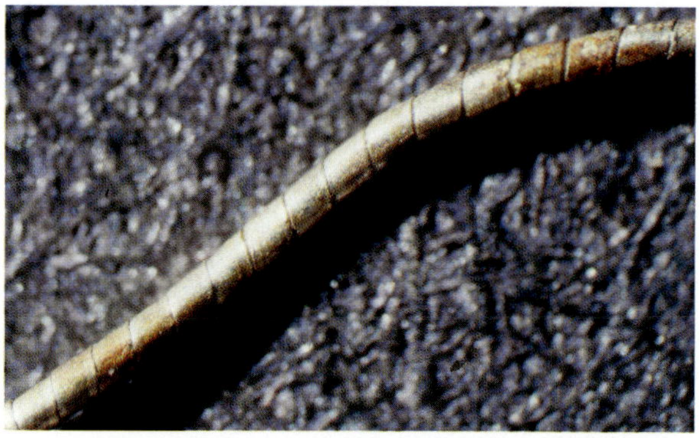

Fig. 4.2. Photomicrograph of gold thread wrapped with metallic strip.

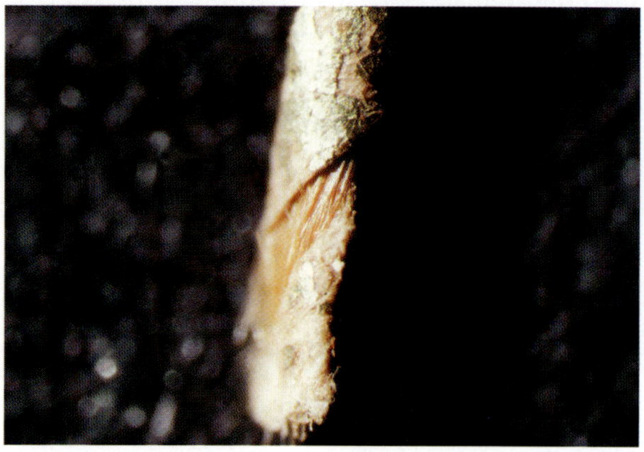

Fig. 4.3. Photomicrograph of paper-wrapped gold wrapped thread, showing abraded gold leaf.

establishments to strip the metallic-wound gold thread from damaged textiles and weave it into new cloths. This may have been a holdover from the days when gold thread in Palembang was nearly pure gold. Weavers acknowledged that clients were not satisfied with the appearance of the reused thread.

After a textile woven with a metallic-strip thread has been folded in the same way many times, as the costume is similarly refolded for each successive ceremony or event, the cloth develops unsightly permanent creases along the fold lines. Further, folding and unfolding cause the edges of the metallic strip to rub against ground threads, resulting in cut warps and producing breaks in the fabric that may lead to its destruction.

Most of the types of metallic thread discussed above are no longer available, but contemporary weavers do have substitutes for them. Gold-colored Mylar strips have found their way into many weaving shops. These plastic threads are readily available, but they are characterized by a glossy, glassy, reflective surface that shouts "plastic!" In the commodities market, where ceremonial use of textiles is not the sole motive for purchase, use of strip-wrapped gold-colored or silver-covered thread made of less expensive materials makes decorated garments available to more people. Some contemporary thread of Indian origin is made of silver that is dipped in gold. It is less expensive than thread made with higher gold content, but the thin plating wears off with repeated use. Much of the metallic thread available today breaks easily, frustrating the weavers, and there is a trend to use readily available gold-colored silk, Mylar, or polyester. Unlike songkets with metallic-wound thread, those with synthetic gold-colored thread are washable, a distinct advantage in a tropical climate. Although it is not commonly found, silk supplementary weft was substituted for the more traditional gold supplementary weft in textiles from the early 1800s or before. See the shoulder cloth textile from Batu Sangkar discussed in chapter 6 (fig. 6.15, p. 101).

Bast Fibers

Bast (plant-based fiber) has long been commonly used to make garments in Asia. Abaca or banana fiber blouses from the Philippines and fine, white ramie kimonos from Japan are among the most beautiful bast garments still produced. In Sumatra some centuries ago, a fine unspun fiber stripped from inside the outer bark of soaked stalks of *Boehmeria*, or stripped from the debarked stem, appeared either as decorative threads or, rarely, as the complete warp structure in handwoven ceremonial garments. Local weavers say that this particular bast fiber, called ramin, has not been used for weaving for roughly 150 years.

Handbags (fig. 4.4) are made by macramé of a different bast fiber, *si cantung*, from plants that grow wild on the mountainsides in West Sumatra

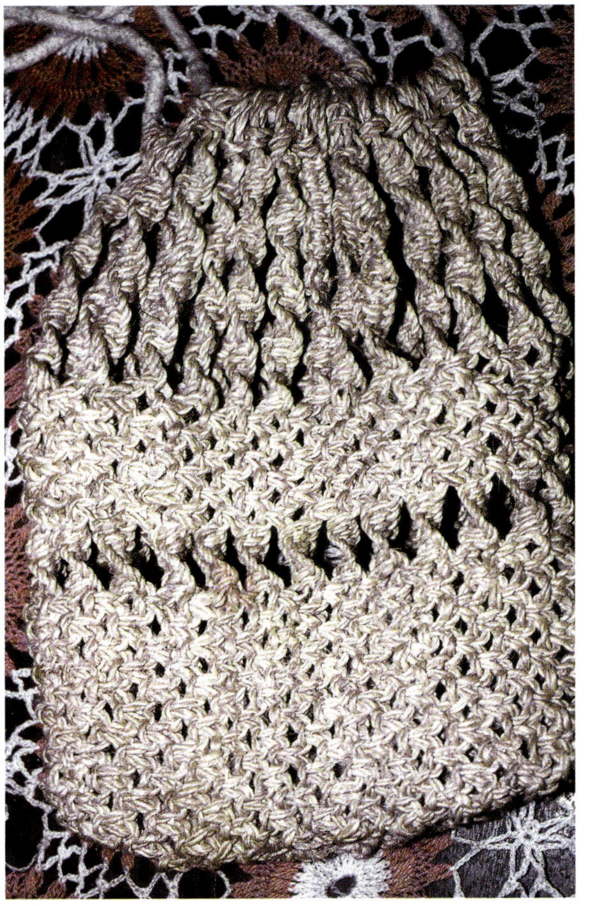

Fig. 4.4. Macramé handbag made of bast fiber from the si cantung plant.

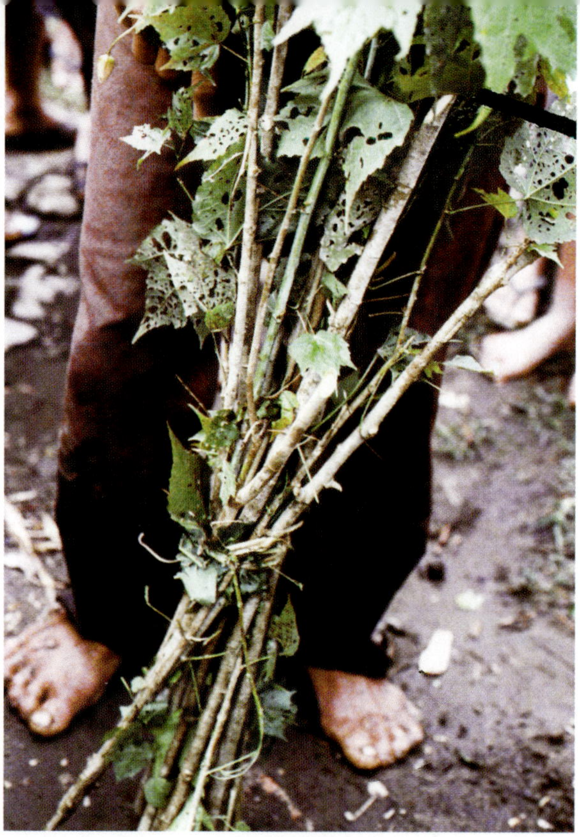

Fig. 4.5. Newly harvested si cantung.

(fig. 4.5). This fiber is stripped from the plant and twisted together to form long strings. These are plied by women in the village of Telang Dasun to make decorative bags.

Use of unspun ramin as a fine bast fiber in ceremonial garments was more widespread than the use of the coarser *si cantung*. Four different kinds of *Boehmeria* grow in central Sumatra, and it is not known if more than one of the four, *Boehmeria nivea*, was used to provide bast found in the spectacularly beautiful centuries-old garments. Although it grows wild along streams and beside wet rice paddies, ramin is also fragile and requires time-consuming preparation. It was obviously a treasured fiber. Its use presents problems as well. Ramin dries and becomes brittle with age, even in the moist tropical climate, leading to warp breaks that could easily destroy a textile. Folding and friction caused by brushing against other objects also causes breaks, exposing holes and gaps in the structure of a garment. But in spite of these difficulties, the fiber from a shrub that grows wild along waterways was treated as a material of special importance. Time and care were lavished on it. It was patterned into exquisite ceremonial textiles, and when used as the sole warp fiber, it served as the base for some few exceptionally splendid ceremonial cloths. In keeping with its origin as inner-bark fiber, ramin is often referred to in Sumatra as *kulit kayu*, literally, "skin of the wood."

Boehmeria nivea today is harvested in quantity commercially to make a twisted and often plied thread called ramie. By contrast, the bast used in songkets is neither spun nor plied. It is definitely not ramie, but is a thin, fragile, flat strip of light beige color, thinner than fine silk (fig. 4.6), most often left undyed. An exception is the shoulder cloth headdress from the village of Tanjung Sungayang, for which most ramin warps are dyed with indigo.

Because the plant is a shrub, the stalks used to supply ramin are seldom longer than six feet. To produce enough fiber to warp a loom for a traditional headdress (see the textile from Pitalah with all ramin warps, chap. 6, fig. 6.1), as many as twenty-five hundred lengths of fiber must have been knotted or twisted together (fig. 4.7). Weavers also used ramin as a delicate warp or weft patterning line on textiles made mostly of cotton or silk (fig. 4.8).

In addition to its function as a patterning element, what is the impact of the use of ramin on the quality of a textile? Ramin fibers in ceremonial textiles are substantially smaller than silk fibers (see again fig. 4.6), thus contributing to the sheerness of a weaving. Because the fiber is not as flexible as silk or cotton, ramin adds a mild stiffness to the hand of a fabric, the degree depending on the amount of bast woven into the cloth.

Ramin was not limited to use in weavings. It was often plied to make a stronger thread or string for purposes more mundane than weaving ceremonial textiles. It was not uncommon in the 1970s and 1980s to see a woman standing near the side of the road holding a long string of knotted lengths of ramin in each hand, the two strings being joined in a knot that was firmly anchored at a fence post. She would cross her hands repeatedly to cross the fibers, twisting or plying the two strings together. Fish traps and tote bags were made of these plied fibers. Multiple plyings were used to produce strings of larger and larger diameter. In fact, in the past, multiple plyings were used to form ramin fibers into ropes adequate to serve as a ship's hawser.

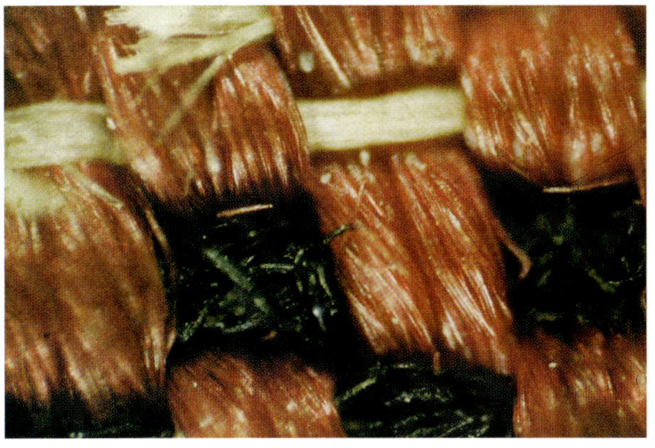

Fig. 4.6. Photomicrographic detail of textile containing cotton, silk, and ramin.

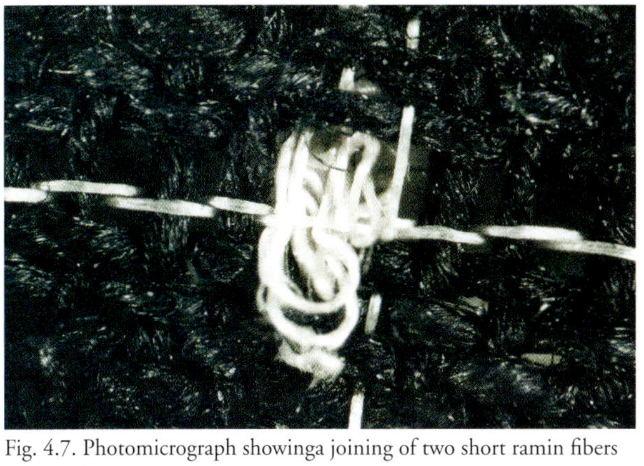

Fig. 4.7. Photomicrograph showinga joining of two short ramin fibers in a weaving.

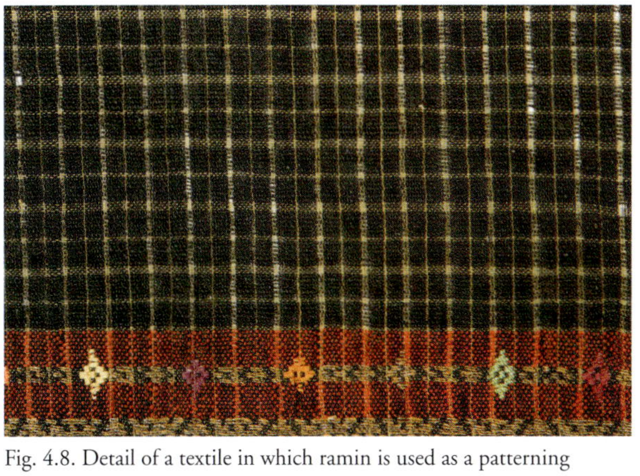

Fig. 4.8. Detail of a textile in which ramin is used as a patterning thread.

Silk

The poetic tale of the legendary child empress of China, Hsi Ling Shi, who allegedly first discovered how to unreel the silk cocoon and is now known as the patroness of silkworms, places the beginnings of sericulture in late Neolithic China, circa 2650 B.C.E. Over the following centuries techniques were perfected for raising the worms, unwinding the filamented cocoons, degumming the filaments, and forming multistrand yarns used to produce lustrous and brilliantly colorful court garments. The first recorded evidence of the existence of Chinese silks is found much later, in the annals of the Han dynasty (206 B.C.E. to 220 C.E.), marking the export trade of silk fabrics with the Greco-Roman world (Hitchcock 1985:7).

Syria played a role of intermediary in the transport of the knowledge of sericulture and silk weaving between China and the Mediterranean area. Nestorian monks brought eggs of the silk worm in hollow canes to Justinian, leading Syria to plant mulberry trees and raise a portion of its own silk. The ancient Persian Sassanians conquered Syria, supposedly to import skilled silk weavers to Persia.

Muslim conquest of the area brought new life to the established silk trade.[2] The prophet Mohammed himself was a merchant who traveled by camel caravan and did not object when pilgrims came to Mecca for the obligatory haj laden with textiles to sell.[3] Many brought gifts of textiles to Mohammed, who apparently loved the strange textiles from remote places and thus became one of the world's first textile collectors.

Processes involved in producing silk yarn from domesticated silkworms (*Bombyx mori*) are labor intensive. First, worms must be selected to be disease free. They are bred, and their eggs are deposited on a bed of leaves from the mulberry tree. Mulberry trees do not grow in northern climates, and thus the practice of sericulture is limited to warm or tropical regions. Worms develop from the eggs and feed on young, tender mulberry leaves that are torn into shreds. Fresh leaves for food must be picked, destemmed, and shredded daily. After about forty-five days the worms are ready to spin the cocoons in which they will turn into pupae, and from which they will later emerge as silk moths

The cocoon's fibers, two filaments of protein, are formed from a liquid excreted from two large glands inside the insect. Two other large internal glands secrete a gummy substance, sericin, which holds the two filaments together. The liquid protein hardens on contact with the air. This silk is formed in a single usable strand more than a half-mile long. If the moth were allowed to exit from the cocoon, it would destroy the cocoon in the process, breaking the long strand of silk in many places. To prevent such damage, the cocoon is steamed or boiled to kill the larva. Filaments that make up the cocoon are much too small, too fine, to serve as thread or yarn. It is customary when unreeling the cocoons to combine filaments from several cocoons, unreeling them together with a slight twist into a strand large enough to be useful. Finer yarns are woven into sheer, clinging fabrics. Heavier yarns are used for sturdier cloth that is suitable for elegant robes or similar garments subject to hard use.

Sometimes silk is reinforced with a heavier thread such as cotton. Silk songket headdresses in the province of West Sumatra are generally made of fine silk, but the center sections, which are frequently folded into complicated shapes, are often woven with cotton wefts to prevent damage by repeated abrasion. No such consideration is given to men's ceremonial waist ties. The plain center sections of these exquisite belts are made of silk only, and they often have been so severely damaged by tying that the center section have been replaced by commercial cotton.

The gummy cement sericin is usually left in silk fibers for protection during processing, up to the thread or yarn stage. Silk that contains sericin is called raw silk and is often used for drapes and other furnishing fabrics. Sericin is removed by boiling silk thread or fabric in soapy water. This degumming results in a lustrous, strong, soft material. Silk can be stretched by 1 or 2 percent of its length without serious damage. It is lighter than most competing fabrics, such as wool, cotton, or rayon; it is readily dyed and absorbs up to 30 percent of its weight in moisture without feeling wet, a distinct advantage for garments to be worn in tropical climates

Spun silk is made from short lengths of what are considered waste fibers—that is, fibers taken from cocoons damaged by exit of the moth—and from the cocoon's outer filaments, often rejected as too coarse for making fine yarn. Tussah silk, a heavier wild silk, comes from a cocoon equipped with a special exit channel, allowing the moth to emerge without damaging the silk fiber.

Cotton

Cotton, a seed fiber grown by various plants of the genus *Gossypium*, is native to most subtropical countries. It is thought to have originated in India, where it has been used for yarn and fabrics since before recorded history. Cotton is sometimes classified by the average length of fibers harvested from the plants. There are roughly three categories: long staple (2.5 to 6.5 cm or 1 to 2 1/2 in.), medium staple (1.3 to 3.3 cm or 1/2 to 1 5/16 in.), and short staple (1 to 2.5 cm or 3/8 to 1 in.). Long-staple cotton is silky and luxurious. This category includes the most expensive and highest-quality cotton fibers, including Egyptian and Sea Island cotton. Because of its comparative rarity, long-staple cotton is usually reserved for production of fine fabrics and hosiery.

The short-staple group is restricted to coarser applications such as carpet and cheaper fabrics. Short-staple cotton, a European variety, grows wild in the far eastern part of the Indonesian archipelago and is harvested to be made into yarn for weaving. It is difficult to weave because the ends of the short fibers give a fuzzy effect to the yarn, making it difficult to pass a shuttle through the warps. Garments woven of this coarser fiber are thick and warm, however, a particular advantage in the region's higher altitudes. Cotton grown in other areas of Indonesia tend toward the longer staples, as evidenced by the ease with which the fibers are separated from their seeds by a two-roller-type cotton gin.

Cotton grows from seed into a bush. The bush blossoms with a flower that lasts only a single day. After the petals have fallen, a structure known as a boll develops. The mature boll ruptures, revealing a fluffy mass of soft, usually white fibers still firmly attached to the seeds. When first exposed, the fibers are moist and must be dried in a rather short time to avoid damage to the quality of the fiber. It is not uncommon in the regions where cotton grows wild in Indonesia to see rows of small cylindrical packets of white fluffy cotton laid out on house roofs to dry in the sun.

The process of separating cotton fibers from their seeds is facilitated by the use of a machine called a cotton gin, first invented by Eli Whitney. The type of gin found throughout the villages is a simple structure composed of two rollers compressed together, resembling a wringer from an old-fashioned washing machine. Much of the cotton grown in Indonesia is of a long enough staple to be easily separated from its seeds by being hand-cranked through the two opposing rollers. The fibers move easily through this wringer, but the seeds are kept back and fall to the ground.

Mature cotton has a natural twist, 150 to 300 twists per inch. Dry, mature cotton is a flattened fiber twisted about its axis. This twist makes it relatively easy to spin mature cotton staples together to form a thread or yarn. Two simple tools are used in Southeast Asia to spin cotton: a drop spindle and a spinning wheel. The drop spindle is a round stick less than a foot long with tapered ends. It is weighted with a wooden disc or a stone whorl near one end. A mass of cotton fibers that may have been loosened somewhat by being beaten with branches or strummed into separation with a bowstring is formed into a loose rope and wrapped around a distaff. One end of this "rope" is fastened to a drop spindle, which is spun around by the fingers and then let fall. As the spindle falls, it pulls fibers from the distaff and spins them into a twisted thread.

The spinning wheel is a simple machine to provide spin to a spindle without dropping it. A large wheel is fastened to a horizontally fixed spindle. The spinner turns the wheel with her right hand while feeding fibers to the spindle with her left. We observed spinning wheels in use in central Sumatra as late as 1995. A third way of producing cotton thread is to join tufts of fibers together, place them on one's thigh horizontally, and roll them by hand down the length of the thigh. By adding tufts and rolling, this technique produces thread of widely varying diameter, depending on how tightly it is rolled, and twists that may range from slight to one that is at almost a ninety-degree angle to the length of the thread. Unevenness in diameter occurs also in commercially manufactured cotton thread, but not to the extent that it is found in handspun threads. Many handwoven fabrics are considered more valuable if they contain handspun cotton thread, partly because of the inordinate amount of labor required to prepare enough handspun thread to warp a loom. Evaluating the degree of unevenness in diameter is a useful way of identifying handspun thread.

Because the ends of cotton staples tend to lie on the surface of the thread, the thread is fuzzy, and it offers resistance to the shuttle that carries weft threads across the warps during the weaving. One way weavers have tried to deal with this difficulty is to hold the fuzzy ends in place by painting warps with water in which rice has been boiled. The starch that boiled rice has imparted to the water binds the ends and results in a relatively smoother thread and eases the shuttle's passage. Usually any rice starch is washed from the fabric after it is woven, but in certain ceremonial songkets it may be left in. This starched fabric is scraped with seashells until it acquires a shine almost as glossy as chintz. The material is identified as *polished* cotton. Note the high shine on the dark cotton portion of the chieftain's shoulder cloth (*salempang*, fig. 4.9).

A process first discovered accidentally by an English fabric printer named Mercer was later developed into a commercial chemical treatment that made cotton thread softer, smoother, and more receptive to dyes. Mercer filtered sodium hydroxide through cotton and found that the cotton shrank and became translucent. He worked with the process of subjecting cotton to short periods of exposure to cold concentrated sodium hydroxide and finally patented it. Later work showed that if the cotton were placed under tension it would not shrink and had increased elasticity and a smooth, lustrous surface. Mercerized cotton thread has been commercially available ever since.

An interesting aside is that Mercer's early experiments led to the production of parchment paper. For this, paper with sufficiently high rag content is exposed to cold sodium hydroxide for short times. This renders it translucent and resistant to water and to grease. Although cotton can withstand exposure to strong alkalis, it is destroyed by exposure to acids. Acid reacts with the cellulose to form hydrocellulose, an easily powdered material. Obviously acid salts should not be used with cotton, but basic salts are not harmful. Many mordants used to increase the absorption of dye are basic (i.e., alkali) salts.

How does the use of cotton affect the quality of handwoven textiles, especially songkets? Songkets are seldom made of an all-cotton-ground fabric, except in the Sumatran region of Lima Puluh Kota (literally, fifty cities), especially in the village regions around Payakumbuh. There, some cotton shoulder cloths are ornamented with silk and gold- or silver-wrapped thread. In songkets containing cotton, the ground threads are usually a mixture of cotton, silk, and/or ramin. For these cloths the cotton should be fine enough and supple enough to blend well with the other, finer fibers. Where cotton is used as a weft to reinforce the center section of a woman's headdress, the fiber should be strong enough to provide silk warps the required protection against strenuous folding without making the fabric appear coarse.

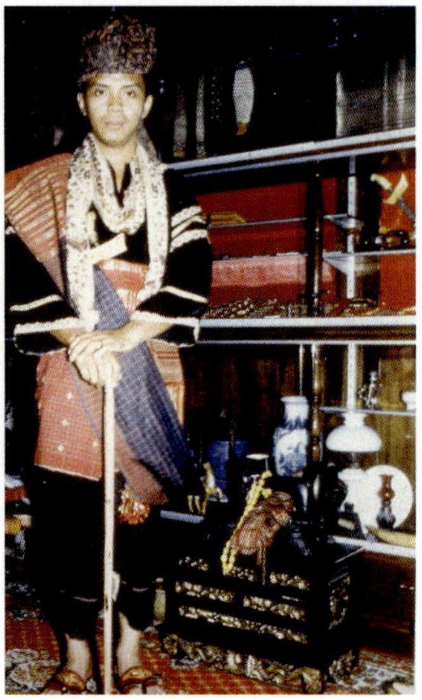

Fig. 4.9. Young chieftain wearing a shoulder cloth in which the starched dark cotton fibers have been polished to shine with a sea shell.

Other fibers found in songket weavings

In addition to the commonly used gold- or silver-wrapped thread, ramin, silk, and cotton, discussed above, man-made fibers, notably rayon and polyester, have found their way into handwoven fabrics in Sumatra and Malaysia. Rayon is seldom, if ever, used for weaving songkets, but polyester is ubiquitous. Polyester comes in many sizes and configurations—from flat to rounded, from single thread to single ply to multiple ply, and mixed with cotton. It has a distinct advantage of being available in many colors. Wool cloth is also found in Indonesian ceremonial textiles. It is a tribute to the Dutch that they were able to sell wool cloth to a community living on the equator. Wool cloth was couched with the gold-wrapped thread to make it suitable for ceremonial wear. Wool yarn was apparently not sold in Sumatra. The weaver's responsibility is to choose the appropriate form of thread for the immediate use.

Decorative techniques used in songket weaving

Patterning with color

Perhaps the simplest means of patterning a handwoven textile is inclusion of warp stripes or weft bands of different colors. Warp stripes are

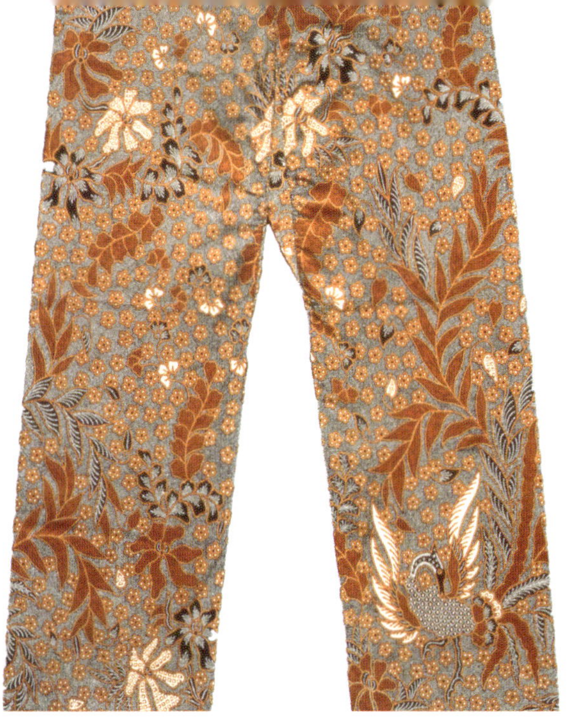

Fig. 4.10. Trousers, made of hand-drawn batik.

formed by the simple act of including enough warp threads of chosen colors to produce stripes of the desired widths when the loom is warped. Weaving is done with a monochromatic weft. Weft bands are formed on a monochromatic warp woven with bands of selected widths in different-colored wefts. Checks or simple plaids are formed by combining warp stripes and weft bands in a single fabric. Complex plaids are produced by mixing stripes and bands of various widths and colors. These patterns are made in the over-one-under-one weaving technique known as tabby, basket, or plain weave. When the number of warps per inch is the same as the number of wefts per inch, the weave is said to be balanced plain weave. Songkets often contain stripes and/or bands or plaids in addition to the defining patterns formed with gold- or silver-wrapped thread.

Resist dyeing: weft ikat

More complex color patterns using only ground threads, warp and weft, are produced with a complex dyeing technique known universally by its Indonesian name, ikat, which means "to tie." Warp ikat refers to a color pattern already dyed in the warp threads before they are put on the loom. The technique is described below. Weft ikat patterns have already been dyed in the weft threads before weaving begins. Weft ikat is used to pattern songkets, especially in Palembang and in the weaving centers in Malaysia. Warp ikat has been known in Indonesian weavings since the late centuries B.C.E.

Sometime between the eighth and second century B.C.E. the Neolithic peoples of Indonesia came into contact with the Dong Son culture[4] of Vietnam and the somewhat less widespread culture of the late Zhou dynasty of southern China. The backstrap loom and the dyeing technique of warp ikat were introduced during this period. Today ikat dyeing in all forms (warp, weft, and double) exists almost universally in world cultures except for Australia and parts of Oceania (Warming and Gaworski 1981: 53-4).

As noted in chapter 3, ikat dyeing is resist dyeing, that is, protecting that part of the cloth or fiber not to be colored with material that prevents the dyestuff from acting. Familiar forms of resist dyeing include batik (fig. 4.10), in which wax or paste covers the material not to be dyed; *pelangi* (tie-dye; fig. 4.11), in which sections of cloth are so tightly tied with string or cloth that the dye cannot penetrate; and *tritik*, in which sections of cloth are stitched so tightly that the dye cannot penetrate. These techniques are used to dye patterns into woven cloth.

Ikat, on the other hand, is a technique employed to dye each element of a pattern into a separate group or bundle of individual threads before they are woven into cloth. This process is more

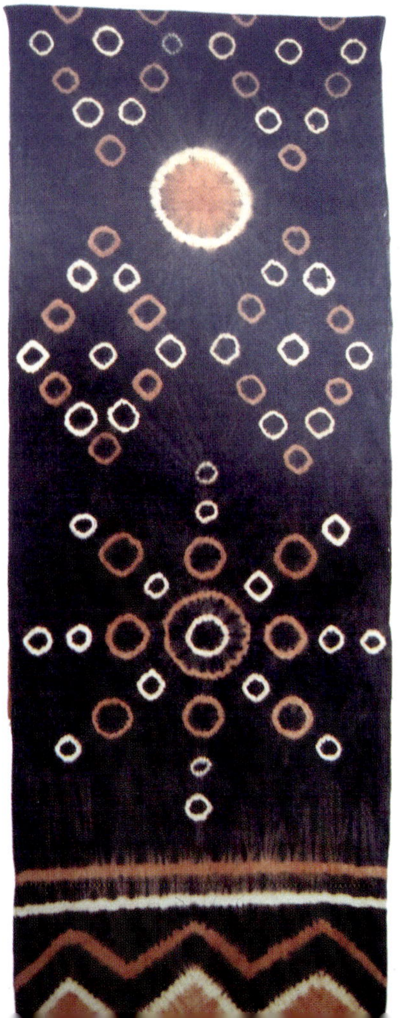

Fig. 4.11. Example of cloth patterned by tie-dye (pelangi).

Fig. 4.12. Double ikat textile from Tenganan, Bali.

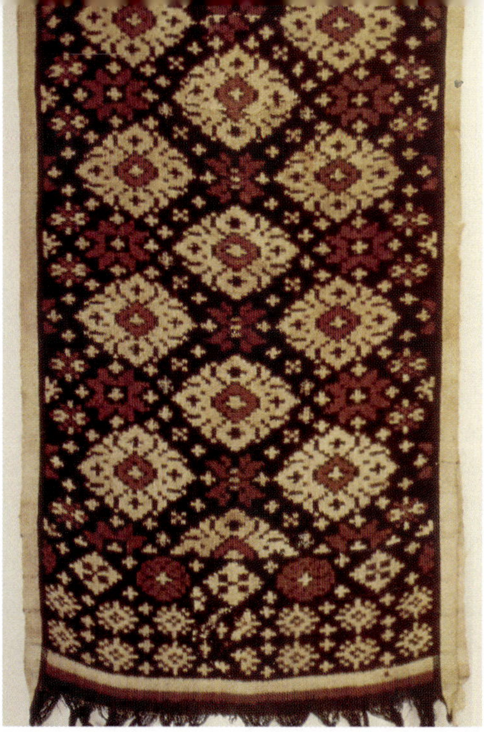

time-consuming, complex, and difficult than the process of dyeing whole cloth. Threads or yarns must first be assembled in the length and order that they will have on the loom. They are then grouped into smaller bundles, the fewer threads in a bundle the finer or more detailed the pattern. A mechanism must be provided to keep the bundles rigidly in position so that all elements of the pattern are kept in place. Those lengths of a bundle that are not to be dyed are tightly wrapped with bast or plastic strips to prevent the dye from coming into contact with the covered threads. At the end of the wrapping process, an image of the undyed pattern is formed by the tied sections.

For warp ikat, a tying frame with the same dimensions as the loom is made to hold the thread bundles firmly in place during the tying process. When the process is complete, the tied thread bundles, kept in order by a connecting thread or some other mechanical means, are removed from the frame and put into the dye pot. When the desired color has been attained, the threads are removed from the pot and dried. The ties are removed, and the loom is warped with the dyed warps. If more than one color is required, the whole process must be repeated: secure the threads on a tying frame, securely tie the bundle areas not to be dyed, provide a mechanism to keep the bundles in order, remove from the frame, and put in a dye pot. Three- or four-color warp ikats may require months or years to complete.

Dyeing weft ikats introduces further difficulties. Although the weft threads could be wound on a frame built to the same dimensions as the loom, this approach is not used for at least two reasons. First, if the weft pattern is repeated, it is inefficient to retie the pattern each time it occurs when bundles could be grouped and dyed together. Second, because of irregularities that necessarily occur during weaving, the position of individual wefts may have to be adjusted slightly to keep the pattern intact. If there were no extra lengths in the wefts to permit this adjustment, the pattern would soon be disturbingly out of register. Different ikat-weaving centers have developed their own methods of managing this difficulty, based on the experience of many generations of weavers and the tolerance of the culture for inexactness in patterning.

Precise weft patterning alone requires highly skilled tying, dyeing, and weaving. When both the warp and the weft of a fabric have been ikatted, the difficulty of weaving is multiplied many times over. Not only must the weft pattern be kept in register, it must also register properly with the warp pattern. Ordinarily every weft thread has to be adjusted. It may take as long as ten years for one of these handloomed cloths to be completed (Van Gelder 1980:11). As noted in chapter 3, this technique, known as double ikat, is practiced in few places. In the village of Tenganen, Bali, ceremonial costumes are made of double ikat (fig. 4.12). The cloths are thought to have magical properties. A double ikat is worn during the tooth-filing ceremony to protect the subject. In Gujarat, India, saris are made in multicolor double ikat. A sari is some eighteen feet long. The tying and dying processes are of almost unimaginable difficulty. It is no wonder that these fine ikats are so treasured that, when they are damaged beyond wearability, pieces are saved for other uses. Some are burned, and the ashes are given to the sick for healing. Very small fragments are rolled into short, thin, stemlike tools used to dip into the black cosmetic kohl, used in India to outline women's eyes.

Many traditional songkets, especially those from Palembang and Malaysian weaving centers, are patterned with weft ikat (fig. 4.13). They are especially valued and are cared for as carefully as the family wealth. The majority of contemporary weavings with weft ikat are understandably not as intricate or as precisely executed as the surviving older cloths. The skills undoubtedly exist to reproduce exquisite weft songkets, but the availability of quality materials is a problem. The quality of gold-wrapped thread is inferior. Silk is very expensive, and the extra cost cannot be justified in view of the inferior quality of gold thread. Few weavers and dyers can spend the long periods of time required to duplicate antique treasures.

Songket weaving and woven patterns

The basic structure of handwoven songkets is produced by plain weave, as described earlier. Gold- or silver-wrapped thread patterning, called supplementary-weft patterning, is indeed supplementary. If all the metallic thread were pulled out of a songket, there would still remain a complete textile made up of plain woven ground threads. What should we look for in the plain weave to help us judge the quality of a songket? If there is no ikat patterning in the textile, a balanced plain weave is appropriate. If the cloth has been patterned with weft ikat, balance between the warps and wefts is no longer desirable. To achieve optimum visibility of a weft ikat pattern, warp threads should not be visible in the ikat area. To hide the warps, a weaver packs the weft threads tightly across the entire width of the cloth. She takes the exposed ends of the sword in her hands, and with several strokes firmly pushes the new weft into the already-woven threads. If this is done properly, the wefts are so tightly packed together that no warps are visible to the naked eye (see again fig. 4.13). This technique results in what is called a weft-faced textile.

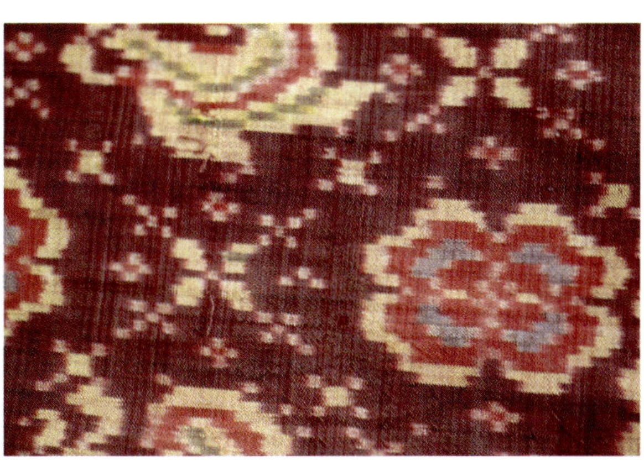

Fig. 4.13. A weft ikat motif. Probably 20th century.

Gold or silver panels of supplementary weft are often limited to the warp ends of the songket, sometimes with smaller motifs scattered throughout the midsection. Sometimes gold or silver motifs cover the entire surface of the fabric. In either case, the rhythm of supplementary-weft weaving is one or two passes of ground thread, a pass of the shuttle carrying supplementary thread, one or two passes of ground, a return pass of supplementary, and so on.

Guiding the ground weft by trying to maneuver it manually over and under a few hundred warp threads to get to the opposite side of the textile would be an exercise in futility. A tool has been developed to speed the process. To visualize how this tool works, consider the warp threads to be numbered consecutively. Fasten each odd-numbered warp with a loop of string to a small rod, called a heddle, so that when the rod is lifted all odd-numbered warps are raised above the even-numbered warps. This creates an opening, a shed, between odd and even numbered warps through which a shuttle can be passed to move the weft across the cloth over one, under one, over one, and so on. Similarly, even numbered warps are fastened to a second heddle. Lifting this second heddle creates a different shed through which the weft moves back across the textile, this time above the odd-numbered warps and below the even-numbered ones.

How can a weaver make a shed that allows a proper pass of gold or silver patterning threads? This path is irregular and is dictated by the pattern itself—that is, where the gold thread should appear on the front of the textile in order to produce the desired motif. Before weaving begins, the desired paths through the warps are picked out, in successive order, by thin, flat sticks called *lidi*. Lidi are stored, in order, in the warps, at the back of the loom. When the time comes for a weaver to

Fig. 4.15. Detail of a weaving showing gold pattern made of 2 and 3 threads per lidi.

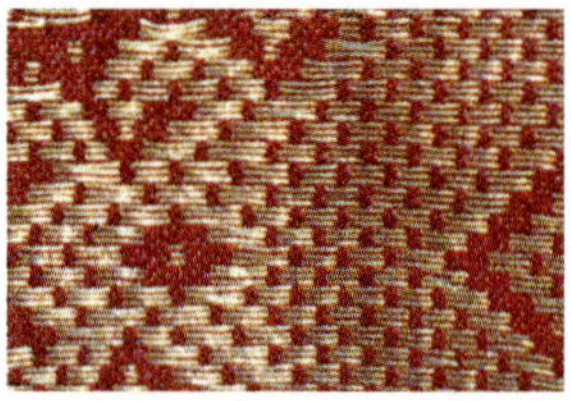

make the supplementary-weft pattern, she draws the first lidi toward the front of the loom and inserts a pointed, thin, flat board a few inches wide in the same path under and over the warps that the lidi follows (fig. 4.14). This thin, very smooth board is called a sword. When it is turned up on edge, it forces selected warps up, making a shed for the shuttle carrying gold thread to pass across the textile. The pattern pass is followed by a weft or two of ground thread. If the lidi is to be used only once, it is discarded. If it is to be used again to double the path of the earlier supplementary weft, it is left in place, and the sword is used again to make a shed for this second pass. If the gold-wrapped thread is very fine, it may require two or three identical passes to make a heavy enough line on the surface of the textile to form the desired visual image (fig.4. 15). Duplication of successive paths is referred to in shorthand terms as "three per lidi". Some coarsely woven contemporary cloths are patterned at 8/lidi (fig. 4.16). If fineness of weave is a criterion of excellence, the number of threads per lidi must be small.

If the path of gold-wrapped thread occupies the full width of the textile and the shuttle is passed across all the warps, the technique is called continuous supplementary weft. If the pattern calls for only a few small figures distributed across the width of the fabric, a different technique is used to avoid wasting long strands of precious thread on the back of the textile, where they may easily be snagged and pulled, damaging the fabric. Instead, several small bobbins are used to carry the pattern thread. At the appropriate place thread from a bobbin is fed under and over the warps as required to create a line of the image. If there are five small motifs to be woven across the cloth, there will be five small bobbins resting on the warps, readily available when needed.

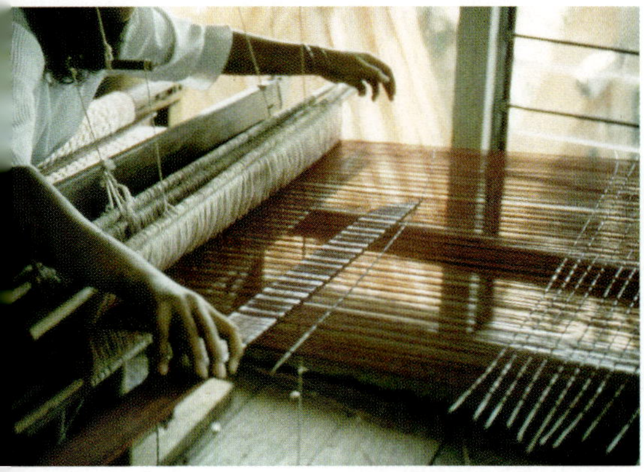

Fig. 4.14. A weaver threads her sword in the same path through the warp threads as the nearby lidi.

Songket patterning is often designed as a series of contiguous supplementary-weft bands, each band containing motifs different from those of its immediate neighbors (fig. 4.17). In Minangkabau textiles especially, these motif bands are made easily and quickly distinguishable to the viewer by weaving different-colored ground wefts in adjacent bands. Red, purple, blue, and black are commonly used weft colors. The color sequence for a series of bands might be red, purple, red, blue, yellow, black, red, and so on, giving the viewer an instant capture of the overall design scheme. Without some such device the viewer would be faced with an entire panel of undifferentiated gold images, distinguishable only by close and careful inspection

Clear recognition of the pattern format is important for Minangkabau songkets, not only for aesthetic appreciation but also because the discrete images carry proverbial references. The multitude of gold and silver motifs woven into Minangkabau songkets over the centuries have individual names

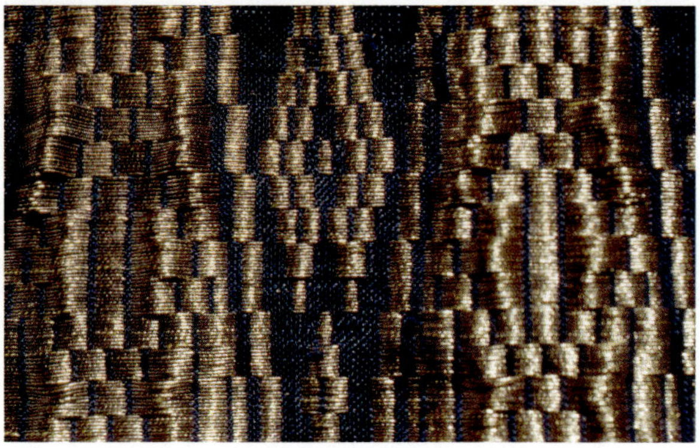

Fig. 4.16. Example of coarse weaving made with 8 threads per lidi.

such as mangosteen calyx, ducks going home in the afternoon, bamboo shoot, snake, split peanut, and so on. In most instances the shape of the motif does not even remotely resemble the shape of the named object. The name refers to a proverb or saying involving the named object, however, and is intended to teach proper Minangkabau behavior. For example, the name *mangosteen calyx* evokes the image of the mangosteen fruit. The fruit is about the size of a medium grapefruit. It has an ugly mottled red skin that covers a thick, woody shell protecting a delicious delicate, white, sectional fruit about the size of a mandarin orange. The teaching is that just as one should not judge the fruit of the mangosteen by its shell and skin, so one should not judge a person by outer appearance.

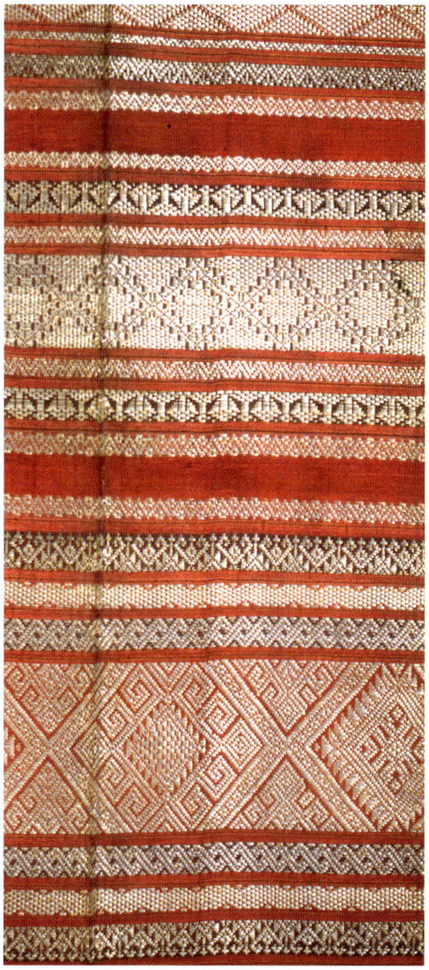

Fig. 4.17. Textile patterned with multiple bands of supplementary weft.

The split peanut name is meant to remind one that if the nut of a peanut is split, the two halves are the same size. The teaching is that if one is asked to make a division of property for another person, one must make certain the portions are equal in size and, by extrapolation, one must be honest in business.

Many Minangkabau traditional songket pattern formats have stayed the same over a period of at least two hundred years. Some speculate that there must be a message contained in this overall arrangement of motifs. Otherwise why would the order have survived so long without change? With the passing of songkets from ceremony to commodity, that persistence of order has disappeared.

What skills must a weaver display to produce an excellent or even great songket? The answer to that question depends in part on the type of loom she uses. Most songket weavers in places like South Sumatra work with backstrap looms, controlling tension of the warp thread with their bodies. Uniformity of the textile depends on the consistency of pressure the weaver exerts by leaning against the backstrap. If there is too little tension, the warps tend to separate and the textile becomes wider. Too much tension, and the warps are drawn in toward each other and the textile narrows.

If a songket contains weft ikat patterns, the wefts must be beaten sufficiently to produce a weft-faced cloth. Because weft ikat patterns must line up precisely, individual weft threads may have to be adjusted by hand. Motifs must be structured carefully so that they can be easily identified. This means using the right number of threads per lidi; it is also crucial to make the motifs as fine as is consistent with identification and with the size of warp and weft ground threads. Coarse ground threads obviously lead to coarse motif elements

In central Sumatra and Malaysia songkets are made on frame looms, in which the warp tension is controlled by the loom. The weaver is relieved of responsibility for body control of warp tension.

We should note that this discussion does not address the question of whether textiles are "art." That involves the philosophy of aesthetics, not a proper subject of this chapter. Because textiles as art is a perennially lively topic we refer interested readers to a valuable older volume: Conrad Fielder's *On judging works of visual art* (1949). Fiedler judges not skills or techniques but the creative process that produces a work of fine art.

Subjective judgments of excellence

Subjective judgments of the value or excellence of a songket are usually not as universally acceptable as the more objective evaluations of material excellence and skilled weaving and dyeing. Subjective judgments may be classified by type: they may be highly personal, based on an individual's experience and taste; they may be culturally based, reflecting social or religious preferences for color or belief-instigated preferences for motifs or pattern formats. The paragraphs that follow explore a few categories of subjective evaluation of excellence in songkets to highlight differences of opinion that may arise between foreign collectors and members of the culture of origin. What is considered a great songket in one region may not, for subjective reasons, be valued as highly in another.

Suitability has to do with the function for which the songket was originally made. In the culture of origin a shoulder cloth is expected to drape easily over the shoulder. It should not be so stiff that it hangs awkwardly. A sarong also should drape well, but it should have enough body to withstand the wear and tear of long ceremonial processionals over dusty roads and long hours of sitting during ceremonial speeches. Head ties should be sturdy enough to withstand the frequent folding and manipulating required to form elaborate shapes, especially in Minangkabau villages. Generous use of gold-wrapped thread helps to strengthen a songket's end panels. Sparsely decorated center sections of many silk headdresses are often reinforced with cotton wefts instead of silk. Does dense patterning or a coarsened center detract from the excellence of a handwoven textile?

Men's silk ceremonial belts, which are often exquisitely executed songkets, are subjected to much the same twisting and tying as headdresses, but the undecorated silk centers are typically not reinforced with cotton wefts. A worn silk belt is often found with its songket ends cut from a damaged center and resewn onto a length of red commercial cotton. How does this susceptibility to severe damage affect the valuation of the belt?

Trousers, shirts, blouses, and tunics should be sturdy enough to withstand dust, dirt, and perspiration. Because gold-wrapped thread is not washable, many shirts and other tops are not songkets. Those decorated with gold are usually protected by undergarments. Recent expanded use of silk floss to replace gold-wrapped thread in traditional songkets is a deliberate attempt to improve ease of maintenance of ceremonial wear. Because songkets are not used as wearable garments in regions outside that culture, the question of suitability does not enter the evaluation deliberation.

The importance of color in a songket may also be a matter of subjective judgment. In some Islamic societies, brightly colored garments are considered immodest and therefore inappropriate. Excessive use of bright and shining gold and silver is also considered immodest, and use of metallic threads is limited to discreet motifs (see Terengganu sarong, fig. 6.19, p. 110). The Minangkabau tend to think of their ceremonial garments as adat ceremonial wear rather than as Islamic clothing, and the colors are often bright. Again, in non-Islamic communities color limitations imposed by religious taboo are not a deterrent to judging a brightly colored songket as excellent.

Evaluation of a contemporary Minangkabau songket

This cloth (fig. 4.18) was allegedly commissioned to be sold to Minangkabau as a partial replacement for family heirloom textiles that were sold, lost, or destroyed. The textile is relatively narrow and long, approximating the shape of a pre-twentieth-century headcloth weaving or shoulder cloth. The images are all motifs that can be found in traditional ceremonial weavings, consistent with the concept of a replacement textile.

Consider first the materials. There is no cotton, ramin, or silk. The gold-wrapped thread is of

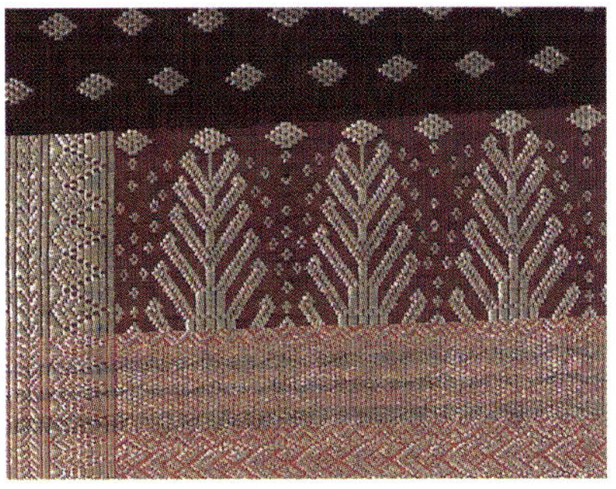

Fig. 4.18. Contemporary textile woven as a replacement for a traditional ceremonial textile. Larger image is fig. 6.6, p. 93.

excellent quality. Warps are two-ply red polyester, larger and heavier than single-strand polyester warps. Wefts in the decorated end panels are single strands of an unusually heavy black polyester thread. In the undecorated center of the songket, wefts, made of heavy black polyester thread, are plied and doubled. Perhaps this heavy weft is a nod to the traditional use of cotton wefts to strengthen silk warps in the plain centers of headdress textiles

The weaving is generally excellent. Motifs are constructed with repetitions of two and three threads per lidi. Although expertly reproduced, these motifs seem somewhat coarse, probably because of the bulk of the plied warps over which the motif threads must pass. There is a tendency for selvedges of the textile to ruffle, probably because heavy plied and doubled wefts make the turnaround at the selvedge doubly bulky. This does not occur when thinner polyester threads are used for warp and weft. In the exhibition that this book accompanies, there is a contemporary set of sarong and shoulder cloth woven with warp and weft of single-stranded polyester. Motifs in that set are very finely woven and compare favorably to the finest traditional textiles (see Summerfield and Summerfield 1999: p. 114).

Horizontal bands of traditional motifs make up the patterning style of the decorated end panels of this weaving. The color of ground wefts in successive bands alternates between red and black, providing the viewer some assistance in quick recognition of different motifs, but not as much help in recognizing the overall pattern as that provided by wefts of red, purple, blue, and black found in traditional weavings. Incidentally, some viewers claim that they see green in traditional textiles. In these pieces the black dye has faded considerably, and faded black juxtaposed to red is interpreted by the eye as green, even in photographs. Examining either the textile or its photograph under magnification clearly shows that there is no green thread, only faded black.

This textile was represented to us a "Pitalah" textile, but not all motifs are traditional Pitalah motifs. Omitted here is the variation in weft band width found in the end panels of traditional Pitalah songkets. The overall pattern here is less interesting than the traditional Pitalah pattern formats because it is less varied. The cloth is not a traditional Pitalah ceremonial textile, but it may not have been intended to be.

If this songket is seen as a contemporary weaving rather than as a contemporary rendition of a traditional textile, other considerations become relevant. When the concept of a "Pitalah" textile is dropped, the weaver's choice of traditional motifs from several different villages instead of from just one is, in a sense, innovative. Contemporary weavers often combine motifs from different villages but not in a traditional pattern format, and they usually include motifs that are not traditional. Because of its weight and stiffness, this songket appears to be suitable only for hanging on a wall, but the headdress/shoulder cloth conformation seems too long to be hung on the walls of many Minangkabau houses. According to the criteria for excellence discussed above, this songket qualifies in some respects, but not in all.

NOTES

1.,2. See exhibition catalogue, *2000 Years of silk weaving*, 1949, New York, E. Weyhe, p. vi.

3. See again, *2000 Years of Silk Weaving*, 1949:vii. A magnificent man's silk cloak from Syria, probably purchased by an Acehnese person on the Haj and brought back to Aceh, is in the exhibition "Gold Cloths of Sumatra."

4. *Encyclopedia Britannica*, Micropedia, vol. 3, 1974, p. 183.

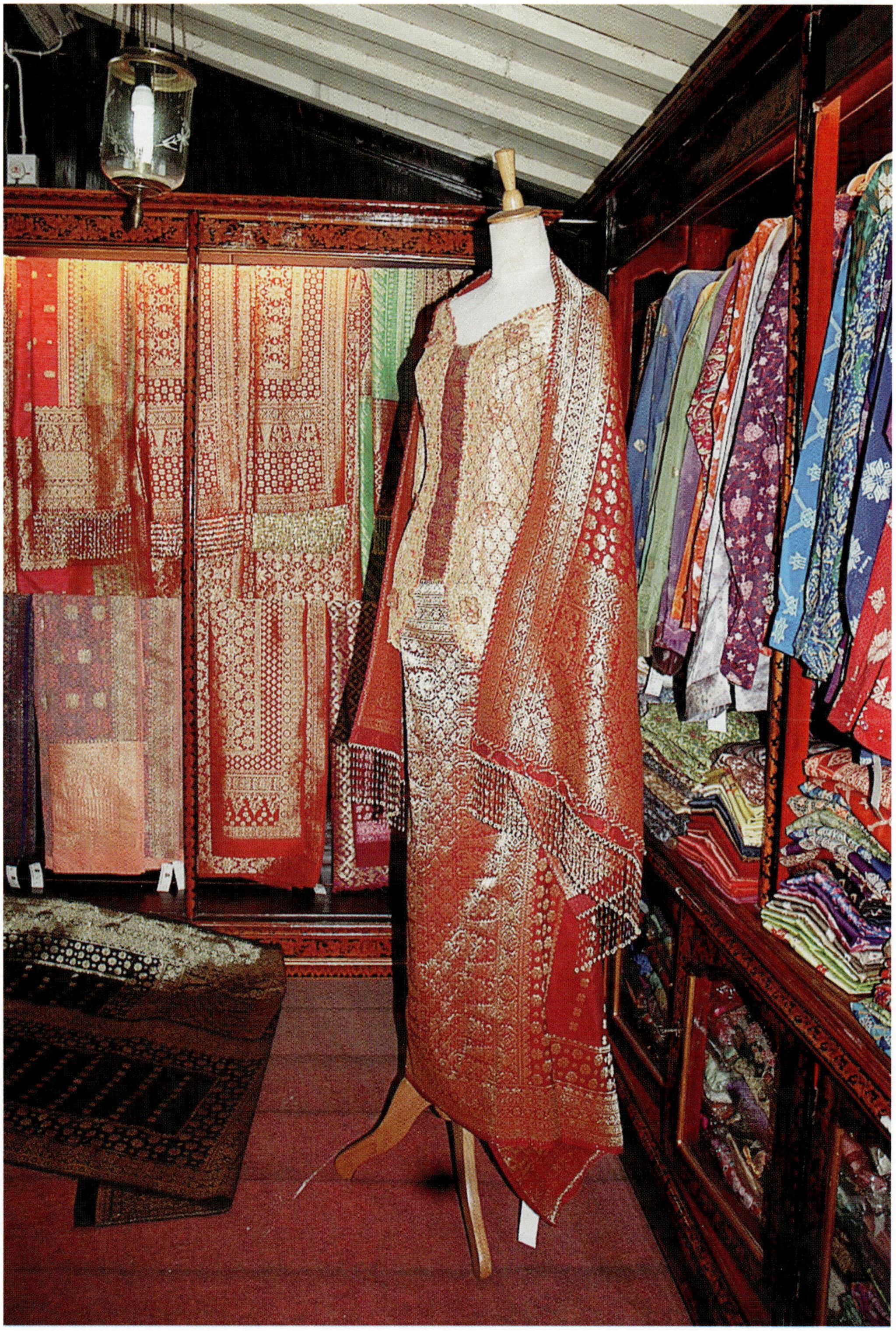

Fig. 5.0. The interior of Pak Zainal's songket emporium in Palembang, 2006. The shop is located in his family's ancestral home.

5. Commerce and creativity: Sumatran songket business families, marketing, and innovation in contemporary songket weaving

Susan Rodgers

As anthropologist Andrew Causey has noted in *Hard bargaining in Sumatra; Western travelers and Toba Bataks in the marketplace of souvenirs* (2003), the cultural event of shopping has important effects on Indonesian indigenous arts today. In his ethnographic study Causey looked at wood carvings executed in "traditional Toba style" (fig. 5.1). These were created in the 1990s by Toba master craftsmen with whom he worked as an apprentice and participant observer on Samosir Island, North Sumatra. Causey reports that marketplace demands by international and Indonesian domestic tourists for this or that "old Toba style" in priests' staffs, medicine jar stoppers, or treasure chests pushed carvers to make objects that they anticipated would be especially popular and profitable. In this way, Causey found, the contemporary marketplace of souvenirs influenced notions of "traditional Toba art" (fig. 5.2). This was so for the craftsmen themselves (Toba carvers are often impoverished and desperate for sales and so readily adapt their art to meet market demand) and for buyers too. The latter included émigré Toba living middle-class lives in Jakarta but eager to have what would be construed as a token of tradition from an ancestral land in Sumatra in their urban homes. A curio version of a nineteenth-century priest's magic staff could fit the bill, although the Bible-focused Protestant Christianity preeminent in Toba has long made relics of Toba's animist past highly problematic. Even souvenir replicas of old objects of worship once used in preconversion times can carry a soupçon of idolatry.

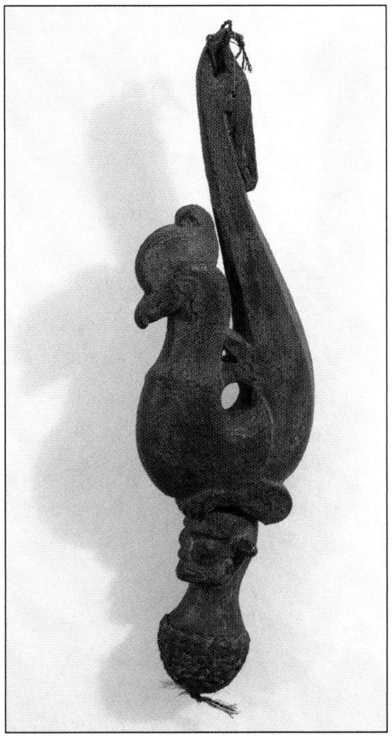

Fig. 5.1. Toba Batak *manuk-manuk* protective figure, for alerting householders of dangers arriving. Circa 1920, Samosir Island.

Causey reports that other consumers of these Toba souvenirs of old beliefs were German, Swiss, and Scandinavian tourists interested in transportable exotica to take back to Europe after a stay in the hostels on scenic Lake Toba. This is Southeast Asia's largest volcanic lake, and its landscapes are dramatic; before the downturn in international tourism from Western countries since 1998, visitors flocked there. Targeting an even more upscale market of potential customers, the Toba carvers sometimes used close-up photographs of actual nineteenth-century Toba antique carvings as guides to their finer work. These illustrations had been published in lavishly produced international museum catalogs or glossy art magazines.

Toba carvers employed these images as templates for creating new but also supposedly authentic pieces. These carvings were generally presented to buyers quite forthrightly as recently created objets d'art. This was a replica art of ingenuity but also integrity, Causey asserts: an expertly done, well-thought-out craft modeled on imagined ethnic traditions, designed

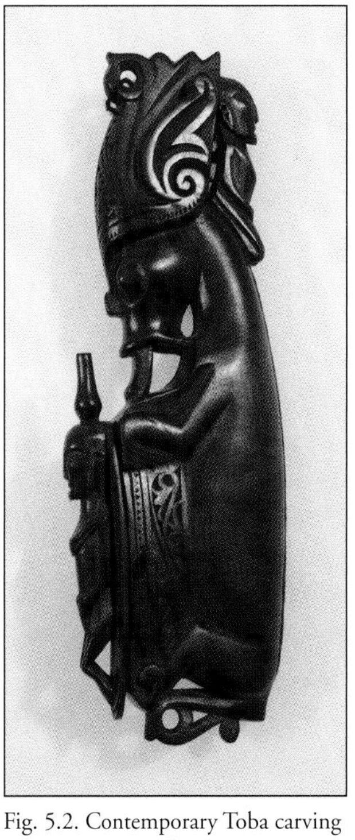

Fig. 5.2. Contemporary Toba carving "in the old style," for the tourist market. 1996.

for indigenous and international consumer publics living very much in 1990s Indonesian and global presents.

Local, national, and international economies of desire—for cultural authenticity, for "genuine" relics of fondly imagined ethnic pasts—empower both the making and the marketing of many Indonesian heritage arts, beyond the Toba Batak wood carvings that Andrew Causey has studied. Sumatra's songket-weaving traditions today also participate in these dense symbolic markets, which are also monetized, real-world mercantile spaces.

In important contrast to Toba's old-style but newly made wood carvings such as souvenir bottle stoppers, however, West Sumatran gold-thread songket textiles and those from Palembang, South Sumatra, are woven today largely not as souvenir craft but as heritage clothing—that is, as wearable craft to be used as emblems of *tradisi*, traditions, primarily by peoples from the songket weaver's own ethnic society. Such textiles are worn as signs of "being traditional" in ritual events such as weddings, boys' circumcision celebrations within Islam, and during the installation of new chieftains.

Another core market for West Sumatran and South Sumatran songkets are individuals and families from other Sumatran and also Malaysian societies who admire the surpassing excellence of highland Minangkabau, Palembang, and Jambi gold-thread textiles and who wish to don their purchases from these regions for their own rites of passage, within Malay adat (inherited custom), southern Batak adat, and so on. Thus, Palembang red silk and gold-thread songkets are bought and used today by Palembang Malays but also by Batak from Angkola, South Tapanuli, North Sumatra (fig. 5.3). This is a region that does no songket weaving. Angkola Batak who wish to outfit their own brides in what they have long considered to be the "traditional Angkola style" often venture into southern Sumatran songket wear. They buy these cloths from shops in Medan or Jakarta, or from textile brokers in local Angkola markets. The Angkola bridal mode for both Muslims and Christians (this southern Batak region is religiously mixed) calls for gold spangly headgear similar to Malay and southern Sumatran court regalia, deep red Palembang songket sarongs, and a pair of narrow Palembang songkets to be crossed over the chest of a bride. This splendid costume (an obviously composite one) denotes her "noble status." Angkola Batak brides are described in the Angkola-language ritual oratory of weddings as "queens for a day," although many of these young women come from modest antecedents.

In West Sumatra and South Sumatra today, songket buyers, songket weaver women and adolescent girls, and the Muslim Minangkabau and Palembang business families that supervise these regions' exuberant songket trades and their fashion fluctuations all engage through objects in multilayered conversations about heritage, art, and time. Songket cloth is their medium of discourse. These textiles "talk" about being traditional and adat-conscious, within Islam, within Indonesian modernity. These are tropes found in much Sumatran public thought, throughout art and textualities, since at least the 1870s.

Songket weaving today in these two locales, Minangkabau and South Sumatra, produces much heritage art of great integrity. Newly woven songkets evoke ethnic pasts and index "traditional" moral stances in the world for populations experiencing swift social change. Moreover,

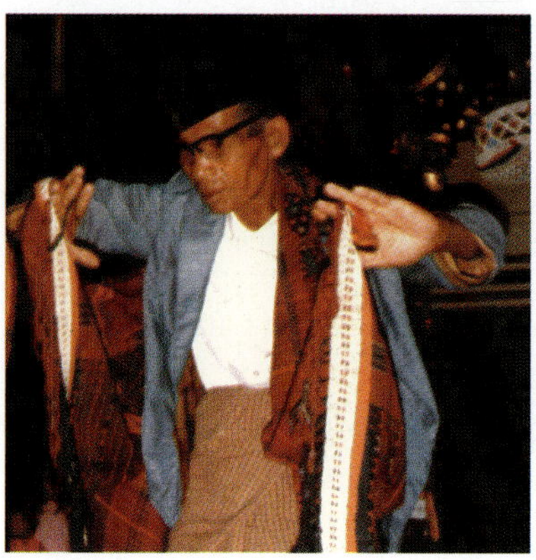

Fig. 5.3. An Angkola Batak raja in a ritual tortor dance, 1970s, in ulos cloak.

Fig. 5.4. Inside Pak Zainal's songket shop in Palembang. 2006.

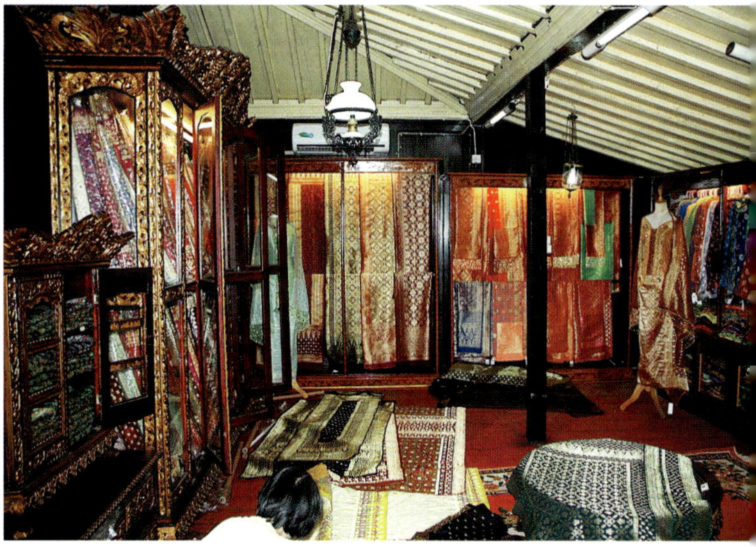

far from being mere curios, West Sumatran and South Sumatran high-end songket cloths today evince considerable artistic creativity while still upholding tradition. This is the focus of the present chapter.[1]

Of particular salience here will be how creativity at the level of the individual songket cloth has operated recently in relation to some of the craft's commercial settings. I shall be looking particularly at one of songket textiles' most typical shopping venues: the weaving craft emporium, managed by old-line weaving families. Contemporary commercial settings of this sort have been relatively little studied in the scholarship on Indonesian heritage textiles. New forms of "old songkets" are coming alive in such ornate, delightful, even heart-stopping shopping spaces (fig. 5.4).

Sumatran songkets on the move: Fieldwork settings

Songket cloths in Sumatra are often conceptualized by Minangkabau and Palembang residents through a rosy haze of nostalgia, as fully traditional objects that supposedly preserve ancient, unchanging Minangkabau or old Malay heritages. In this conceptual framework, certain motifs and ways of arranging design elements on a growing songket on the loom are sometimes held to have lineal, direct connections to textile formats from hundreds of years ago. Some motifs definitely have great stability, but the particular form of rhetoric just noted can falsely veil elements of cloth change over time.

When specific weaving houses' output is examined closely for even so short a period as fifteen to twenty years, much variation in textile form is evident. This creativity takes place within a delicate way of talking about cloth on the part of weavers, cloth co-op entrepreneurs, and songket shopkeepers. They all assert that they are very much keeping tradition in their cloth work. Tradition sells, in some Sumatran contexts. Yet in Minangkabau and Palembang the marketing of luxury textiles demands frequent subtle stylistic changes to entice customers to buy new cloths. The wealthier customers often have many songkets already, from earlier ceremonial occasions. In fact, some have virtual collections of songket sarongs and shoulder cloths, including examples that reflect every slight new variation in color, thread type, and design format.

Ironically the merchandising of "traditional" songkets fosters innovation. The shopping scenes where families acquire new, high-level songkets in places such as the Bukittinggi area of West Sumatra and the 30 Ilir Malay weaving neighborhoods of Palembang, South Sumatra, are constitutive of conversations about traditionalism. But these shopping venues are also animated by undercurrents of constant textile change.

Drawing on Indonesian-language interviews and multiple site visits to selected songket shops in Pandai Sikek (1995 to 2006) and Palembang (2003 to 2006), in this chapter I present sketches of two remarkable songket business families whose traditional-style weaving houses have overseen and in part created an array of new songket textile design ideas since the early 1990s, when I began this study. These two houses' innovative accomplishments may well long predate the time period of the present inquiry. I document only the most recent changes, offering the reader a kind of snapshot in time of Sumatran songket traditions on the move.

These weaving establishments have pushed songket craft to strike out in creative ways in terms of dye color, thread choice, and alignments of motif bands. Within such weaving craft shifts, though, the motifs per se (such classics as Minangkabau's split-peanut design) seem to have remained stable. Additionally, certain motifs that had long fallen into disuse among weavers have also been consciously brought back by these weaving establishments as part of management decisions about both art and commerce. Also crucial have been management's visions of the buying public's perceived desire for traditional songkets.

Important to note too is the fact that individual weavers who are caught up in these marketing currents have themselves subtly altered the overall textile design settings into which they place their regenerated antique motifs—motifs put there at the behest of their bosses. This is particularly so of weavers in their thirties and beyond: self-confident women who have acquired reputations as especially fine craftswomen. At times, they do not have to follow the exact textile design dictates of the cloth shop entrepreneurs who market their songkets.

One business family to be introduced here is Minangkabau. They run the well-known and highly regarded Pusako Weaving House (Rumah Tenun Pusako) in the craft village of Pandai Sikek, West Sumatra (fig. 5.5). Ibu Sanuar, a retired master weaver, and her son Bapak Adyan manage this establishment together, with Ibu Sanuar acting as a songket designer (her word, in English) in her dealings with the numerous fine craftswomen who give her songkets on consignment to sell. The Pusako Weaving House also has a weaving pavilion off to its left side. This is a large, airy structure where employees (women and sometimes adolescent girls) weave songkets for Ibu Sanuar's business on typical Minangkabau frame looms.

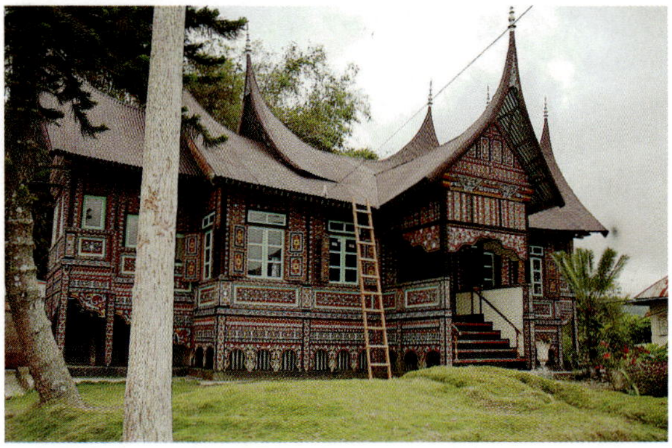

Fig. 5.5. The Rumah Tenun Pusako in Pandai Sikek, West Sumatra, 2005.

The second entrepreneurial family to be discussed here are Palembang Malays. The family is headed by its patriarch, Agus Haji Hussein Rahmat (age seventy-four), and includes his seven sons and two daughters. All these grown children are in the songket business. This extraordinary set of siblings run several weaving houses in the 30 Ilir district of Palembang. The eldest son, Pak Zainal, has established a prominent songket heritage shop in central Jakarta as well. In Palembang the shops have weaving pavilions in the back or off to the side and under the house. There women and older adolescent girls from village backgrounds weave especially luxurious songkets in bright colors and also in the traditional dark reds. They use southern Sumatra's prototypical backstrap looms.

All these shops sell notably high-end songkets, which are most typically bought by Minangkabau, Sumatran Malay, or other Indonesian peoples who are knowledgeable about fine weaving and who wish to purchase especially lovely and well-woven cloths for their families' ceremonial clothing needs. These buyers are generally middle-aged or older and are aware that the best newly produced gold textiles can generally be had close to the source—close to weavers whose work has been vetted by cognoscenti such as Ibu Sanuar, Bapak Adyan, Agus Haji Hussein, and his remarkable progeny.

A trip to one of these songket emporia is an event. The customer is swept into a great room ringed by glass-fronted cabinets filled with glistening rolls of gold cloth. One by one these are unfurled in front of the rapt customer. The cloths

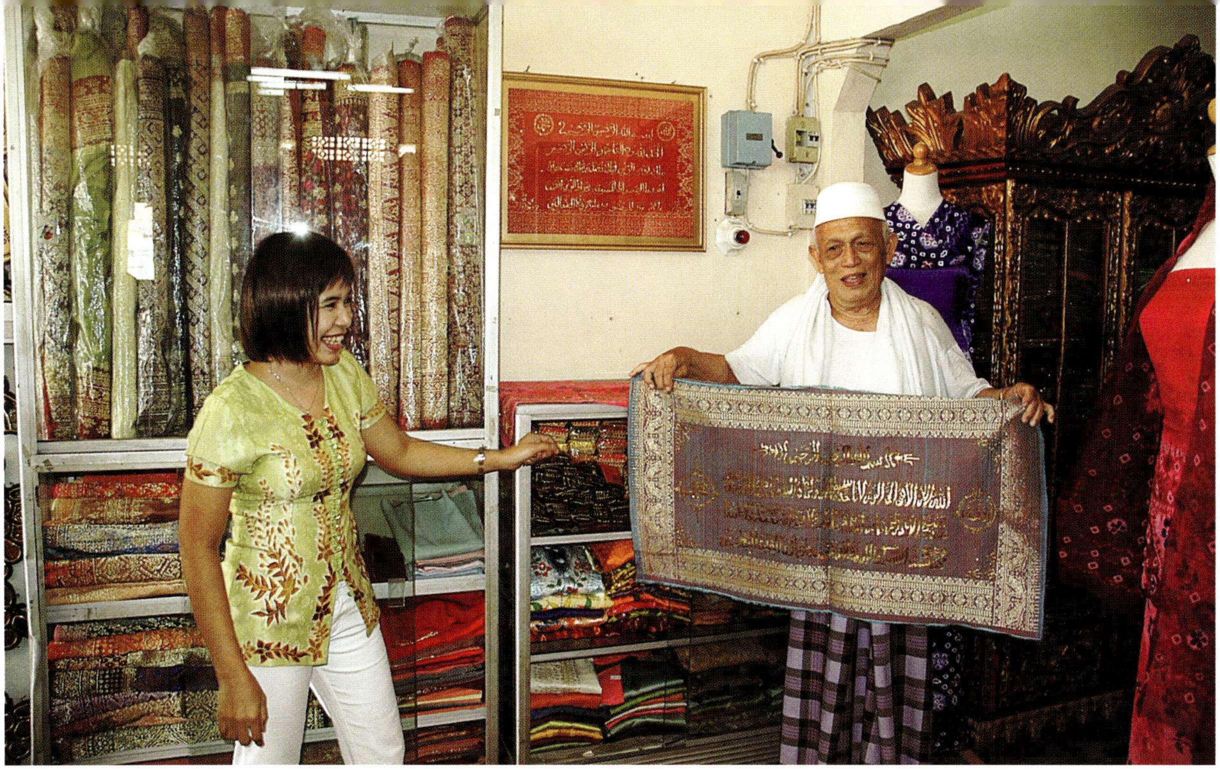

Fig. 5.6. Agus Haji Hussein Rahmat, in the Fikri Koleksi, Palembang, 2005.

are draped in gentle heaps on the carpet; the chamber begins to glow. The shopper stands amid this bounty, awestruck at songket artistry—and heritage.

By examining specific songkets that have been offered for sale since 1992 by the Minangkabau Pusako establishment and since 2003 by the Palembang Malay shops owned by Agus Haji Hussein's family (fig. 5.6), one can witness, in some detail, change within tradition in heritage art. By listening to the stories that West and South Sumatran business families tell about their cloths and about songket craft and songket history in general, we can also begin to hear some of the recurrent vibrations of Sumatra's longer history of what has perhaps been near-constant songket textile change. Of the full range of Indonesia's and Malaysia's heritage cloths, after all, Sumatra's songkets are most fully fabrics of commerce. They are interlaced at every level of their material and ideational existence with the push and pull of interregional and international trade, and with the ups and downs of running family businesses.

Rumah Pusako, Pandai Sikek, West Sumatra: A managed heritage textile arts renaissance

A case study of a Minangkabau songket business as it operates today can offer insight into the nexus of commerce and gold-cloth creativity at the level of individual textiles. The Pusako Weaving House is an apt focus, for it lies at the center of a thirty-one-year-long planned renaissance of songket weaving in the village of Pandai Sikek (fig. 5.7). The business's owners have been prime movers in this successful effort to regenerate fine songket weaving in West Sumatra.

Pandai Sikek weaving has historical ties to gold-cloth home production in Pitalah, whose weavers did exemplary craftwork as early as the 1700s. Today Pitalah and the nearby old weaving village of Pariangan produce no cloth. Pandai Sikek weavers and those in Tanjung (an extension of the village, up the hillside) contribute the

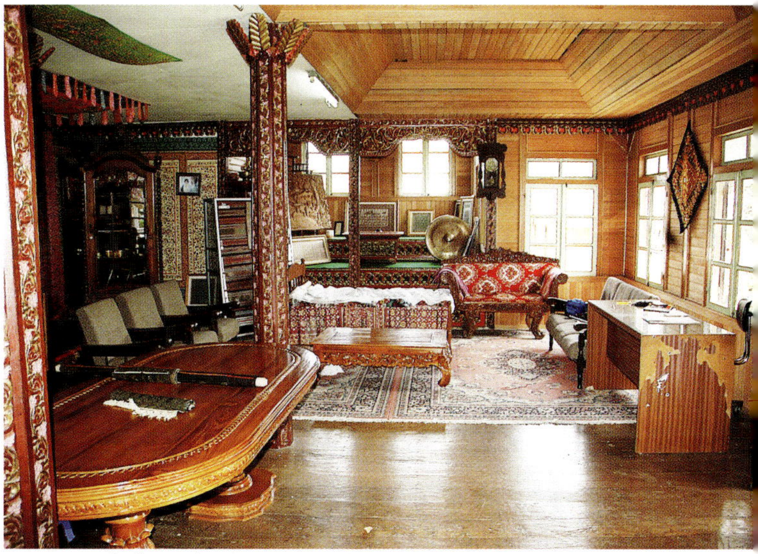

Fig. 5.7. Inside the Pusako Weaving House, 2005.

province's greatest songkets today. A larger town called Silungkang, near Lake Singkarak, also does a significant amount of songket weaving, but cloths from there are more roughly done than are the Pandai Sikek and Tanjung textiles.

Pandai Sikek lies a short distance from the main Bukittinggi-Padang road, at the turnoff for Koto Baru, near an imposing mosque. Pandai Sikek has a striking look of prosperity to it, which is not surprising, given its many thriving craft businesses. These include sandalwood carving (for home decorative plaques, Koran book stands, and small boxes), embroidery work for Muslim fashion wear for women, and songket weaving. Numerous craft shops selling all these luxury goods line the main road into Pandai Sikek. Also adding income to household coffers is the settlement's vegetable farming. The soil is black and volcanic; red peppers, carrots, leafy greens, and beans grow in abundance. A weekly market in Koto Baru offers this produce for sale.

Customers come directly to Pandai Sikek to buy some of the finest songkets, although good-quality gold textiles made in this village are also available for sale in Bukittinggi's own large number of songket businesses. Some of these are located in the multistory main marketplace in town. Other shops lie in rows of buildings lining the main highway. While it is possible to purchase Pandai Sikek songkets in Jakarta, at major department stores (on their Indonesian heritage floors, in fact), Minangkabau families who are knowledgeable about weaving will often combine a shopping trip to Pandai Sikek with their yearly trek back home during the Idul Fitri holidays following the Muslim fasting month of Ramadan. These visitors are part of the widespread Minangkabau diaspora in Java and beyond. Other songket shoppers include Malay families who come to West Sumatra from Kuala Lumpur and Negeri Sembilan. Some come specifically to call on Ibu Sanuar and to savor her songket riches for sale. Indonesian songkets are largely prevented from being exported to Malaysia legally by Malaysian law. Some of the Malaysian visitors hail from Minangkabau families that migrated to Negeri Sembilan, Malaysia, in the late 1800s.

Ibu Sanuar's songket emporium sits atop a slight rise in the very center of the craft-making village. This is a strategic location chosen for the structure in 1975 by her late husband, A. Ramli Dt. Rangkayo Sati. He was alert to the spot's marketing possibilities and also its symbolic impact. As they walk toward the weaving emporium, customers have a sense of approaching a grand noble's house. In the 1970s Ramli Dt. Rangkayo Sati was enmeshed in efforts to regenerate the old Minangkabau arts of wood carving and songket weaving. Indonesia's widespread political unrest following the violent change of national regimes in 1965 had calmed by this period; a degree of prosperity was returning to West Sumatra. He saw his wife's textile brokerage in her home village as integral to the sort of broad-scale arts renaissance that he hoped to bring to the province as a whole. Ibu Sanuar was a superb weaver herself; at the time she was also turning her attention to brokering crafts. Her husband was a trained oil painter, writer, and arts promoter. He built the songket emporium/house in 1975 by hand with the aid of carvers and decorative painters he had helped train.

Looking toward the Pusako Weaving House from any of an array of vantage points, villagers and visitors get a full view of this impressive home-cum-songket-shop, with its weaving pavilion alongside. The main house resembles nothing so much as a grand Minangkabau traditional house, with painted and carved wooden wall panels, soaring gables, and a spacious front porch. This imagery was deliberate on the family's part; they were fabricating an ideal old-style Minangkabau great house.

In the front courtyard are a traditionally decorated rice granary and a stocked goldfish pond. These are classic signs of family wealth and

Fig. 5.8. Master weaver Ibu Sanuar and her son Pak Adyan, in the Pusako Weaving House, 2006. The interior bespeaks elegance and wealth, in Malay World style.

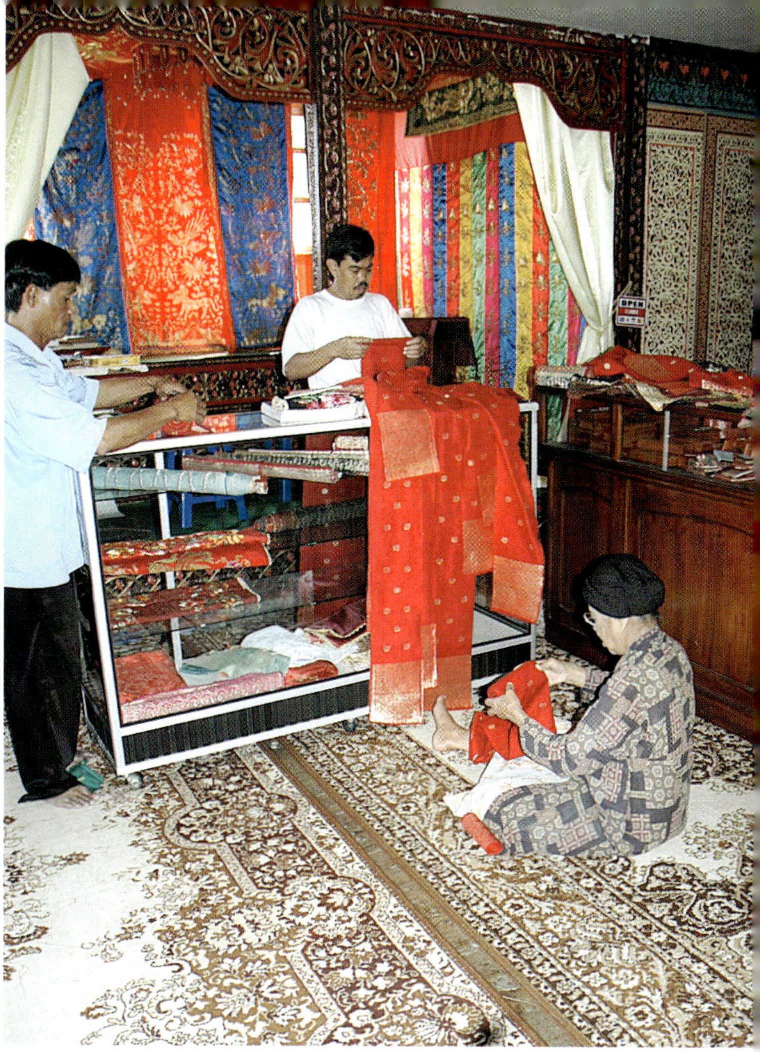

well-being in the Malay world. The gracious home of the high nobles is lauded often in the court poetry and village oratory of this entire region. Familiar from the Malay chronicles, Minangkabau *kaba* story-sagas, and village folktales is an iconography of an aristocratic house's orchard trees spilling over with jambu fruits and mangoes, comely maidens peeking out of windows in full adat headdress, and noble-born visitors flowing in from the ramparts toward the home to attend the village chiefs' grand ceremonies (fig. 5.8). Ramli Dt. Rangkayo Sati evoked this iconography of Minangkabau royal bounty and lifestyles in his design of the weaving house. His widow continues this architectural and landscape vision of the past by keeping the property in pristine shape and cultivating banks of colorful flowers all about. When songket customers approach the home/shop, she is sometimes kneeling in the front gardens, tending flowers.

As much as it is an allusion to a distant Minangkabau past, the Pusako Weaving House is much more than a so-called traditional regal home. The house was and is a songket shop, and proudly so—this is a family that relishes its reputation for business acumen in the heritage cloth trade. And the house is a dwelling for the family itself. Ibu Sanuar lives there today, sometimes accompanied by a granddaughter or two.

The wide main room of the shop images the long house form of the old-style village Minangkabau noble home but is smaller than this standard typically demands. This is a store, so glass-fronted cabinets full of rolled songkets predominate, along with an ornate carved wooden sofa and chairs set out for tired customers to rest upon. A classic Minangkabau long house has numerous small bedroom chambers off to the sides of the long central passageway. These are stereotypically for the grown daughters of the ancestral house to share with their young children and visiting husbands. Minangkabau adat for the high aristocracy valorizes the mother-daughter bond and posits the idea that the family line continues through generational time via female links, from a founder-matriarch through her daughters and their daughters and so on. Men belong to their mothers' ancestral houses and participate in the care and financial upkeep of their sisters' children. In the Pusako Weaving House, however, the bedrooms, off to back, are the places where the especially fine songkets are kept for special customers. This is a pattern found in high-end art dealerships worldwide, needless to say.

In sum, this grand house/shop is an example of national-era Indonesian heritage art writ large and made into a carefully designed, deftly Minangkabau-themed, high-toned commercial space. The weaving house's embedded visions of "Minangkabau traditions" resonate softly with the ideological claims of the craftwork that is sold inside.

These goods consist mostly of excellent songket textiles designed for wear as sarongs and shoulder cloths. Most of the songket merchandise is presented to viewers in long, upright gold-toned tubes, which are clustered behind the

Fig. 5.9. Sampler-size songket, for the upscale tourist market. Pandai Sikek, 2006.

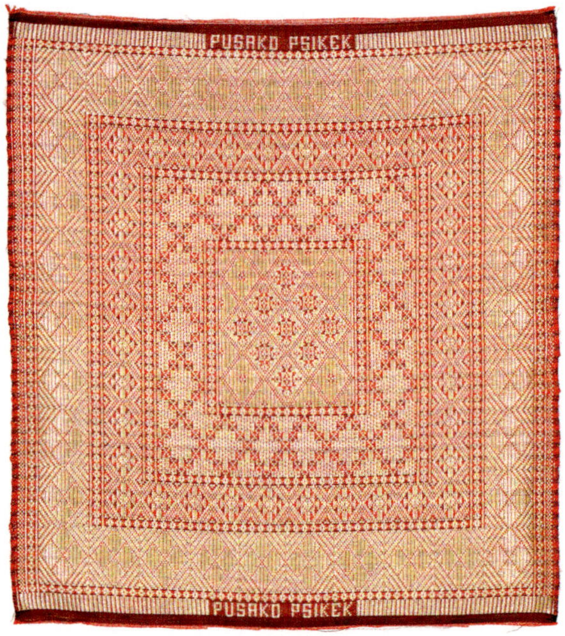

glass doors of the heavy carved wooden cabinets. (See figure, page iv). The lengths of songket are wound around long tubes. These are lined up in glistening banks in front of the buyer. Out in the back room are the pure silk songkets, woven in antique patterns, sometimes on commission. Off to the right side is a raised area evoking a wedding display of cloths and cushions, along with a rack for showing more songkets. To the left are glass cabinets and a desk and a computer.

The Pusako Weaving House also offers a few less exalted forms of songket for sale, probably because the many other weaving shops in Pandai Sikek uniformly carry this sector of the trade and customers have come to expect it. That is, there are small, sampler-size songkets (fig. 5.9), clearly meant as tourist curios (although these are expertly woven pieces and offer an abundance of traditional motifs in a small square, suitable for framing). There are also wallets, purses, and key chains made of the fabric, for the tourist and Minangkabau souvenir trade (fig. 5.10). The Pusako Weaving House also offers one of the village's best-selling items: little carved wood boxes made of sandalwood with songket inlays. These are for fanciers of wood carving, but also apparently for customers who may not have the money for a major songket purchase but who still wish to have a serious souvenir of their visit to the Pusako Weaving House. A tiny box of this sort went for the rupiah equivalent of about $3.25 in 2006.

Far up the price scale is a relatively new product, this one woven by men: songket versions of phrases or holy names in Arabic calligraphy, from the Koran and the Muslim prayers. Sampler-size Arabic-letter songkets of the sort shown in fig. 5.11 are notably expensive. This piece cost the rupiah equivalent of $50. Sellers say that it is technically challenging to make the curvilinear shapes of the calligraphy in metal-thread supplementary-weft work. These small textiles are intended as wall hangings for pious homes.

Many of these items can also be glimpsed on the Pusako Weaving House's Web site.[2] This attractively designed site has pages on the history of songket and the history of the weaving house (with a color photograph of Ibu Sanuar that shows her charm at age eighty). There is also an extensive list of the house's products (under "Katalog produk"), along with color photographs of several sample contemporary weavings.

This adroitly managed songket and old traditions business fosters several sorts of creativity in songket weaving and design in terms of fabric and thread level, three of which are discussed below. All these innovations are

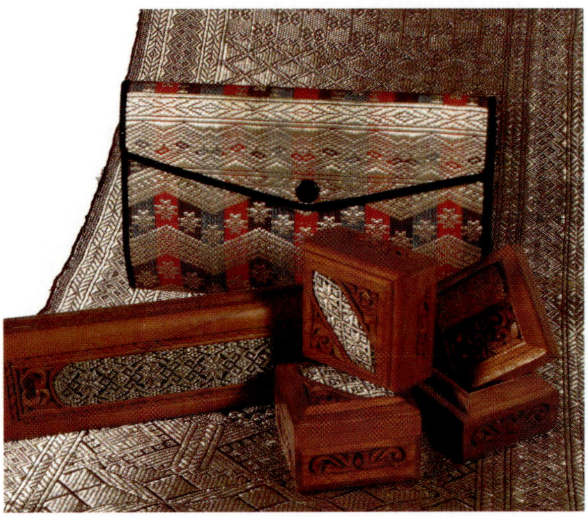

Fig. 5.10. Trinkets, but finely made of songket. Pandai Sikek, 2006.

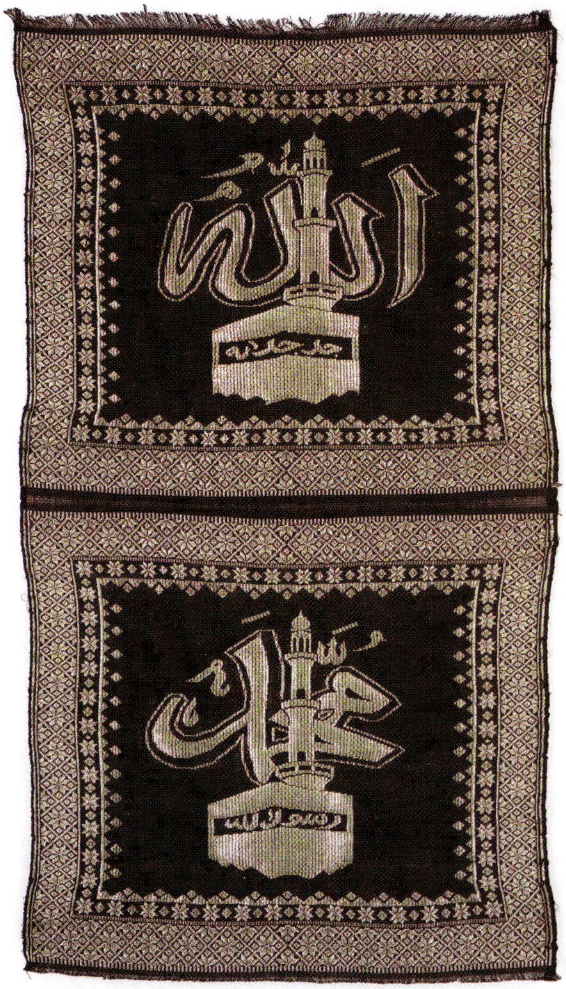

Fig. 5.11. Arabic calligraphy, in songket. Pandai Sikek, 2006. The top script, "Allah," and the second one, "Muhammad," are also decorated with minarets.

executed within a discourse of remaining faithful to Minangkabau traditions and to Minangkabau weaving heritages.

First, motif bands are being recombined in innovative and markedly quick-changing ways, under the firm managerial oversight of Ibu Sanuar in her role as songket designer. She talks of her activity here as being one of preserving old weaving traditions, but she is also a forceful innovator whose business actions speak to both the artistic and the commercial aspects of the resultant songkets.

The five songkets shown in the following pages (figs. 5.12-5.16) have all enjoyed considerable popularity with West Sumatran and Minangkabau diaspora buyers since 1995. All are shoulder cloths and were typically sold as part of sets, with matched sarongs. Each set was generally woven by the same weaver, although that can vary as sometimes mothers and daughters work together at their home looms in the village. As is evident, these five songkets vary in several respects. All are "traditional" in the sales and art history rhetoric of the Pusako Weaving House. Yet weaving creativity abounds in these cloths and across them from one to another through time.

A red songket (fig. 5.12), purchased in 1995, is of a type that is a perennial favorite. It is available even today, though finding it may require some digging through the Pusako Weaving House's stock. Its bold scarlet color is deemed a classic of Minangkabau weaving by craftspeople and customers. Any Minangkabau woman with a supply of songkets for ceremonial occasions will have a shoulder cloth closely resembling this one. It is suitable for a range of ritual events and is always in good taste; it shouts out Minangkabau tradition. It is also a good example of the Pandai Sikek weaver's art. Particularly notable, as one scans the textile from top to bottom, is the fact that the weaver has included a veritable sampler of major Pandai Sikek weaving motifs. The "problem," though, with this dramatic and quite excellent red songket is exactly its classicity. In Bukittinggi and Padang, everyone who knows anything about Minangkabau songkets from Pandai Sikek will probably have one of these. In this sector of Minangkabau society—with a customer base of women from families of means and old money but also women with paid jobs in the school sector, the government bureaucracy, health care, and small shops in town—consumption patterns tended toward a desire for novelty in the 1990s. Ibu Sanuar was acutely aware of this trend among her longtime customers (families keep coming back) but also among the new songket consumers whom she wished to attract. Therefore, she urged her most favored and expert weavers to create *new* traditional songkets—textiles that would use the old motifs but would arrange pattern bands and combinations of motifs in innovative, eye-catching ways.

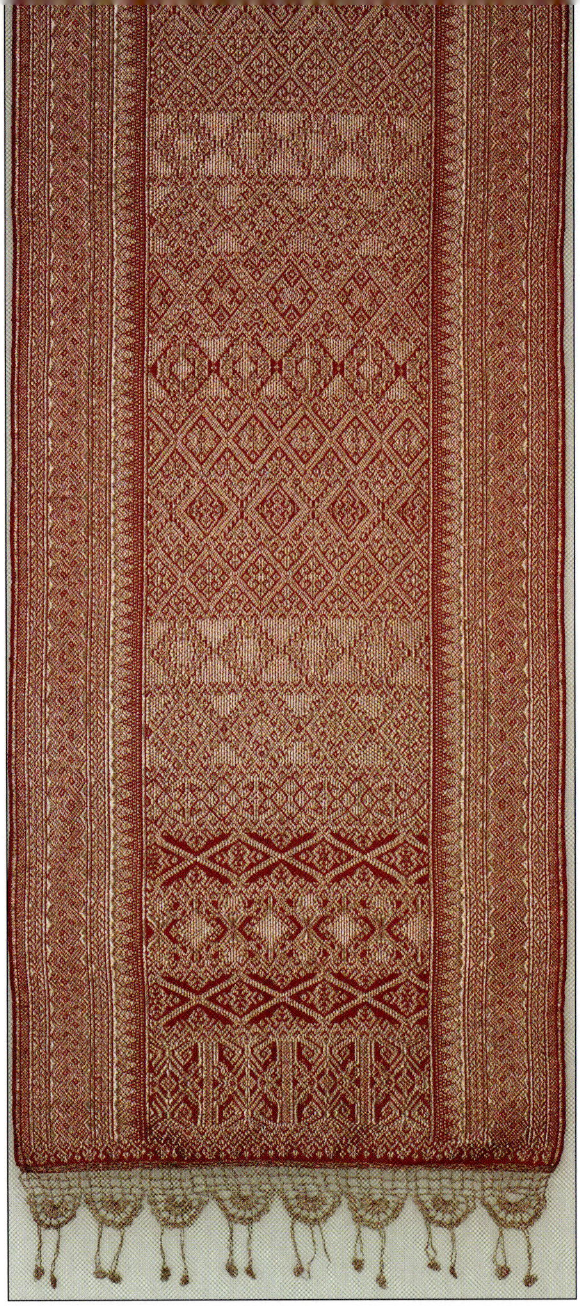

Fig. 5.12. Finely woven songket shoulder cloth, 1995, Pandai Sikek.

The black-and-gold-thread shoulder cloth (fig. 5.13) is of a style that was reaching its ascendancy in popularity at the Pusako Weaving House at the time the red songket was purchased. This black textile is bordered with motif bands along the selvedge that are familiar favorites of Pandai Sikek weavers. The relatively open field all along the center of this cloth, though, was its main selling point during this period. This clearly was a different sort of songket than the more uniformly patterned "motif sampler" red one. For this open-field design, weavers would sometimes leave the center blank (as shown in the dark blue shoulder cloth [fig. 5.14]), or, as in fig. 5.13, the weaver could decorate the center with small stars, boxes, or blossoms (prominent in Palembang weaving far to the south). The blue and the black songkets are still recognizable as Pandai Sikek weavings, most

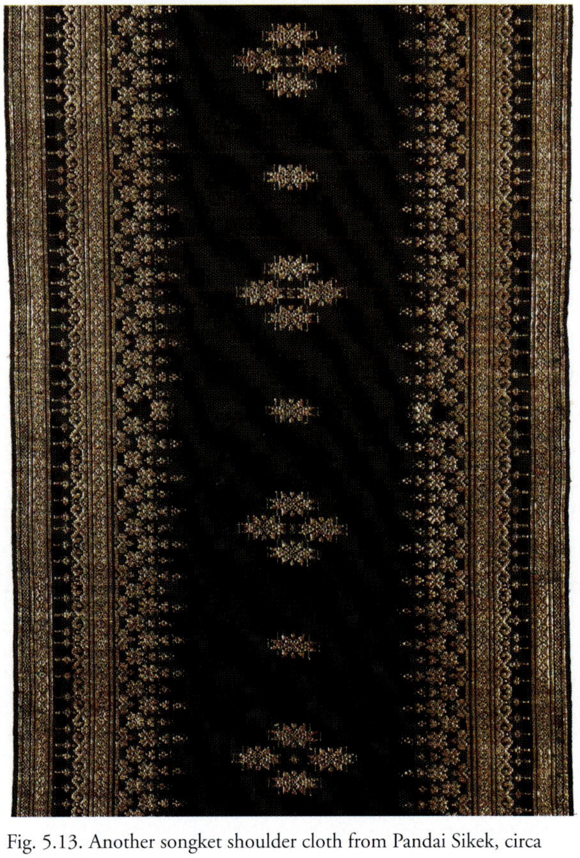

Fig. 5.13. Another songket shoulder cloth from Pandai Sikek, circa mid-1990s.

Ibu Sanuar also encouraged the use of high-end silk thread and silk blends, moving the weavers away from their heavy reliance on cotton blends. These managerial suggestions on her part, done overtly to reinvigorate Minangkabau's old weaving traditions, resulted in the manifestly new-looking shoulder cloths shown here. Ibu Sanuar's profound knowledge of the compositional tool kit of nineteenth-century weavers from her home village but also from Kotogadang, Pitalah, Pariangan, Padang Magek, and on through a range of other old weaving centers aided her in overseeing weavers' work. As is still the case today, Ibu Sanuar would reject a weaver's offering if the textile at issue did not meet her exacting standards.

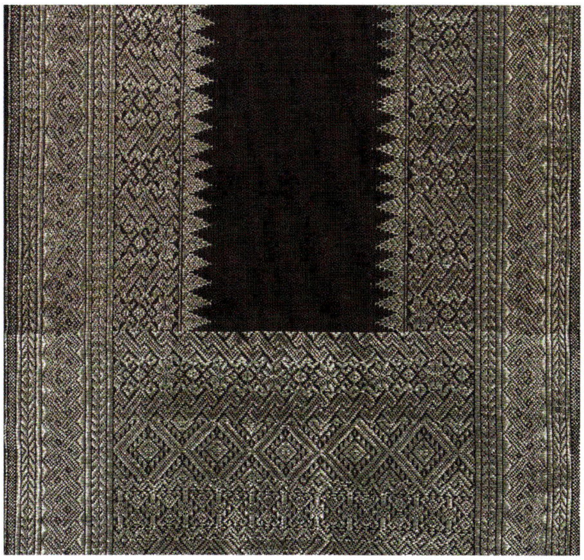

Fig. 5.14. Songket shoulder cloth, Pandai Sikek, mid-1990s.

notably thanks to their selvedge bands.

Close on the heels of these "open-center" songkets was another hotly marketed and much-sought-after style, available from about 1996–97 through 2002–3, exemplified by a cream-colored example (fig. 5.15). In these cloths the intense blanketing of the entire fabric field with close metal-thread work made the resulting songket resemble a patterned sheet of gold. This shoulder cloth was also a step up in price from the open-center ones. The cream cloth cost approximately $90, whereas the others were in the $70 to $80 range. The "gold sheet" songket type recalled a classic antique songket form from Kotogadang Village, called *balapak*. This reinvigorated (though not perfectly replicated) style quickly caught on among prosperous Minangkabau customers and became a must-have for ceremonial occasions and for brides.

By this point Ibu Sanuar's customers were happily entangled in a quick-changing fashion scene, albeit one that was rigidly traditional in one sense: the songkets could not be cut into pieces for reassembly into high-fashion shirts or suits. The latter treatment of Indonesian traditional cloths had long been common in the Javanese, Jambi, and Bengkulu batik industries, but songket's physical nature as a relatively stiff loomed cloth made of metal-wrapped yarns made this approach unwieldy.

The bright aqua and blue stripe-upon-stripe shoulder cloth (fig. 5.16) is a more recent incarnation of Pandai Sikek songket weaving. Interestingly, this precise type was also shown on the opening page of the Pusako Weaving House's Web site in 2006. Clearly this one is a star of the present-day songket shopping scene. Songkets composed of small pattern bands are offered in a variety of pastel colors today, with this particular blue combination being one of the top sellers. These jaunty songkets are suitable for all adat occasions.

By 2006 the Pusako Weaving House's march of new yet traditional songkets had moved on to new styles, with no sign of abatement in the rapid turnover of style formats. Part of this was likely due to the Pusako Weaving House's special status as the shop that sold the finest goods in the village. Other weaving emporia were offering excellent songkets as well, and Ibu Sanuar had to strive to maintain her house's position at the top of the weaving pyramid. Throughout all this, many of Pandai Sikek weavers' favorite old motifs remained stable, as did the village's predictable,

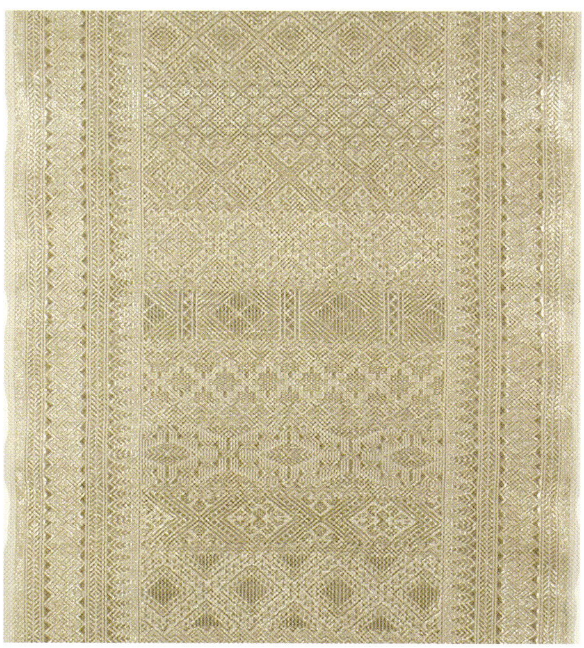

Fig. 5.15. An additional recent Pandai Sikek shoulder cloth, this one echoing the balapak style of Kotogadang textiles of the 1800s.

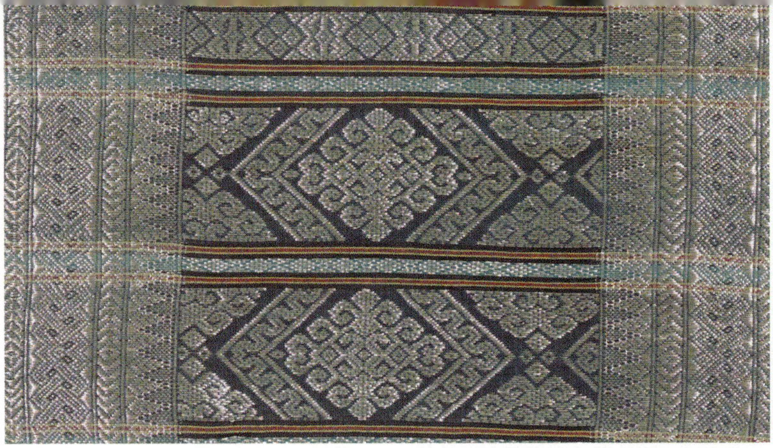

Fig. 5.16. "The latest thing": a new style of songket shoulder cloth popular among Pandai Sikek weavers, dealers, and the public, circa 2003-06.

diagnostically local selvedge bands.

A second trend that has led to new forms of traditional songkets relates to mundane, practical concerns about what type of songket wears best in Indonesia's hot, humid climate. Certain new types of cloth are trumping traditional metal-thread choices for both a textile's ground and its decorative supplementary wefts. As a result, a number of songket houses are beginning to produce songket cloths without gold thread.

Ibu Sanuar and her son Bapak Adyan know that this is a growing sector of the market, and they have some of their more expert weavers experimenting with songket weaving without metal thread (fig. 5.17). This type of weaving is uncommonly difficult since silk or silk-blend supplementary wefts are harder to work with than the stiffer metal-wrapped yarns (figs. 5.18, 5.19). Ibu Sanuar and Bapak Adyan are still not completely satisfied with the results of their collaborating weavers' experiments, so they are not yet marketing this type of textile. But they see promise in this approach to creating songkets and know that it can produce impressive cloths, as the example illustrated here—which was woven in Pandai Sikek, though not for the Pusako Weaving House—demonstrates.

Intricate designs of all the traditional metal-thread sorts can be essayed in this form of cloth, and the wearer reaps the benefits—that is, most importantly, the songket looks like a standard songket, yet it can be laundered. Metal-thread songket dulls when washed with soap and water, yet the tropical climate of West Sumatra and

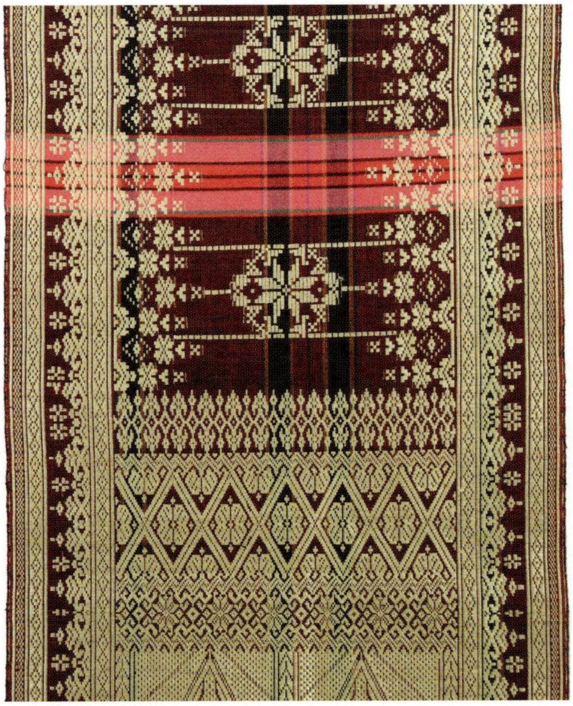

Fig. 5.17. Songket shoulder cloth made without metallic thread. The supplementary wefts are silk. Purchased in a shop in Bukittinggi, 2006.

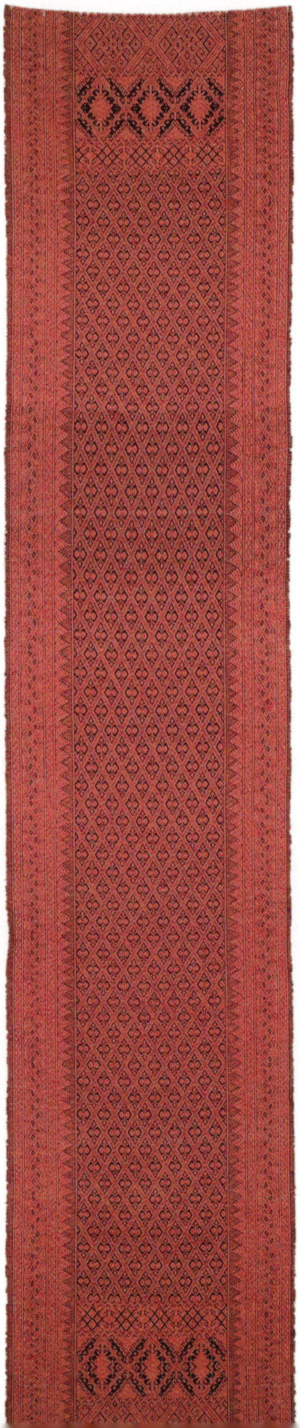

Fig. 5.18. Another unusually fine contemporary silk supplementary wefts songket shoulder cloth. West Sumatra, circa 1990s.

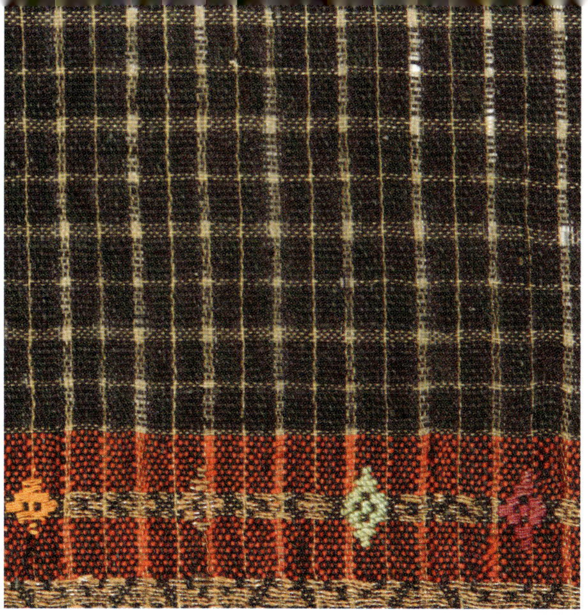

Fig. 5.19. Shoulder cloth woven in Batu Sangkar, before 1850. Songket work at the bottom edge is done not in metallic thread but in pink silk embroidery floss.

Jakarta means that wearers often sweat down their ritual finery in just one wearing.

Songkets like the ones pictured here also make for ease of wearing: they are not rigid like standard songkets, nor are they heavy and stiff. A closely related sector of Pandai Sikek weaving today is producing songkets in metal-wrapped thread as supplementary wefts paired to pure silk warps and wefts. Customers aver that this expensive approach yields lighter-weight, more pliable sarongs. These cloths, however, can run to $1,000 or more for a set.

A third instance of innovation is taking place at the Pusako Weaving House. The very high-end heritage cloth market in the Minangkabau highland cities and among the upper middle class in the diaspora is generating demand for old-style songkets from villages such as Kotogadang and Padang Magek, where looms are no longer found. Customers from these former weaving villages who have no inherited antique songkets to wear for their important ceremonial occasions come to songket brokers such as Ibu Sanuar, who commissions her Pandai Sikek weavers to create versions of the old songkets, sometimes entirely in silk and gold thread.

These "replica" cloths (fig. 5.20) are not so much perfect copies of the nineteenth-century songkets from ancestral villages as they are imaginative reworkings of them. These cloths are subject in small but intriguing ways to the taste of individual weavers and to Ibu Sanuar's own highly developed sense of songket propriety and excellence. Once again she keeps an eye on art as she attends to the marketability of these cloths. This purple-brown shoulder cloth that was

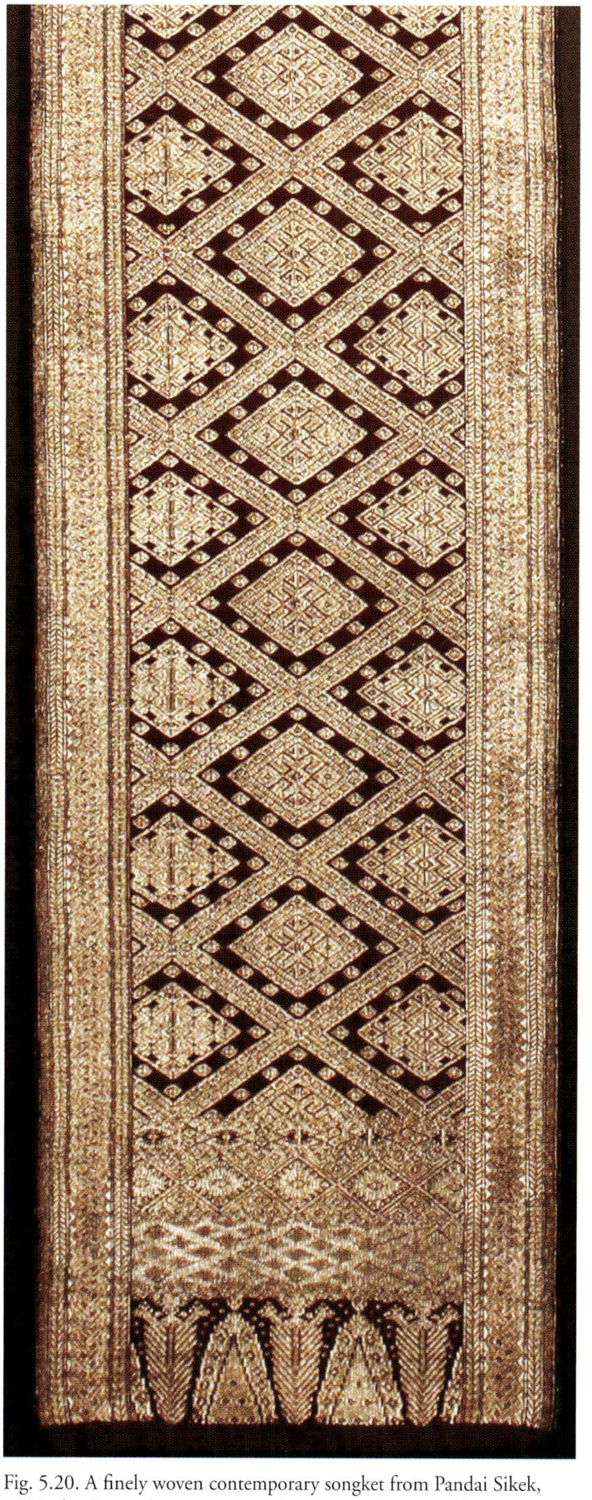

Fig. 5.20. A finely woven contemporary songket from Pandai Sikek, 2006. Ibu Sanuar has encouraged the weaver who wove this textile to mine old motifs, from throughout West Sumatra.

available for sale at the Pusako Weaving House in 2006 illustrates this trend. Its center-field motifs are ones that Ibu Sanuar and her son identify as coming from the old weaving traditions of distant settlements. Ibu Sanuar gives favored weavers fragments of old cloths from such villages to use as pattern templates. In this cloth the weaver has combined these old motifs with several diagnostically Pandai Sikek-esque features, such as the selvedge bands. In such ways, Ibu Sanuar and the weavers who produce such cleverly designed heritage textiles keep antique motif repertoires alive in contemporary songket craft. As a songket designer Ibu Sanuar mediates past and present to great artistic, and commercial, effect.

Palembang Malay songkets in transition

The southern Sumatran city of Palembang is located near the possible site of the Buddhist trade kingdom of Sriviyaya, the late 7th century mediator of commerce between this part of the Indonesian archipelago, China, and India. Palembang's locale also has ties to several key Malay sultanates of the late 1700s and early 1800s. These ambitious Malay polities of that latter period supported luxury arts (decorated wood carpentry, gold work, fine weavings) associated with the sultan's court and mid-level but still prideful aristocrats. The sultanate of Mahmud Badaruddin II, who came to power in 1803, was linked to great songket weaving, in fact. Some of the gold cloth production may have been done in the kraton, the palace (Uchino 2005: 209). Following Sutan Mahmud Badaruddin II's usurpation and exile by the Dutch authorities in 1821, Palembang songket production probably moved beyond the circle of noblewomen to a near-professional class of weavers (Uchino 205: 211-213; see also B. Andaya 1989 for the older linkage between songket weaving and the women of the sultan's court).

From approximately 1830 to 1850, gold cloth weaving in Palembang intensified and reached heights of artistic excellence (Uchino 2005: 211-213). Although the formal sultanate had come under Dutch administrative control by this point, mid-level noblewomen tied to the old kraton social hierarchy probably continued to acquire and wear elaborate songket finery (Uchino 2005: 211-212). In addition, Arab merchants from Hadhramaut (southern Arabia) had moved to Palembang in the late 1700s to profit from trade opportunities there (Uchino 2005: 212-213). They became close to the sultanate's core Muslim, Malay high-ranking families. Some of these Arab traders married Palembang Malay women. The mestizo class of Arab-Malays that resulted became an important customer base for the songket weavers.

Uchino describes the 1850-1900 period as one of alternating stability and minor decline for Palembang songket weaving (2005: 213-215). The 1900-1960s period was one of definite decline in this craft sector, in part due to the difficulties of obtaining the fine materials so central to songket weaving excellence. Uchino reports that (2005:218),

> Around 1965 a Palembang woman of noble descent, Ibu Sity Bambang Utoyo, inititated a project for reviving songket weaving. The silk thread came from Sulawesi as the import of Chinese silk had not resumed. *Benang emas jantung* [actual gold thread] was still unavailable, but synthetically coloured gold thread was imported from Japan, India and Europe (Proyek RPM 1977/1978). The artificial gold thread was much cheaper than benang emas jantung, and reasonably attractive. Furthermore, synthetic dyes were becoming popular in Palembang.
>
> Ibu Sity Bambang Utoyo realized that the surviving songket weavers were old and no longer active. She recruited experienced weavers to teach ten young men and women

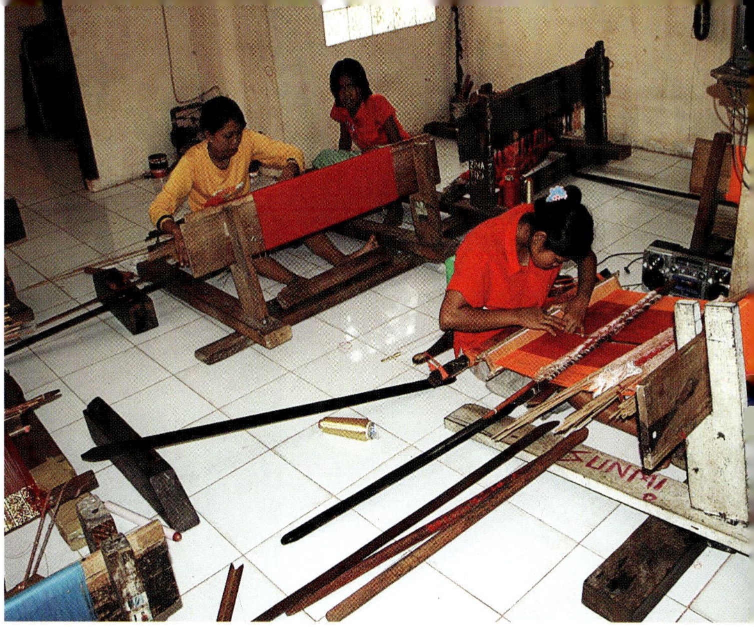

Fig. 5.21. Weavers at work, Fikri Koleksi, Palembang, 2005.

> the techniques of songket weaving. She invested in a shop in Daerah Suro [the weaving district of town]; this was the first songket shop in Palembang, but was soon followed by two others.

Today this managed renaissance of songket production (so similar to the efforts of Ibu Sanuar and her late husband Ramli Dt. Rangkayo Sati in Pandai Sikek in Minangkabau) has come into full flower. The 30 Ilir neighborhood of town has a contemporary songket-weaving industry that combines an overt traditionalism with much innovation, keyed to marketing demands. The economy and history of this revivified songket craft district (presented to visitors as an old Malay kampong) revolve around the weaving and selling of especially fine, high-end songket cloth.

Palembang as a whole is dominated by the oil business and oil-related manufacturing. A sprawling metropolis, Palembang has numerous traditional markets and new-style malls, museums, and universities. There are also new housing estates, old business districts, and Minangkabau restaurants galore (many West Sumatran immigrants live in Palembang). The city also has the Chinese shops with apartments atop familiar throughout urban Sumatra, as well as a colonial-era residential neighborhood of imposing villas. The 30 Ilir area is near this, and as one enters this weaving kampong, a grand archway announces that travelers are coming into the songket-weaving center of the city.

Palembang is laid out along the Musi River, which is famous throughout Indonesia for its long-span bridge. Even the latter has been caught up in the city's songket business. In the Fikri Koleksi emporium, one of our foci here, the proprietors offer brightly colored wall hangings portraying this familiar bridge, done in prada gold-leaf work.

The Fikri Koleksi in fact offers numerous home decorations for sale. There are other wall hangings in prada work presenting well-known verses of the Koran suitable for mounting in front parlors. There are also purses, shoes, hats, and fans in songket, which is definitely this large shop's stock-in-trade. As was the case with Ibu Sanuar's establishment in the Minangkabau highlands, the Fikri Koleksi shop offers exquisite high-end handloomed songkets to a notably upscale clientele. The owners take care to offer both the most "traditional" Palembang red silk songkets and new versions of the cloths.

This shop is a particularly large one and is in essence a spacious villa-type house with a big, airy weaving pavilion in a separate building in the back (fig. 5.21). Some twelve or so young women work there most days, sitting on the floor and weaving songkets in glaringly bright silk yarns on Palembang's signature backstrap looms. The pavilion is well lit, and a television set (a common feature of Palembang weaving-shop floors) hums in the background. According to interviews with the owners, the workers are generally villagers who have come there to earn a salary, live in the big city, and, for those who are still of school age, to try to get an education.

The shop itself consists of several expansive, interconnected rooms, fronted by a large, open entranceway near the concrete driveway. The generally quite well-off customers typically arrive in their own sedans or Land Rovers, or come by taxi. This is an establishment that projects an air of sedate wealth, good taste, and leisurely, unpressured shopping adventures in the songket trade. The family prides itself on being among Palembang's old Malay weaving aristocracy. "We are," they proclaim, "*orang Palembang asli—Melayu*"—the original Palembang people, Malays.

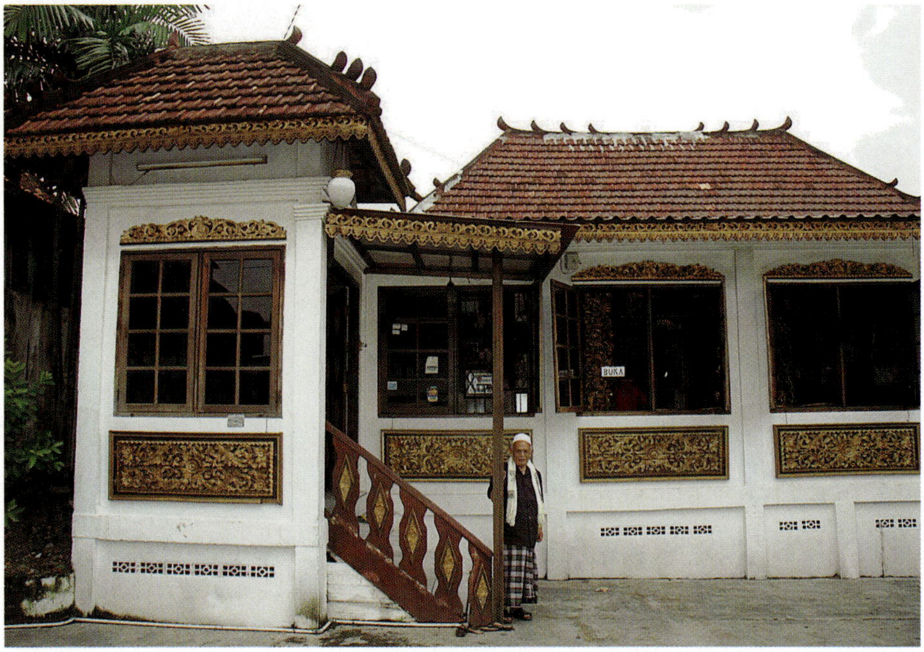

Fig. 5.22. Agus Haji Hussein Rahmat, outside his family's old home. Palembang, 2006.

In the first two main rooms, rolls of songket line the walls inside glass-fronted floor-to-ceiling cabinets. The souvenir goods are displayed on another wall nearer to the entrance, as is a rack of ready-to-wear. A small sitting area with chairs and a sofa is off to the side; behind these front rooms is another chamber with more songkets for sale, along with other fine textiles. These include pelangi silk in long lengths (mostly for ritual dress for wedding attendants) and cloth coffin covers.

The Fikri Koleksi has the architectural style of a modern-day, upper-middle-class urban home. Another major house-shop owned by the same extended family, however, is quite literally an old Malay house (fig. 5.22). This is the ancestral manse of Agus Haji Hussein Rahmah's grandparents and great-grandparents: the family's original domicile, located a few streets away from the Fikri Koleksi. Owned by one of Haji Hussein's sons, this house-shop is now managed by Haji Hussein's eldest son, Pak Zainal. 5.35). It is Zainal's Palembang base, although he is probably better known in Indonesia as a whole as the proprietor of Zainal Songket in central Jakarta. In fact, his Jakarta songket emporium, which is located in a particularly palatial villa in the Tanah Abang neighborhood, off Jalan Thamrin, is in many ways the public face of Palembang songket for the nation. That shop markets very fine songkets to Palembang émigrés and members of other Indonesian societies who use songket in adat.

The grand old family home back in Palembang is not a reconstructed traditional house, as is Ibu Sanuar's shop, but is the original structure. Wide stairways invite the customer up into the house, into a long enclosed porch, metaphorically transforming them into old-time visitors to a noble Malay great house. The clientele step through tiny doorways inside the home to enter grand halls lined with the requisite carved wooden cabinets stocked with rolls of shiny songkets. Old family photographs of great-grandparents and other Palembang notables hang on the dark wood walls; Dutch colonial-era hanging ceramic lamps softly illuminate the shopping scene (abetted by fluorescent lights). This establishment is subdued and notably upscale in tone, as is the case at the Fikri Koleksi. Young attendants, once again, pull out any songkets that a customer might wish to view. The textiles are unfurled, held up for inspection, and then piled gently on the floor, as the customer mulls over decisions.

The family's several shops offer cultivated buying publics a great wealth of traditional yet evolving songkets. These cloths evince several different types of creativity of form, each shaped in part by the heated competitiveness of the Palembang traditional weaving business. The Ilir neighborhood has twenty or more songket shops, all selling basically similar wares done in Palembang style—that is, brightly colored silk or silk-blend supplementary-weft gold-wrapped thread textiles in solids or in the famous *kain limar* style (fig. 5.23). The Palembang

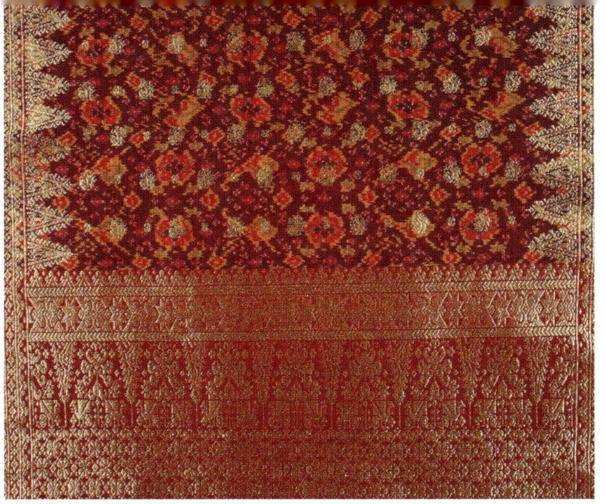

Fig. 5.23. A kain limar-style songket from Palembang, from the Fikri Koleksi. 2005.

style demands a fairly standardized array of songketted borders, plus center fields (some ikatted, some not) decorated with songketted blossoms, stars, or box motifs. With this much uniformity of weaving product, proprietors have to strive hard to differentiate their goods from those of their competitors.

The songkets sold by Haji Hussein's far-flung family members are distinguished primarily by their sheer excellence of weaving quality (tightness of weave, fineness of the silk yarns, the weaver's adeptness in replicating old motifs). Beyond this, however, color, decoration, and what might even be called fashion flair enter the picture.

Color is an important area of innovation. Palembang's signature silk and gold-thread songkets are traditionally a deep, rich red. This is a tone that sometimes shades off into a brilliant red-purple, also an acceptable classic. With the kain limar, the ikatted center field can also show flecks of black, yellow, or blue-purple. But the main background color should be that dark red. This is not so today, however, in emporia such as the Fikri Koleksi, where a color palette encompassing pastels, creams, bright greens, eye-popping purples, and electric blues augments the standard, more subdued classic reds. In 2006 popular colors included one described by the Fikri Koleksi proprietors, using the English term, as "baby pink" (fig. 5.24). Many other color choices jostle with this one, and the range of hues changes with some rapidity from year to year. Ibu Sanuar's shop in Pandai Sikek offered songkets in a range of colors, but Palembang shops such as this one take color choice to even greater extremes.

The owners, who are also the managers who give the weavers their colored yarns to work with, always take care to stock a good supply of classic red silk songkets in kain limar style. So why the alarming blues and greens and purples too? Interviews in 2005 and 2006 yielded two answers: first, the shop owners like to have weavers experiment with all the candy-colored shades of silk yarn now available commercially and, second, customers have a sense of fashion and like to keep up with all the new colors that they see elsewhere in Indonesia's (and the world's) traditional textiles and also in global fashion (fig. 5.25). Indonesian-language magazines like the glossy *Femina* (a women's magazine with features on clothes, food, child-rearing, relationships, and family lifestyle issues) are readily available in news shops to the Fikri Koleksi's customers.

A second creative touch evident in the songkets in one of the extended family's shops is the exuberant addition of "bells and whistles," so to speak, to completed cloths. For example, a cloth from Pak Zainal's shop in Palembang (fig. 5.26) is a striking songket on its own, with its bold

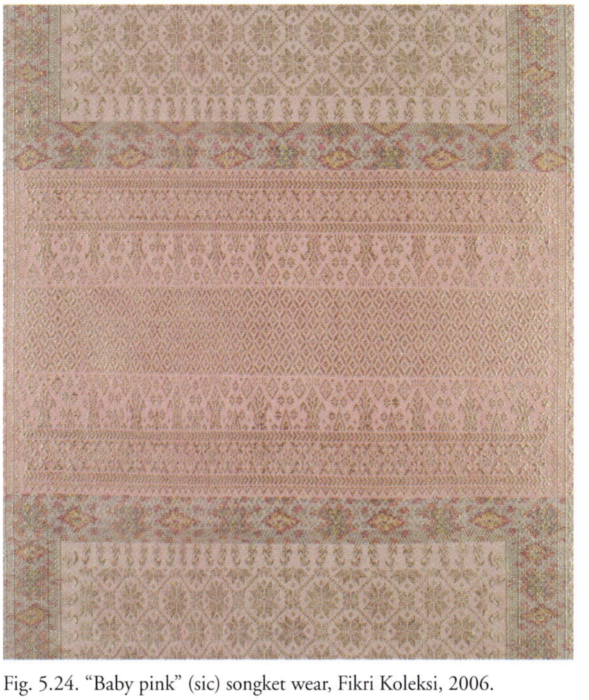

Fig. 5.24. "Baby pink" (sic) songket wear, Fikri Koleksi, 2006.

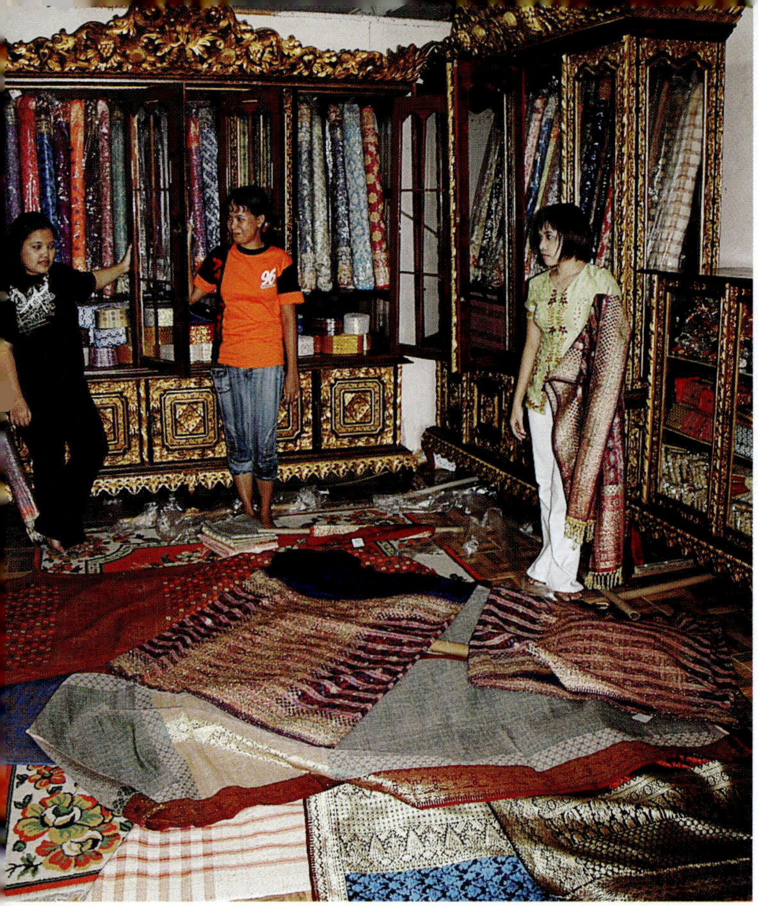

Fig. 5.25. A rainbow array of songkets, in the Fikri Koleksi, 2005.

patterning, tight weave, and pure black color. Yet the manager/owner instructed his weavers to embellish the finished cloth with an edging of tiny gold-toned beads, set off with a luxurious fringe of gold-hued glass beads. Zainal also sells the most conservative, classic, red kain limar textiles, in several price categories, but decorated cloths like this one seem to be establishing a significant foothold in his product line.

Minangkabau cloth brokers also often top off their fine songket shoulder cloths with crocheted fringes in gold-colored filigree. This style may well be a legacy of the considerable influence that European lace-making and fancywork embroidery had in such craft villages as Kotogadang, from the late 1800s through the end of the colonial period (fig. 5.27). A particularly important craft cooperative in that settlement, an establishment called Amai Setia, spearheaded the marketing of this sort of decorative textile work in West Sumatra. Yet Palembang songkets may be far more ornate.

The almost excessive beadwork of these songkets points to an aspect of Palembang songket weaving today that may not be evident to customers who are not familiar with the overall Sumatran songket-weaving scene. That

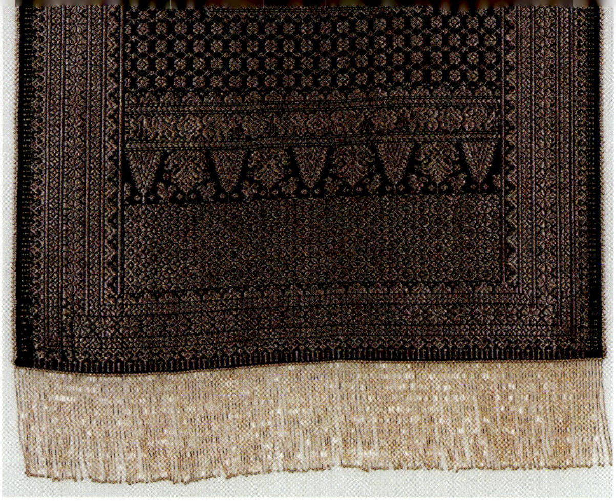

Fig. 5.26. A contemporary songket with much visual and tactile impact. From Pak Zainal's shop in Palembang, 2006.

is, Palembang songket work is excellent in technique, and the overall aesthetic impact of the textiles is certainly alluring, but the motif register and compositional structure of the cloths are fairly static. This stands in great contrast to the remarkable imaginativeness of songket design found in Pandai Sikek shops like Ibu Sanuar's; the studious character of West Sumatran weaving culture, with its interest in discovering and bringing back old motifs, is also not found in pronounced form in Palembang. This situation leaves sellers to differentiate their goods by other means, such as color and ornate decorative flourishes.

A third aspect of Palembang cloth creativity shaped by shopping is the Indonesian high-fashion universe, in the sense of couture ideas radiating from Jakarta ateliers. Can stiff, metal-thread cloth of ritual and Muslim origins be made into upscale fashion wear? Pak Zainal of

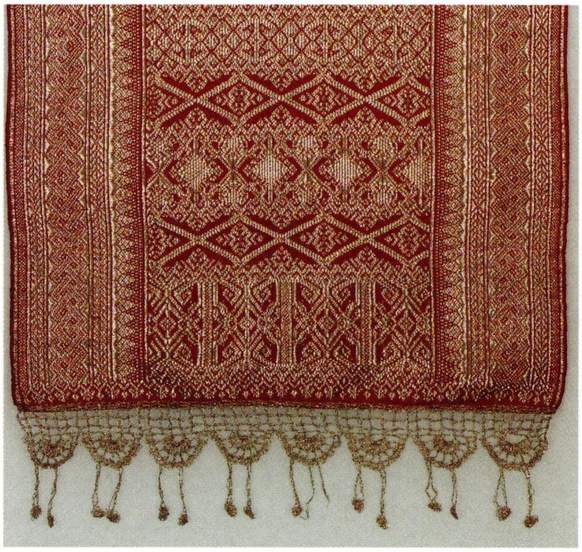

Fig. 5.27. Edgings added to fine songkets intensify a textile's aura of luxury and presence. A Pandai Sikek songket, 1990s.

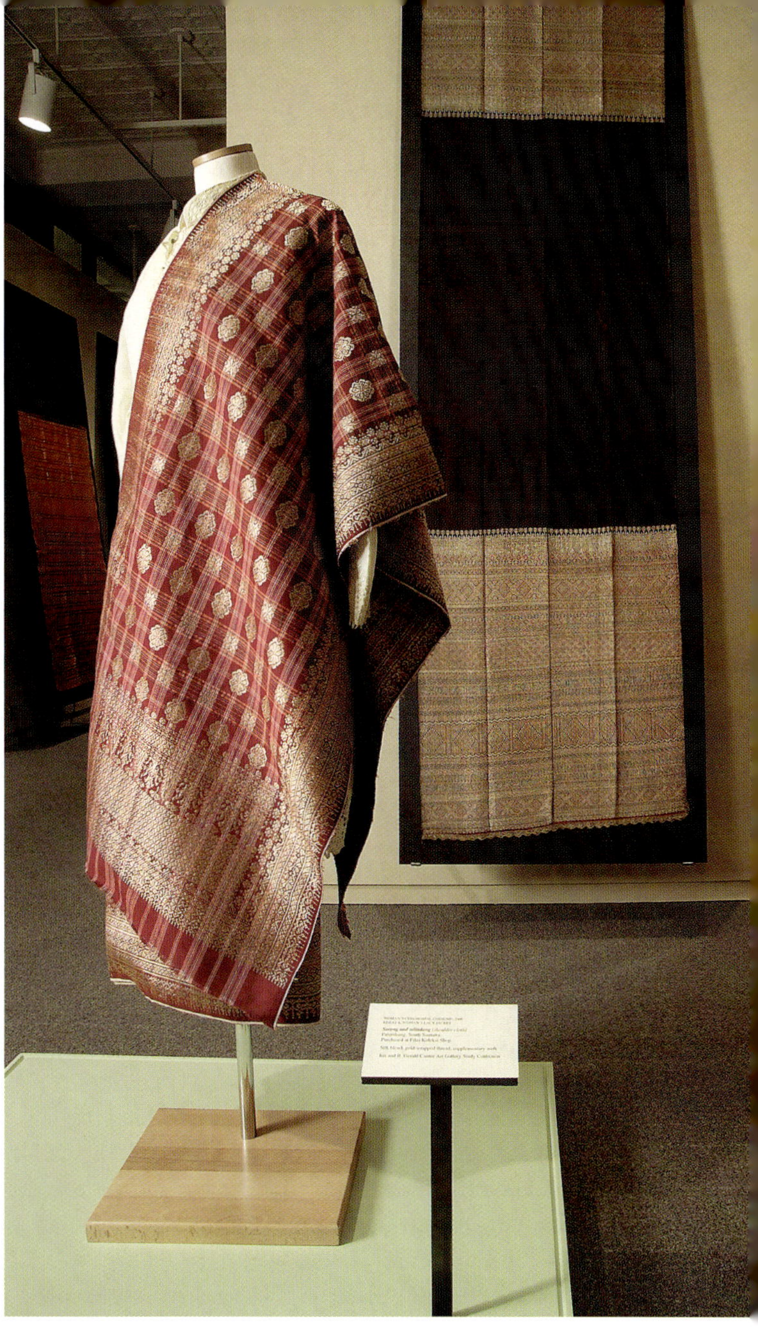

Fig. 5.28. A mannequin in classic Palembang songket attire for a ceremony. The sarong and shoulder cloth are from the Fikri Koleksi, 2005. Iris and B. Gerald Cantor Art Gallery, 2007.

Palembang and Jakarta asserts that it can. His Tanah Abang shop/house in Jakarta sells the full range of traditional songket sarongs and shoulder cloths for standard adat uses (fig. 5.28). He also offers excellent antique south Sumatran songkets for connoisseurs and collectors. But he is vigorously developing quite another part of his business too: elegant sarongs and shoulder cloths that he is fashioning into evening wear for Indonesian high-society women. The songkets used are quite expensive, as are the entire costumes. His full-color brochures and his Jakarta shop's website (Zainalsongket at http://www.zainalsongket.com) present photographs of young women in traditional-looking songket sarongs. But, young women in resepsi-style gold cloth wear were also pictured.

Pak Zainal does not so much cut the songkets into evening gowns and tops (this would violate the stability of the metal thread cloth) as he overlays them with filmy or lacey jackets. The latter, called *kebaya* in standard Indonesian and Malay usage, are notably transparent and soigné in his product line. This creates styles that evoke high-end party wear for city sophisticates.

In Zainal Songket's brochure available in 2006 the comely young women models (most of these styles are for women) wear slinky, open-toed high-heeled sandals. The models all wear elaborate, upswept hairstyles, with cascades of small blossoms pinned into their locks, and ornate, dangling metal-toned earrings that recall the gold headdress ornaments of royal Palembang brides of old. The entire costume evokes many imageries of female beauty: international evening wear, Palembang brides, and the sort of high couture styles associated with more mainstream Indonesian elite batik designers such as Irwan Tirta. The latter and other designers in Indonesia's large community of high-fashion couture often work in cotton or silk batik, which of course can be cut into pattern fabric.

The Muslim aspect of Zainal Songket's excursions into songket couture is especially interesting. The kebaya tops worn by Pak Zainal's models are notably long, covering the hips modestly. Yet the kebayas are fairly see-through. Songket per se evokes Muslim conservatism among many Sumatrans. Yet the models' hair and heads are totally uncovered. In some photographs in the brochure, the young women wear open-neck kebayas and even off-the-shoulder garb. In other pictures a gauzy fabric covers the models from the upper chest to the neck. In sum, this is a hybrid couture located with some anxiety between the modest styles of Indonesia's nationwide *busana Muslim* (Muslim fashions for women, heavily influenced by current Middle Eastern fashion.

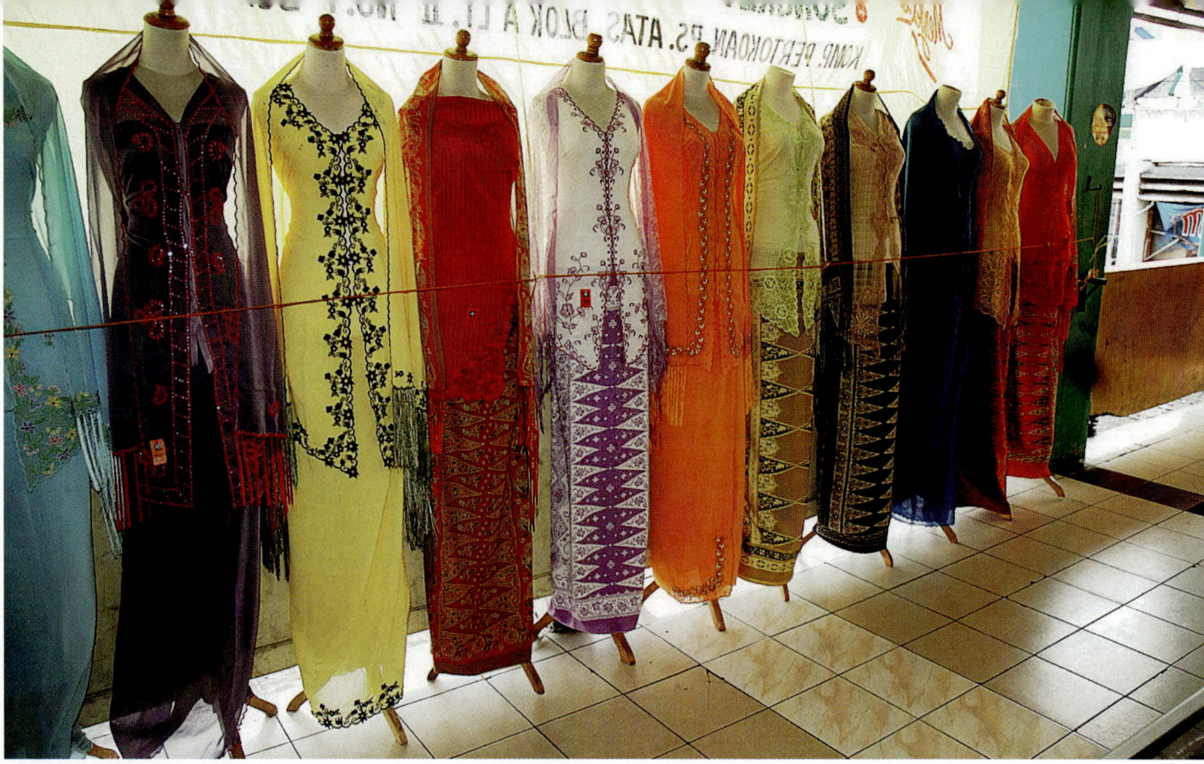

Fig. 5.29. A row of mannequins attired in fine embroidery wear *(bordir)*, on the second floor of the central, multistoried market, Bukittinggi, West Sumatra, 2005. Such bordir wear increasingly competes with classic songket attire.

See, for instance, Taruna Kusmayadi, *Busana pengantin Muslim* [2005]) and the more relaxed, sensual styles found in Indonesian couture based in batik wear.

In "Three Scenarios from Batak Clothing History: Designing Participation in the Global Fashion Trajectory," anthropologist Sandra Niessen documents several ways in which Toba Batak designer/entrepreneurs of *ulos* (the Toba ritual cloth) have cut, folded, sewn, and rethought that cotton ikat heritage textile to render it into business suits and leisure wear for sale on the national market (Niessen 2003). The buyers here are often middle class. A related sector of the "updated *ulos* market," so to speak, is the touristic one of cheap jackets, vests, and totes. This Toba ulos-plus market is fairly large. Not so with couture versions of Palembang songket: this seems to be a narrow, not widely accepted sector of the songket business. The songkets themselves are fairly conservative in terms of motifs and designs, although their metal threads do tend toward shine and glitteriness.[3]

Conclusion: Business, Consumption, and Class within Indonesian Heritage Arts

Even with Indonesia's slow, uncertain recovery from the Southeast Asian financial crisis of 1997–98, some Sumatran families in West Sumatra, Palembang, and rantau cities such as Jakarta have enough disposable income—and enough love of songket—to participate enthusiastically in shopping for new gold-thread sarongs and shoulder cloths (fig. 5.29). They buy this finery for ritual events such as traditional weddings, but also for the type of formal events in Jakarta that call for songket-based costumes, whether of the heritage sort or the experimental couture type. With clothing cabinets stocked with a few antique songkets and numerous examples from the 1970s to the 1990s, the richer Minangkabau and Palembang Malay women of social substance empower this heated, highly competitive heritage textile market. Songket designer/entrepreneurs cater wisely to their clientele by highlighting both subtle innovations in color, thread choice, and motif alignment *and* traditional weaving artistry.

What results is a heritage cloth-weaving universe oriented toward change, but always toward change within tradition. Given that songkets, throughout their long history in Sumatra, have been tied to trade and market demand, this may be seen simply as a continuation of one of this splendid textile's key traditions.

NOTES

1. Fieldwork for this chapter in the Bukittinggi area began in 1995–96 and continued through six additional, shorter visits. Brief visits to songket shops and weaving floors in Jambi and Palembang took place from 2003 through 2006. Especially valuable studies of the history of songket weaving in southern Sumatra are Megumi Uchino 2005 and Barbara Andaya 1989. For a museum staff's version of Pandai Sikek songket weaving history, see Museum Adityawarman, 1998, *Kain songket Pandai Sikek*. See also Sita Demi Razmi et al, 2005, *Pakaian tradisional Kotogadang*. Barbara Andaya's 1993 *To live as brothers; Southeastern Sumatran in the seventeenth and eighteenth centuries* is invaluable in its thorough discussion of the trade history of both Jambi and Palembang. See especially ch. 2, on 1600s pepper commerce, the role of Chinese merchants in the cloth trade, and textiles as gifts. For general references on songket weaving see note 9, ch. 2. On Silungkang weaving see M. Casey 1982. On textile production in Jambi, see Fiona Kerlogue 1995-96, 1999, 2005.
2. Rumah Tenun Pusako, http://www.tenun-pusako.com.
3. For a valuable discussion of fashion theory issues related to Southeast Asian textile market demand and the middle class, see Jones and Leshkowich 2003. See also the essays in Niessen, Jones, and Leshkowich 2003 for case studies.

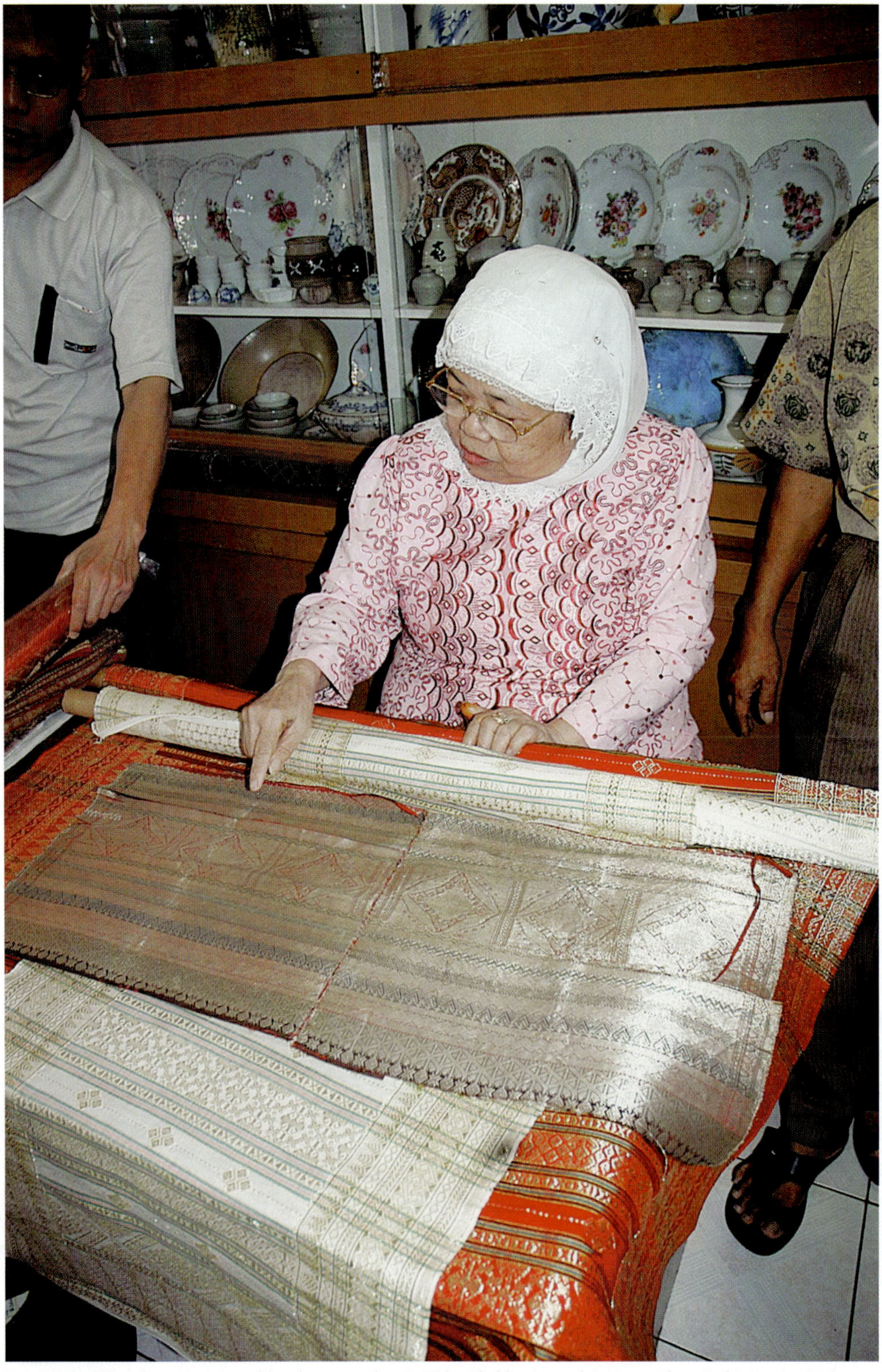

Fig. 6.0. H. Elly Azhar examining old and new songkets in Toko Aladdin Art and Antiques Shop, Bukittinggi, 2006.

6. Biographied textiles

Susan Rodgers, Anne Summerfield, John Summerfield

In her work on Kodi worldviews, anthropologist Janet Hoskins has explored "how things tell the stories of people's lives" (Hoskins 1998, from the book's title). She uncovers muted narratives streaming through this West Sumbanese culture, stories that emanate from what she terms "biographied objects." These meaningful things include a healer's drum and a decorated betel bag that serves as "a sack for souls and stories" (chap. 2). There is also a spindle whose presence in a village woman's life evokes "the loss of romantic love" (chap. 5). Indeed, weaving figures strongly in this lyrical volume, which urges a new methodology for writing about Indonesian village arts.

Hoskins's chapter 4, entitled "The Royal Snake Shroud: Local weaving and colonial kingship," tells of an object whose texture and weaving history are embedded with messages about noble status and kingship in this eastern Indonesian society. Hoskins' approach stimulated our use of the concept of biographied textiles. We shall present short biographies of especially story-filled songkets from Minangkabau, Palembang, and Jambi.

Hoskins notes that the Kodi man's mantle, called a *hanggi nggoko karaha kaboko*, is patterned with motifs called snake's rib. The reptile in the cloth is an uncurled python, termed both an *ular* [snake] *patola* and *ular naga*. The naga is island Southeast Asia's famous serpent/dragon, a world snake represented in some village art as the creature that holds up houses and human society. This supernatural creature is found in myths from Sumatra to Timor. The naga snake also ties Kodi's indigo-dyed mantles to Indian ideas of sacred kingship. And the naga evokes the animal designs in Indian trade-cloth patolas that came into Kodi house treasuries in past centuries.

Other meanings inlaid in the hanggi cloth are more personal. Hoskins explains by relating an incident from her fieldwork (1998: 84):

> In the early 1980s, when I returned to Kodi and stayed as a houseguest in the home of Raja H. R. Horo, his wives showed me a number of very fine snake cloths. One in particular was woven of hand-spun thread and had exquisitely detailed indigo designs and a fine border contrast-dyed in rust. I was interested in buying some cloth to take home, and asked about that one.
>
> "No," my host told me. "This one is a royal cloth—it is a cloth I could wear for my final journey, when I cross over from the world of the living to that of the dead. This is the cloth we are saving for my funeral shroud (*ghabuho*)."
>
> "Why must it be this particular cloth?" I asked.
>
> "These cloths are used only by the highest nobility at funerals. They bear the signs of royal privilege, the mystical power of kings (*kesaktian raja-raja*). For me, this cloth is especially powerful, because it depicts the guardian spirit of my ancestor, Rato Rangga Ramba Deta."
>
> The name was familiar to me as that of the founder of Rangga Baki, the raja's ancestral village.

Hoskins goes on to report that "the python that Raja Horo claimed as his benefactor and ancestral guardian is not Pala Kawata [Sumba's most famous mythical python] but instead a kind of yora or 'spirit wife' (*ariwyei marapu*). She can take the form of a beautiful woman, and has appeared to him most often in his bed. She is the source of his famous medicine to treat impotence, and his power to conjure her up in his imagination has helped him to restore the virility of many other men who have come to him for treatment" (1998: 84-85).

Kodi cloth obviously extends into cultural domains ranging from politics to myth to gender and sexuality. Songkets in Sumatra sometimes also carry narratives: ones about locality and distance, state centers and periphery, personal and family status, and generational time. Songkets also tell stories about Islam, and about bodily glamour within that. In the following pages of this chapter Anne Summerfield and John Summerfield write first about eight old songkets and other textiles, attending especially to technical weaving details and the tales that information can tell about songkets as they exist within Asian textile worlds. In this section Susan Rodgers also offers a biography of a new songket woven "in the style of" an old Pitalah piece. This is the same textile woven by Ibu Us that Anne Summerfield and John Summerfield discuss at the end of chapter 4. We locate this particular biography next to two antique Pitalah textiles. Then, at the end of the chapter, Rodgers presents biographies of seven more contemporary songkets. She homes in on their slightly undercover themes of conflict; for the weavers and brokers who produce and sell them, some of these cloths are lovely things poised anxiously within Islam, Indonesian nationhood, and ideologies of the modern.

Our biographies of specific cloths follow.

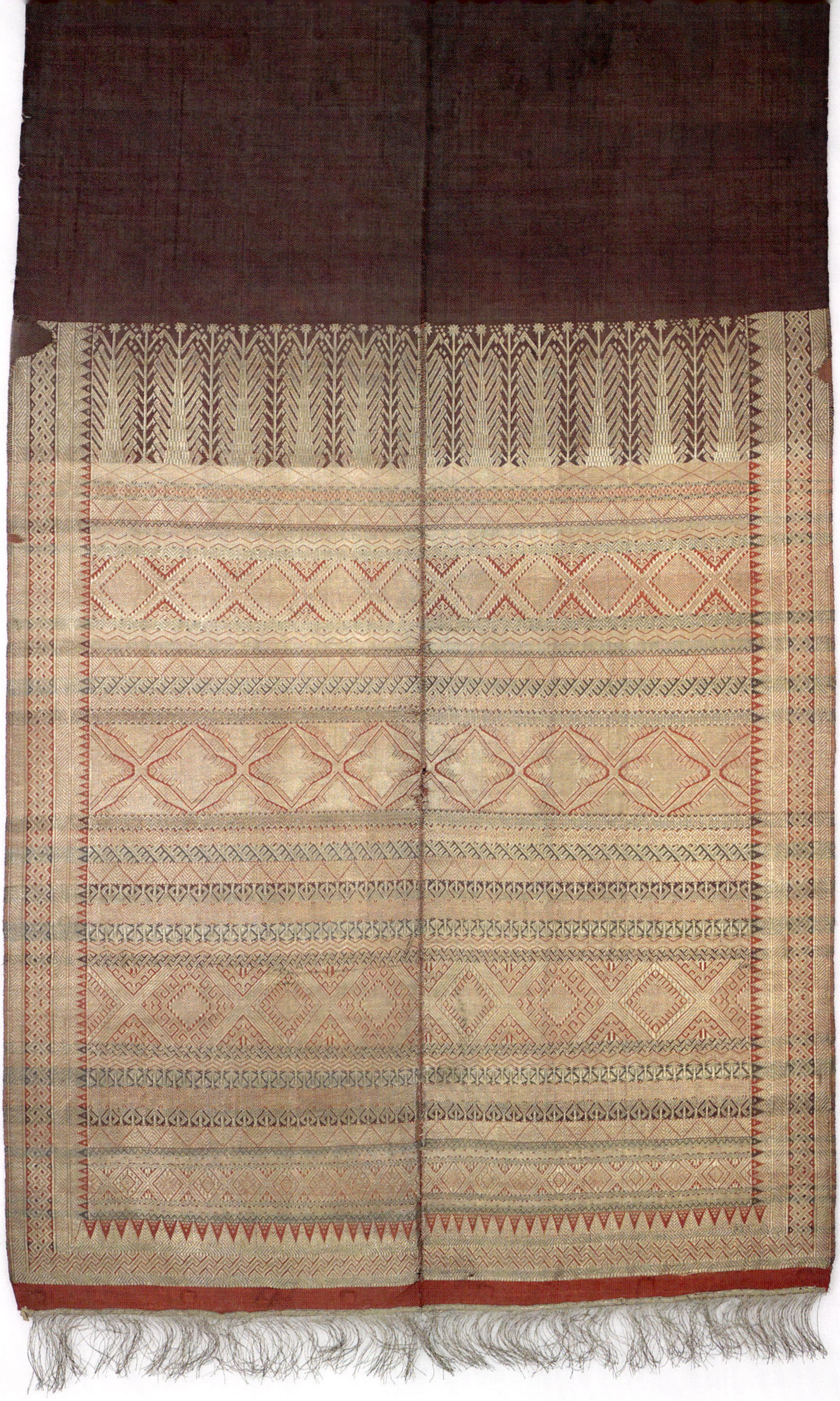

Fig. 6.1

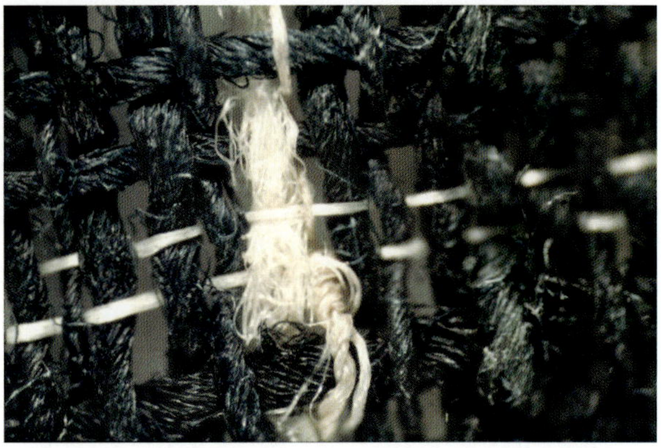

Fig. 6.2. Photomicrograph showing knotting of two lengths of ramin in a woven textile.

Figure 6.1
Tangkuluak (headdress) or ***selendang*** (shoulder cloth), circa 1800
Minangkabau people
Pitalah, West Sumatra
Silk, gold-wrapped thread, ramin
Plain weave, supplementary weft
110 x 29.3", 279.5 x 74.5 cm

This sumptuous textile is a rare relic of the days when Minangkabau weavers used the fine inner bark of *boehmeria* plants as the warps of their treasured ceremonial garments. These bast fibers, as found in Minangkabau ceremonial textiles, are not spun, as are cotton and silk, to form long, continuous threads. Rather, they are flat, thin, narrow strips of fiber peeled from inside the soaked rough outer bark or from the debarked stem of these plants. The fibers, called ramin, are relatively short. The maximum length is about seven feet. Many such lengths must be fastened together to provide enough fiber to serve as the total warp for a long weaving (fig. 6.2). Taking into account the 110-inch length of this textile and the number of ramin warps per inch of width, we estimate that this piece contains some twenty-five hundred knots. Just preparing the warp for this headcloth was a formidable task.

The labor involved in producing the fragile and delicate warps for this beautiful cloth is testimony to the value placed by the Minangkabau on such weavings. Ramin must have ranked with gold-wrapped thread in aesthetic value. Not many ramin-warped textiles have survived over the ages, especially not in good condition. We have found only six in some thirty years of research.

Another stunning aspect of this cloth is the uniquely Minangkabau method of making the densely packed, shining motifs in the gold or silver end panels immediately recognizable to the viewer. To accomplish this, different colors of weft thread are used in neighboring rows of motifs so that individual rows are easily differentiated from one another. If it were not for these differing adjacent colors in the rows of motifs, the glare of light reflected from the densely packed metallic threads would make quick recognition of individual motifs almost impossible. Ease of identifying motifs is important because of their relation to the adat, the Minangkabau traditional system of rules for proper behavior.

The sources of motifs are many. Some of the geometric forms were carved into local megaliths that are thought to be at least four thousand years old. Others have been adopted and adapted from arts and trade items that entered the Minangkabau heartland from other societies. Motifs are identified by names that may have no relation to the geometric forms. As noted in chapter 4, the name given to a motif, rather than describing it, points to a proverb or aphorism from the adat. For example, the motifs in the red band in the center of the decorated end panel in the accompanying picture are shaped like diamonds with slightly concave sides (fig. 6.3). The name of this motif is *balah kacang*, or split peanut. This refers to the fact that the two halves of a split peanut are of equal size. The adat teaching is that if a Minangkabau person is asked to make an equal division of property, he must be very careful to see that the two parts are of equal size. By extension, a Minangkabau must be honest in business dealings.

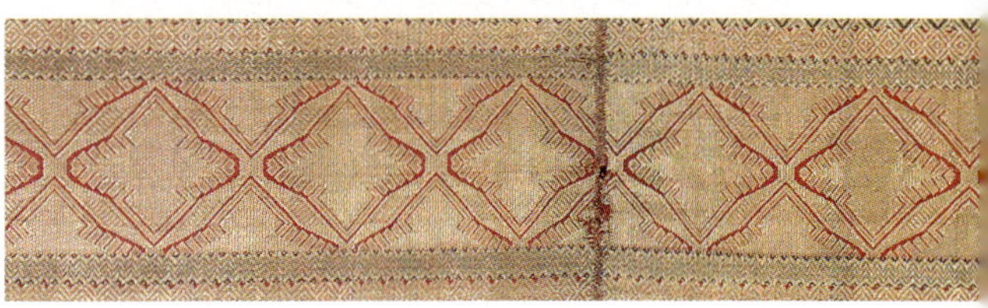

Fig. 6.3. An ancient motif, dating to prehistoric times, found in South Indian pottery, called "split peanut" motif in Minangkabau textiles.

The large collection of teachings that make up today's form of the adat was developed over centuries. Adat sayings and proverbs had to be taught orally; as Amin Sweeney notes, the Minangkabau are "...one of the upland peoples of South and West Sumatra whose societies were, until recently, still radically oral..." (1987:111). In his significant book *A Full Hearing: Orality and Literacy in the Malay World* (1987: 121-122), Sweeney describes how the Minangkabau adat grew and was codified over centuries to include even rules for administering local villages. Before the arrival of the Dutch, village government was subject to the rules of adat administered by a council of clan leaders, or *penghulu*. They met in a special council house with open sides so villagers could observe the deliberations and hear the decisions. Some regular attendees learned so much from these open sessions that they became virtual amateur jurists. Sweeney writes that when the Dutch replaced the adat rules with the Dutch system of constitutional and criminal law, they diminished the area of responsibility of the penghulu. But the Dutch did not do away with the rest of the adat, which encapsulated the wisdom of the oral society. This wisdom was expressed in short, pithy statements that tell the Minangkabau what is correct behavior. These are the sayings and proverbs alluded to by motifs in the ceremonial weavings. Weavers say that their ritual textiles are the skin of adat. Preservation of textiles thus is important to the maintenance of adat history.

Other motifs of interest in this textile include but are not limited to narrow bands on either side of the band of split peanuts. These narrow bands contain motifs composed of slanting lines studded with four equally spaced short, perpendicular lines. The relevant name here is *itiak pulang patang*, or ducks going home in the afternoon. This refers to the practice of rice farmers, who lead their ducks to the wet rice paddies in the morning and then back home in the afternoon. The ducks keep to a line and do not stray into the countryside. The teaching is that just as the ducks do not stray from their path, so a good Minangkabau does not stray from the teachings of the adat. For more about the relationship of motifs to sayings and proverbs, see Anne Summerfield and H.A. Sutan Madjo Indo, chapter 7, "Motifs and their Meaning," in *Walk in Splendor: Ceremonial Dress of the Minangkabau* (Summerfield and Summerfield 1999: 171-199).

The men and women who dressed in these garments frequently participated in ceremonies. They were thus reminded each time of the adat teachings. Today, in-depth knowledge of the meanings of the motifs has diminished among the general population. With the exception of several especially popular images, recognition is limited by and large to weavers, dealers, scholars, and collectors. Ducks going home in the afternoon, the motif just cited, is one of the most widely recognized. It has a life in modern-day Minangkabau. For instance, a few years ago, a large illuminated display appeared above the ticketing desk at the Padang, West Sumatra, airport. Small yellow ducklings were shown in a line across the top of the display. The headline below the ducklings read, "We must learn from them," and the text went on to explain the importance of doing one's work without disturbing one's social ambiance or damaging the environment (fig. 6.4).

Anne Summerfield, John Summerfield

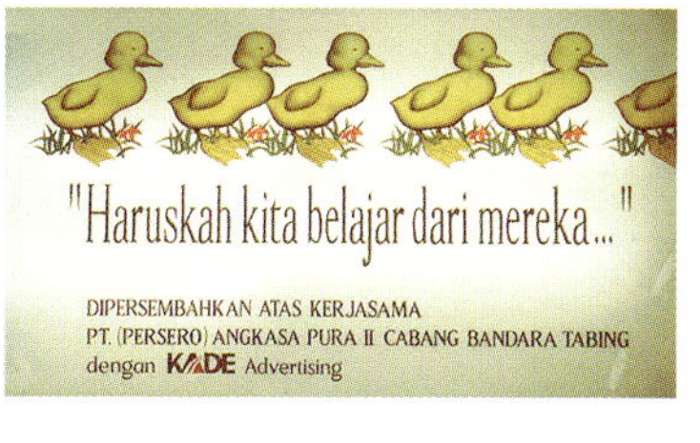

Fig. 6.4. Illuminated panel above the ticket counter in Padang (West Sumatra) airport, referring to motif called "ducks going home in the afternoon."

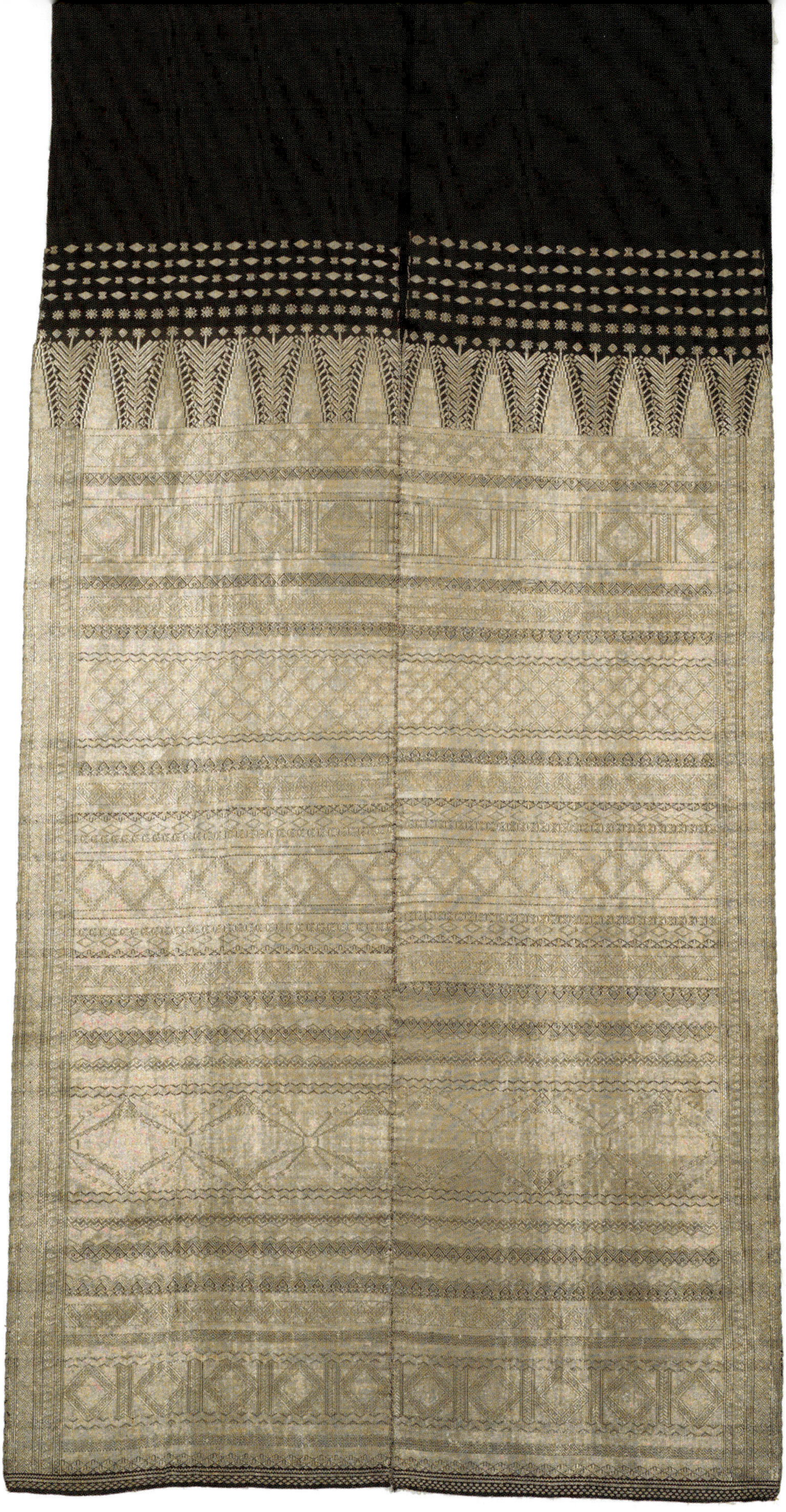

Fig. 6.5

Figure 6.5
Tangkuluak (headdress), circa 1800
Minangkabau people
Pitalah, West Sumatra
Silk, silver-wrapped thread
Plain weave, silver-wrapped thread supplementary weft
113 x 27", 287 x 68.6 cm

This resplendent weaving qualifies technically as a superior or "great" textile. It is notable for the unusually long panel of silver images at each end. A skilled weaver could probably complete only one or one and a half inches of such complex patterning in a day at the loom. Materials in the weaving are fine silk and fine silver-wrapped thread. Warps are dark blue silk. Wefts in the undecorated center are purple silk. Wefts in the decorated panels are red, purple, or black silk, now faded to a dark gray. Faded black wefts often appear to the naked eye to be green because of their proximity to the color red. When viewed under magnification even as slight as two times, however, the faded black no longer appears green. Warps in the center of the textile have deteriorated significantly. This could be due to the presence of iron in the original dye, to folding of the cloth over many decades, or to both.

There are seventy-five horizontal bands of silver supplementary weft in each of the unusually long end panels, displaying thirty-one different motifs. Adjacent motif bands are easily perceived as being separate from each other because the colors of the underlying weft threads differ from band to band and because there is a darker narrow band separating the bands with underlying bright wefts. These narrow bands are similarly densely patterned with metallic thread.

To form a headdress typical of the village of Pitalah with this cloth, the textile is folded in half along its entire length and then folded in half again. This produces a long folded cloth one-fourth its original width. It is then wrapped on the wearer's head so that the length of one of the decorated panels crosses over her forehead horizontally and extends well beyond her face. The finished structure identifies her home village and forms an elegant statement of her importance to the community.

The attributes that mark a weaving as technically superior can be found in many textiles woven over the centuries in Pitalah, a village nestled in one of the valleys in the central highlands of the Bukit Barisan Mountains, which run like a spine down the western side of Sumatra. Pitalah is located in the district that later because known as Tanah Datar (flat or level land). Legend has it that this was the first region in Sumatra settled by the people who came to be called the Minangkabau.

Inhabitants of this region were subjected to a long period of Indianization, during which they came into contact with Indian- and Chinese-made products. These included exquisitely gold-embellished court cloths. Early in the second millennium C.E. the district was already heavily involved with Indian Muslim traders on both the east and the west coasts of Sumatra. Routes to active trade along the Straits of Malacca to the east were developed along rivers that arose in the Barisan Mountains and increased in size and navigability on their way down to the Straits. Ways to the west coast were along treacherous footpaths that wound through dense jungle and over hazardous cliffs to an Indian Ocean port town now known as Pariaman.

By the thirteenth century trade had grown substantially, with Sumatran gold being exchanged for Indian cloth (Dobbin 1987 [1983]: 60). Traders found it prudent to monitor their preferred trade routes to the west coast to prevent banditry and theft of the gold. An Indian settlement was established for that purpose in the village of Pariangan, from which the first parts of the routes could be visually monitored. Later other traders made their way up the rivers from the

Straits to the growing trade centers, increasing the contacts of landlocked villagers with the outside world. The influence of traders was felt not only commercially but also artistically (Dobbin 1987 [1983]: 61). Christine Dobbin speculates that since the Malabar traders came from a matrilineal culture they could have introduced matrilineality to the Minangkabau, or if it already existed, they could have strengthened it.

With the arrival in 1347 C.E. of Adityawarman, the son of a Javanese-Minangkabau marriage at the Indianized court of Majapahit in Java, the process of Indianization was greatly expanded. Adityawarman originally came as an invader with an army in search of the gold for which Tanah Datar was famous. He set up a royal court in Tanah Datar and a lesser one in the neighboring region of Jambi.

The concept of a kingdom was new to the Minangkabau, whose villages had traditionally been administered by the penghulus or clan leaders of the village region. This village system persisted, and Adityawarman's direct political rule was not absolute. Rather, it was limited to sparsely settled areas not under penghulu jurisdiction. These areas, however, were near or at the gold mines. Adityawarman set up outposts of his court in these regions, to be administered by his appointed rajas. Tribute was collected from the outposts, and courtly goods, including jewelry and silk cloths with gold, were provided to the appointed rajas from the main court.

It is highly probable that by the end of Adityawarman's reign the people who later came to be known as the Minangkabau had been exposed to local court textiles. Some Minangkabau women may even have been employed as weavers at the court. It is not known exactly when songket weaving was first practiced by the Minangkabau for themselves. Textiles from this area have not been carbon-dated, but printed cloths and elaborately ikatted cloths from other parts of the Indonesian archipelago have been dated to the fifteenth century (Oxford Asian Textile Group Newsletter 1996). During Adityawarman's reign (1347–75), what came to be known as Minangkabau culture flourished in language and other arts.

With centuries of exposure to foreign goods and to the textiles of Adityawarman's Indianized courts, it is to be expected that the village weavers of Pitalah would develop exacting standards for production of their own arts. This elegant, sophisticated ceremonial weaving and many other equally fine pieces from Pitalah owe a debt to their village's long history of contact with the arts and cultures brought by traders and invaders.

Anne Summerfield, John Summerfield

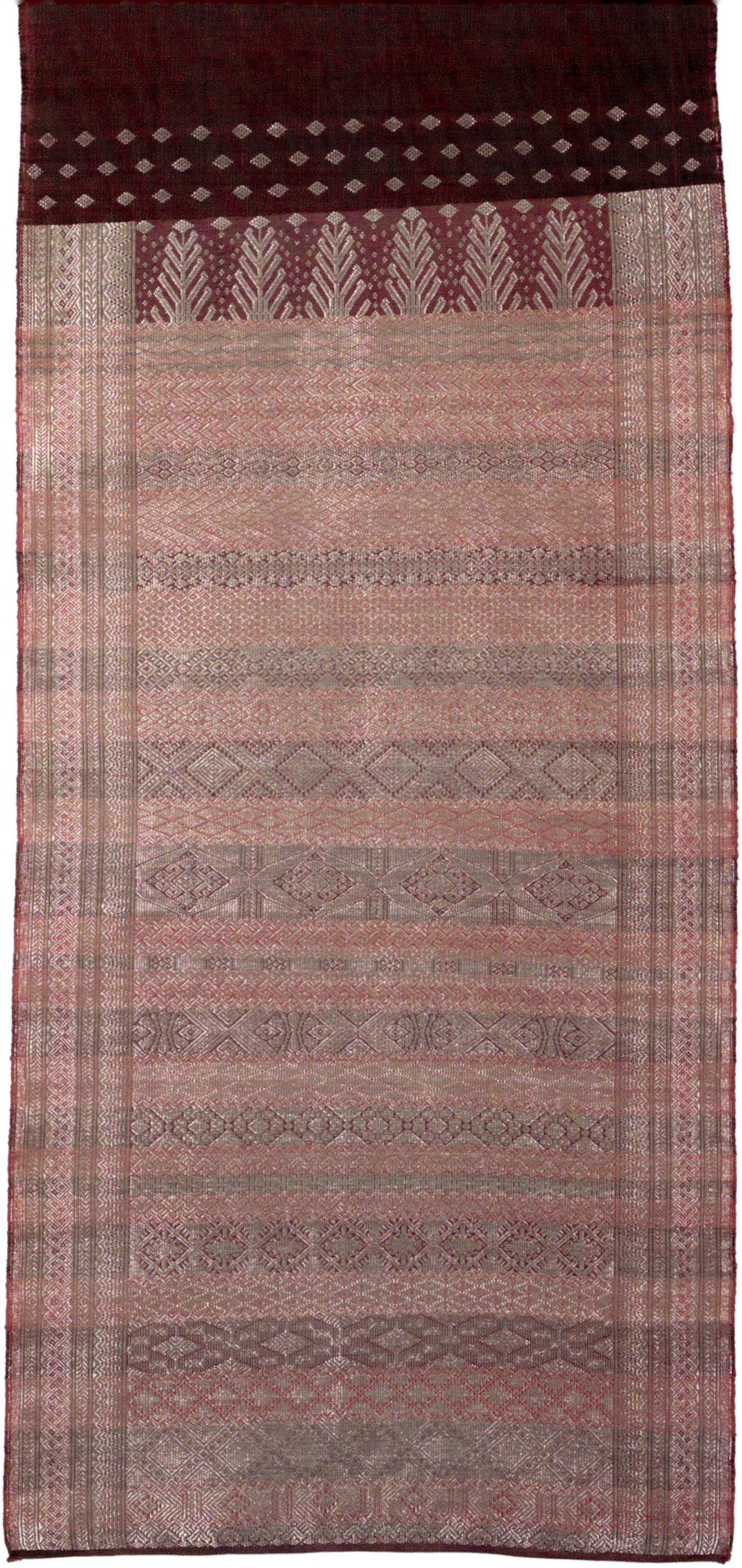

Fig. 6.6

Figure 6.6
Selendang (shoulder cloth) or ***tangkuluak*** (headdress), circa 2005
Minangkabau people
Tanjung, Pandai Sikek, West Sumatra
Linen-polyester blend, gold-wrapped thread
Plain weave, supplementary weft
112 x 20-1/2 in., 284-1/2 x 52 cm

This quite recent cloth was woven by Ibu Us, an accomplished thirty-six-year old craftswomen in the Tanjung neighborhood of Pandai Sikek. She wove it in reaction to and in artistic interaction with old Pitalah weavings such as the ones just described. The materials and weaving skills basic to this contemporary weaving are discussed in detail at the conclusion of chapter 4. Ibu Us's understanding of her textile formed a focus of chapter 2.

Ibu Us brokers her high-end songkets via an art and antique dealership in the city of Bukittinggi; the proprietors there urged her to begin weaving "replacements for" old Pitalah shoulder cloths and headdresses for Pitalah families who need ceremonial wear in their village's distinctive styles but have sold all their old songkets to the national and international art market. The dealers also wanted to encourage fine weaving in general.

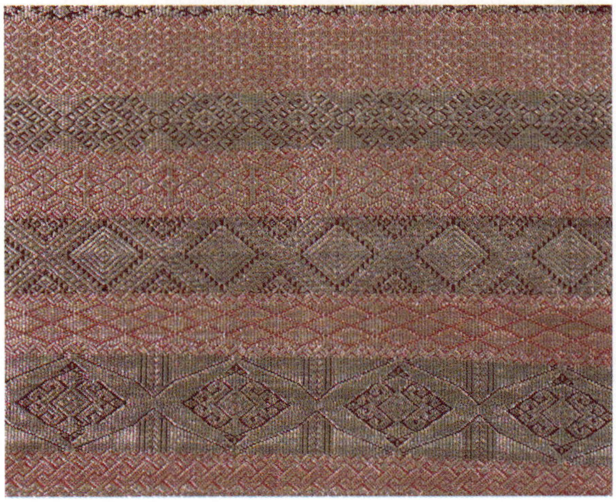

Fig. 6.7. Detail of Ibu Us' textile.

They provided Ibu Us with a fragment of an old Pitalah cloth to follow in her weaving as a motif template. The Pitalah weavings discussed in the preceding two entries are great old cloths of just this sort.

The shop owners' intended markets also included Minangkabau living in cities who are themselves collectors of heritage art, along with wealthy international tourists with a serious interest in the Indonesian arts. Unfortunately, after the downturn of the Indonesian national economy in the years after the Southeast Asian currency crisis of 1997, these markets disappeared. The Bukittinggi shop owners also had hopes of selling Ibu Us's textiles in antique boutiques in hotels in Bali that specialized in high-end Sumatran art; this market had also faded by 2002. Ibu Us has now gone on to weave sarongs and selendangs on commission for wealthy Minangkabau who wish to have cloths that incorporate old motifs.

Ibu Us takes pride in creating new songket textiles by mining her notably rich repertoire of antique motifs. The latter have become familiar to her specifically because of her business relationship with the Bukittinggi art dealers mentioned above, H. Elly Azhar and her husband H.A. Sutan Madjo Indo. Upon examining study fragments of old songkets given to her by the art dealers, Ibu Us learns to weave antique motifs that come from old weaving centers located far from Pandai Sikek in distant parts of West Sumatra. Ibu Us hews to some Pandai Sikek conventions (for instance, the village's selvedge patterns) but goes on to combine motifs from various regions in her textiles' center fields. This is unorthodox. Since her brokers are the ones who commissioned her textiles of this sort in the first place, Ibu Us is generally not subject to the oversight often exercised by more conservative designer-brokers. Ibu Us's songkets are vividly original, while staying in conversation with antique motifs.

Susan Rodgers

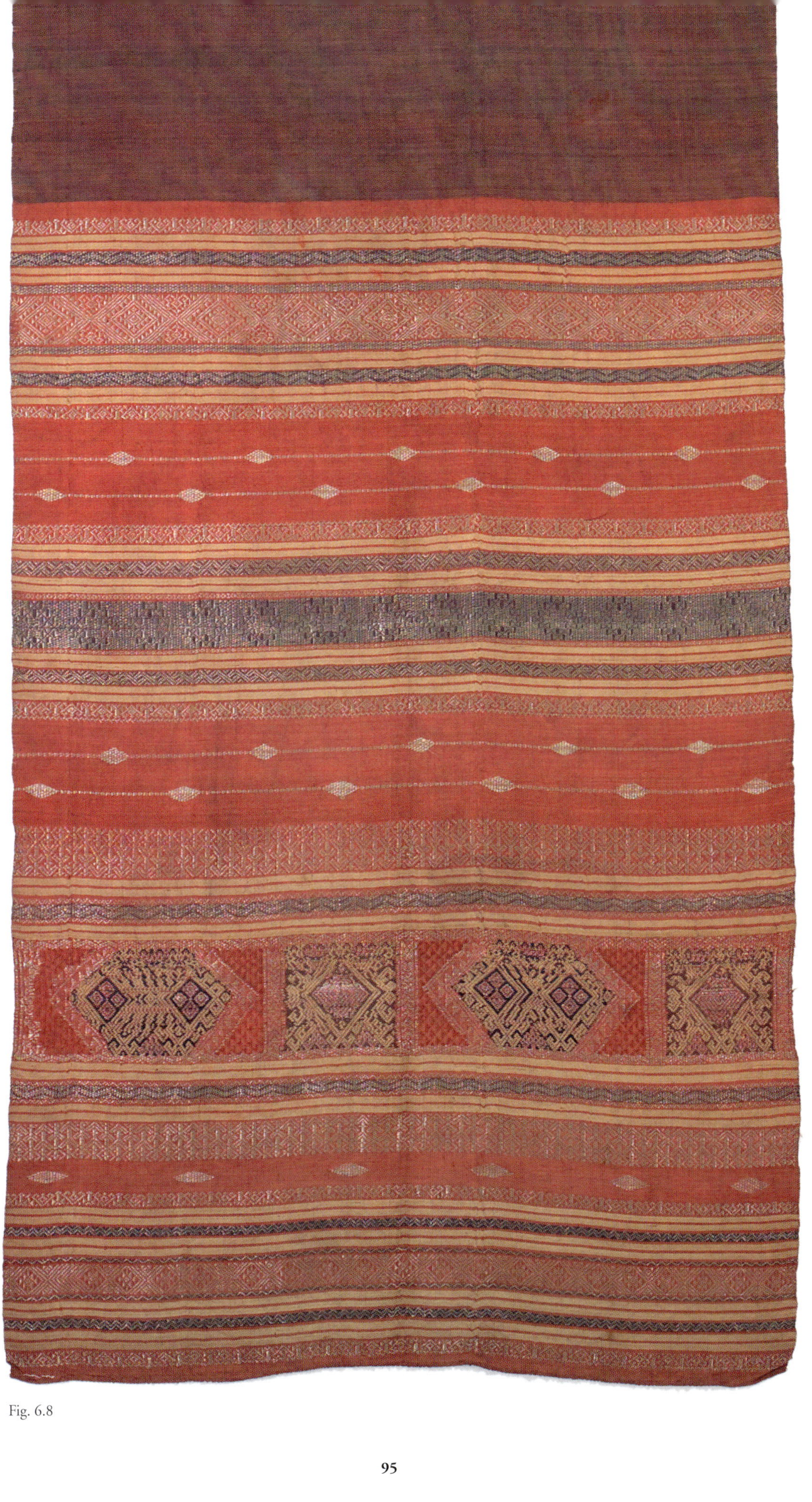

Fig. 6.8

Figure 6.8
Selendang (shoulder cloth), ***tangkuluak*** (headdress), circa 1800
Minangkabau people
Pariangan, West Sumatra
Silk, silk floss, silver-wrapped thread
Plain weave, supplementary weft
101 x 22 1/2 in., 256.5 x 57.2 cm

According to Minangkabau legend, three sons of Alexander the Great sailed to the South Pacific en route to China. One son left the ship to set foot on the top of Mount Merapi, in the Barisan Mountains of West Sumatra, to establish the heartland of what would grow to be the *alam Minangkabau,* the Minangkabau world. He declared himself Maharajah Dirajah, the highest of all rajas. As the story goes, the area was flooded, so the first settlement was on the upper slopes of the mountain. As the waters receded, the people moved down the slopes and eventually established a village in the fertile valley below.

There is indeed geological evidence that the area was once under water, but the rest of the legend remains unverified. The village settlement was named Pariangan. Some oral histories assert that émigrés from Pariangan went out to populate three other highland valleys. As weaving was introduced in the village, Pariangan weavers did not include selvedge patterns in the overall pattern formats on their ceremonial weavings. As a result, the weft bands of motifs cover the entire width of their textiles. Weavers say any side borders on their textiles would have been barriers to emigration and that Pariangan had a grave responsibility to populate the Minangkabau world.

Pariangan offered many advantages to settlers. There are natural hot springs, some of which were channeled into community showers for the populace. Also, the warm waters provided therapeutic baths for the aching and the elderly. The soil is fertile, restored by the frequent volcanic eruptions of Mount Merapi. Coffee, rice, and vegetables flourish. The village was built on steep mountain slopes, and what would normally be village sidewalks are flights of stairs, often very long. These lead from the village center up to the hillside homes of the inhabitants.

The Pariangan shoulder cloth/headdress pictured here is generally judged to be an older textile. That is based on the fineness of the weaving and the density of the woven silk background cloth. As a headdress, the textile is folded into the shape of two horns, with the colorful warp ends of the cloth extending down to the wearer's shoulders (fig. 6.9). Motifs in this textile include one that is named for a ceremonial object, a ritual necklace. Others have names referring to adat teachings. The ceremonial necklace is usually represented by a row of diamonds connected by one or two lines. A traditional motif is frequently found on contemporary songkets, normally as a repeated design element. In the exhibition "Gold Cloths of Sumatra" this textile was displayed next to a contemporary weaving patterned by rows of gold "necklaces" on a bright red ground. A second motif in this Pariangan weaving is named "caterpillars walking in line." It is related to the

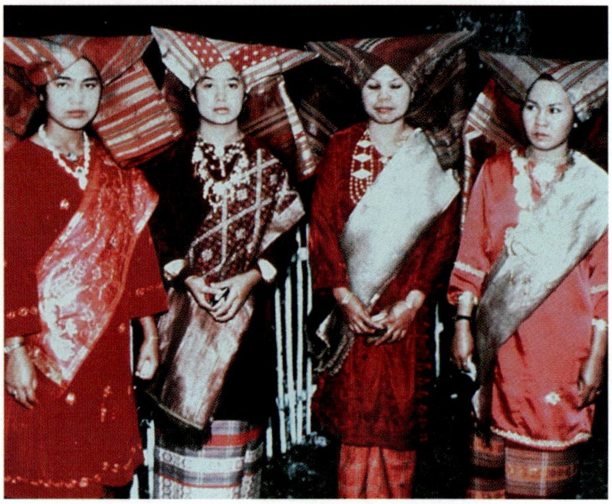

Fig. 6.9. Minangkabau women in ceremonial headdresses.

motif called "ducks going home in the afternoon." The teaching is that a good Minangkabau attends to the work he is doing and does not wander off into the countryside making mischief. A third example, a motif called the mangosteen calyx, is shaped as a diamond formed of small offset verticals. The mangosteen is a delicious tropical fruit whose interior consists of small white sections similar in size to the sections of a mandarin orange. But the mangosteen fruit is encased in a thick, woody, hard shell with a surface of coarse, mottled red skin. The teaching is that just as you should not judge the fruit of the mangosteen by its coarse exterior, so too you should not judge a person by his external appearance.

A distinctive feature of this ceremonial textile is the wide band of supplementary weft of silk and silver-wrapped thread. Motifs in this band are closely related to motifs commonly found in Middle Eastern fabrics and rugs. There is a narrow path approximately one centimeter wide of silver-wrapped thread at the edges of the larger silk pattern (fig. 6.10). Because the silver image is small, it is woven from a bobbin, not with a shuttle, which would carry the silver thread across the entire width of the textile, a wasteful use of precious metal when only a small portion would be visible on the front of the textile. Thread from the bobbin is hand-manipulated by the weaver, back and forth across the narrow band to form the desired silver pattern. To go back and forth implies that the thread turns around to change direction. The turnaround is visible on the back of this textile (fig. 6.11). Similar patterns appearing in textiles made in the neighboring town of Padang Magek have the turnaround on the front of the cloth. This difference in technique is used as an aid in determining provenance.

Anne Summerfield, John Summerfield

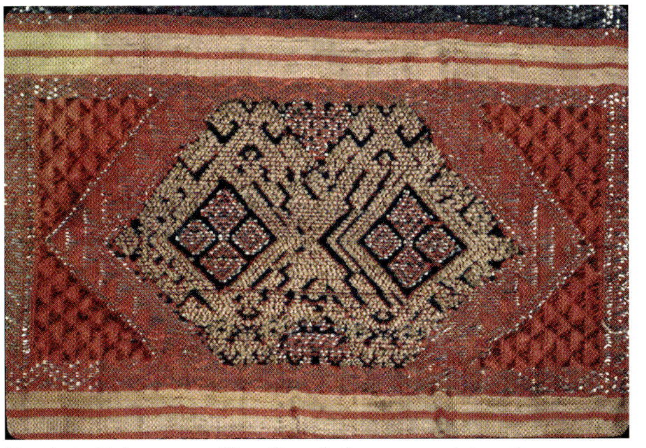

Fig. 6.10. Elaborate motif in silk and silver-wrapped thread supplementary weft, as seen from the front of the textile. Note narrow silver band like a parenthesis around the silk supplementary.

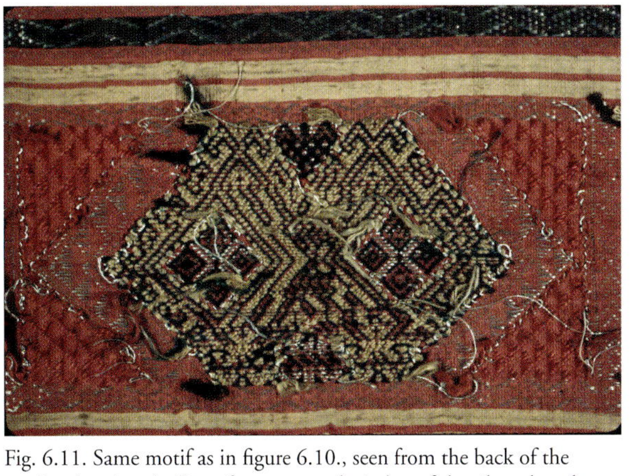

Fig. 6.11. Same motif as in figure 6.10., seen from the back of the textile, showing the line of turn-around stitches of the silver thread.

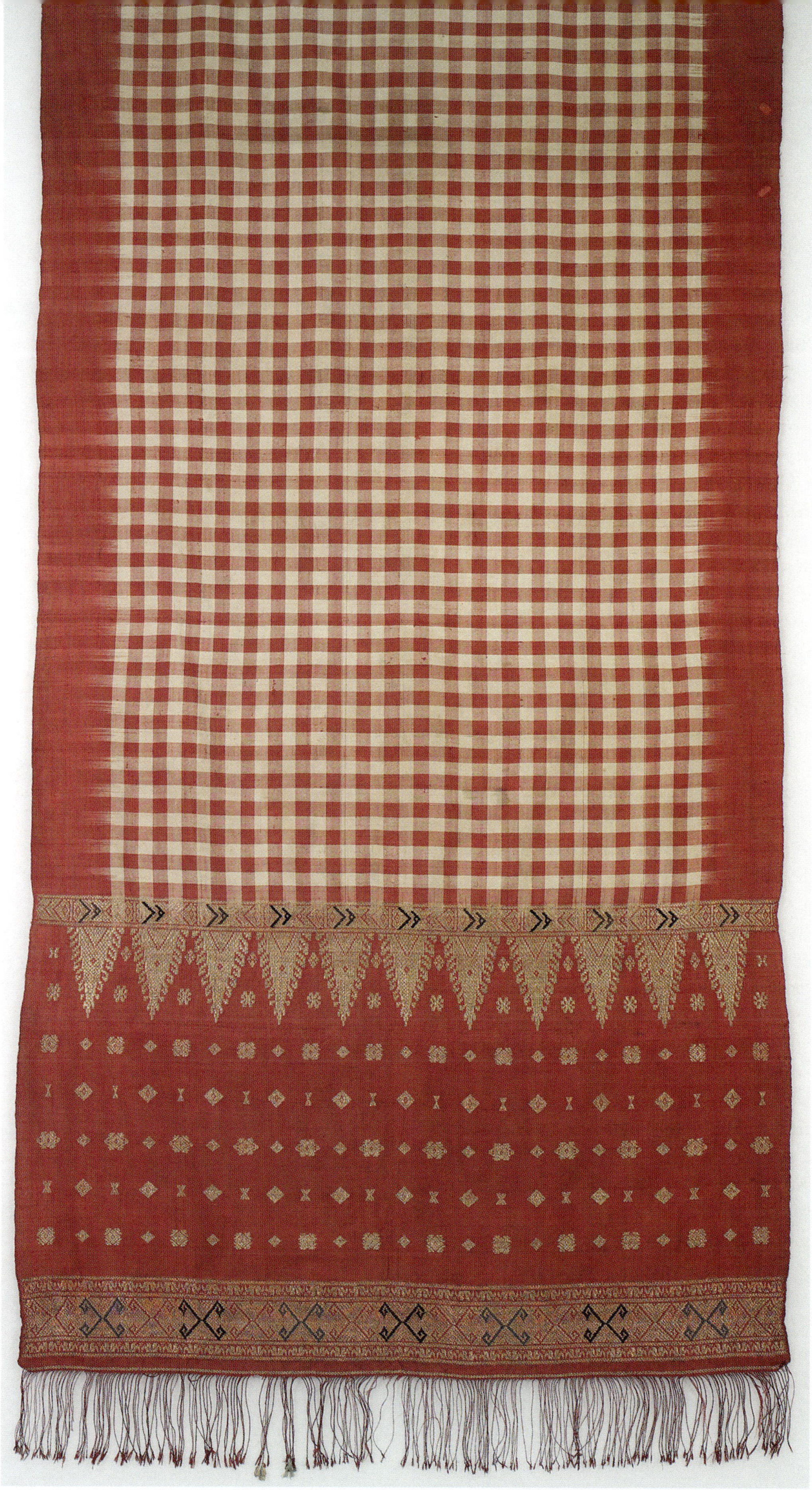

Fig. 6.12

Figure 6.12
Selendang (shoulder cloth), 1850
Minangkabau people
Batu Sangkar, West Sumatra
Silk, gold-wrapped thread, embroidery floss
Plain weave, supplementary weft, warp and weft ikat?
100 x 28 in., 255 x 71.4 cm

There is a mystery about this textile. None of the weavers active in the highlands of West Sumatra today knows where it was woven or just how it was dyed. The colored silk supplementary weft motifs at the ends of the weaving are typical of Batu Sangkar, but the red and white checks in the body of the cloth and the dyeing technique used to produce them are not found in other Batu Sangkar textiles.

There is speculation in West Sumatra as to the provenance of this type of textile. If it had been made in Batu Sangkar, the red dye might have been daubed on the warps after the loom was warped. Such daubing was used in Okinawa to apply color to unwoven threads (Amanda Stinchecum, personal communication). An alternative technique, ikat, was not used in Batu Sangkar. A type of weaving similar to this one but with three-color checks (red, white, and blue) is made in a somewhat distant village, Silungkang, about thirty miles east of Batu Sangkar. Here the tying and dyeing that constitute the ikat process were frequently used to pattern sarongs and shoulder cloths.

Some Minangkabau say that they think this piece was dyed in Silungkang for use in Batu Sangkar. Others suggest that a Silungkang weaver may have married a man from Batu Sangkar and brought her weaving and dyeing skills with her to her husband's village. Whatever the case, this red and white checked shoulder cloth has been a highly valued ceremonial textile. Few extant examples are in good condition, but we find smaller garments made from remnants of what were probably cloths too damaged to be used for their original purpose as ceremonial textiles. For example, a man's ceremonial shirt pieced together from such a remnant is in the Indonesian textile collection at the University of Pennsylvania Museum in Philadelphia. Saving a damaged ceremonial cloth by making it into a smaller ceremonial garment is somewhat unusual.

Another aspect of the patterning of this textile that raises questions is the apparent evolution of the colored silk supplementary motifs found at the very end of the weaving. Colored silk motifs in the end bands of ceremonial weavings is typically found in Batu Sangkar. On this example the motifs are shaped like an X with spiral curls at the ends of the crossed diagonals. This motif is carved into ancient megaliths found in a neighboring district (fig. 6.13). In this cloth, abutting motifs are of different colors, forming a row of red against black, purple, and green. The band of motifs, a series of embellished Xs, is in fact hiding the intended motif. The name given to the motif is *kuruang*, meaning enclosed. The term is commonly found in the expression *baju kuruang*, which is the slipover blouse or tunic that women wear with their sarongs. To find the hidden motif in this textile one must look at the right hand half of an X motif and visually connect it to the left-hand side of the adjacent motif. The resulting image is a lozenge-like shape, open at the upper and lower center

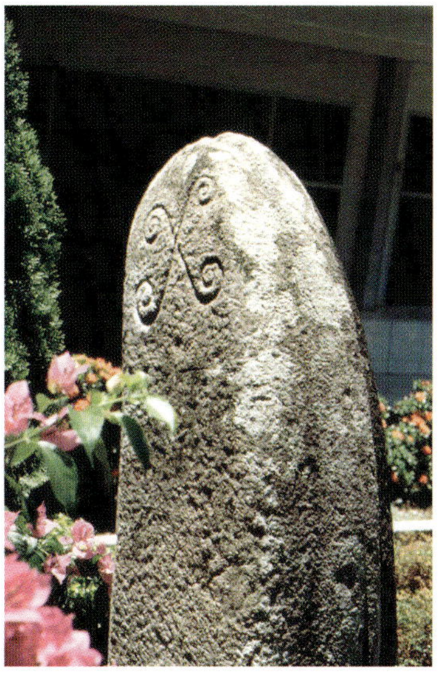

Fig. 6.13. Ancient motif of ornamented figure "X" on megalith. Motifs occurs in warp end border of selendang.

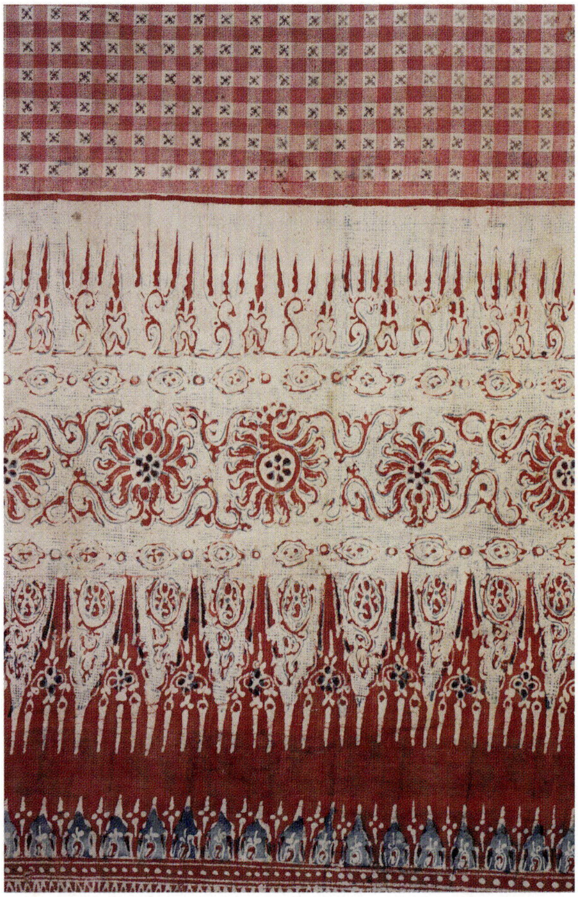

Fig. 6.14. Printed and ikatted Indian cloth with red checks that probably inspired the Minangkabau selendang.

points, enclosing a smaller motif.

The adat, the Minangkabau system of rules for wise social conduct, says that one should never give a direct answer to a question. By extension, it follows that concealing a motif from the uninitiated is fair game. In a much older version of this textile, the bottom row of motifs is clearly a row of lozenges. When did the change occur, and why? The answer to the first question awaits the results of large-scale carbon dating of old Minangkabau textiles. The second question requires serious research into similar changes of motif, if such information can be found. Also important would be the study of how the keepers of the adat might have judged such changes at the time.

Batu Sangkar was a village teeming with traders and gold runners during the height of the Indianization period. It was customary at that time for a woman's loom to be located on the main floor of the house and especially at the front, near windows that provided a view of activity in the village center. As weavers at these exposed looms studied the clothing and goods of visitors to the settlement, they found new motifs and new pattern formats that they could adapt for their textiles. This is the explanation most often heard for the remarkable variety of textiles found in Batu Sangkar.

A non-Indonesian model for this checked shoulder cloth is an Indian cloth (fig. 6.14). The finished textile consists of two panels joined at the selvedge. Centers of the panels are filled with red and white checks; the large triangular tumpals do not appear directly below the checks, as in the Minangkabau piece, but are closer to the warp end of the textile. In any event the similarity is striking. Mary Hunt Kahlenberg found the Indian piece during a visit to Lampung, at the far eastern tip of southern Sumatra.

A similar red, white, and blue checked cloth was made in Silungkang, located several miles east of Batu Sangkar but still within the area where traders regularly passed. Silungkang weavers have long used ikat methods of tying and dyeing warps and wefts, thus determining the dyed pattern of the textile even before the loom is warped.

Warping the loom with patterned warps and wefts requires special skill. Each warp must be carefully aligned with its neighbors to ensure that the pattern will be clear in the finished cloth. During weaving, the weaver must adjust each weft to make sure that it fits precisely with the warp pattern. Inexactness in dyeing the threads that are red along the selvedges but are white in the body of the textile is clearly evident in the photograph of the red and white checked Minangkabau textile.

Anne Summerfield, John Summerfield

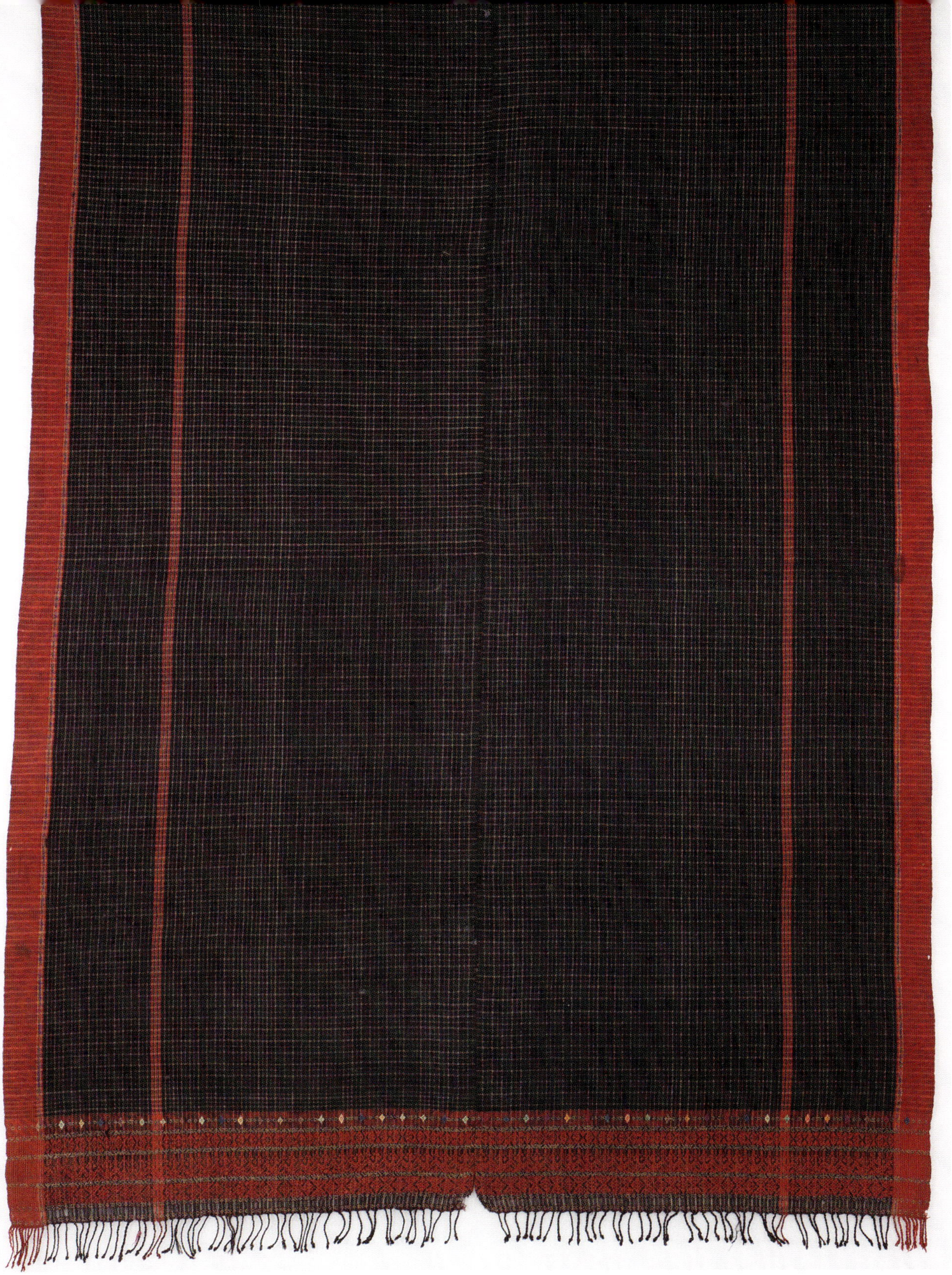

Fig. 6.15

Figure 6.15
Selendang (shoulder cloth), before 1850
Minangkabau people
Batu Sangkar, West Sumatra
Cotton, ramin (bast), silk embroidery floss, silver-wrapped thread
Plain weave, silk supplementary weft, silver thread supplementary weft
86 x 32 in., 218.4 x 81.3 cm

This very sophisticated, subtly patterned cotton, silk, and bast fiber textile was woven no later than 1850. It was possibly produced considerably before that time. Extensive use of bast fiber to achieve the complex patterning of this shoulder cloth has not been commonly found in weaving in the Minangkabau highlands for more than 150 years. This unspun bast fiber is a flat strip much finer than cotton or silk, and its generous use here gives the textile a quality of sheerness, a highly desirable element in garments made for an area that straddles the equator. Bast warps occur every eight cotton warps; bast wefts alternate between every two and four cotton wefts.

Batu Sangkar, the capital of the Tanah Datar district, was a center of trade for centuries. Starting during the early years of Sumatra's Indianization era, the Batu Sangkar area's inhabitants were exposed to materials imported from India and also Arabia. As trade developed, gold mined in Tanah Datar brought outsiders to the highland cities. There was even a settlement of Indians there; they felt a need to protect the perilous trade routes down to the west coast ports, since these were the routes used to transport the gold that was to be exchanged for Indian-made cotton fabrics. The precipitous paths were subject to attack by bandits who stole the gold. The commercially sponsored invasion by outsiders of Tanah Datar and its main settlement of Batu Sangkar affected all inhabitants. Over time the weavers—who absorbed information, use of materials, and cultural themes from the wider world—developed their own sophisticated, eclectic sense of design. Located near the royal court of the Javanese invader Adityawarman, Batu Sangkar became the art capital of the Minangkabau highlands.

In her excellent *Islamic revivalism in a changing peasant economy* (1987 [1983]:
1) historian Christine Dobbin writes:

> "The inhabitants of the Central Sumatran highlands, the Minangkabau, have become famous throughout the Indonesian world for their agricultural skills, for their commercial adaptability, and for their willingness to seize new opportunities and adapt to new mental horizons, whether introduced from India, from the Middle East, or from Europe. Hand in hand has gone the capacity to preserve their own particular identity."

We expect weavings from Batu Sangkar to be especially innovative because of Minangkabau's commerce with the world.

It is clear that this textile was well cared for during its long life. Bast fibers become dry and brittle as they age and tend to break easily, leaving holes in a weaving. There are no bast breaks in this cloth. Also, the tarnished metallic strips that are wound around the core of the silver-wrapped thread can loosen and cut the cotton and bast fibers in a textile when it is folded or otherwise handled. But there are no obvious cuts here.

Not all motifs in Minangkabau ceremonial textiles refer to sayings and proverbs from the adat. Some motifs represent ceremonial objects such as tobacco boxes, a cake that must be served at rituals, or, as in this example, a ceremonial necklace. This ornament is represented by a row of diamonds joined by short lines. A similar motif is found in the shoulder cloth from the village of Pariangan (see fig. 6.8). Some contemporary textiles are patterned with rows of "necklaces," suggesting that there is some continuity between the old and the new.

In another example of continuity between traditional and contemporary weavings, the wide pattern band of pink supplementary weft in this textile is made of silk embroidery floss, not metallic-wrapped thread. A contemporary selendang, in comparison, is covered with pink silk supplementary wefts as motifs. Silk thread has a big advantage over metal threads: it can be laundered. Gold silk thread available today looks almost as rich as the gold-wrapped thread used in older textiles. Unfortunately this traditional shoulder cloth (fig. 6.15) could not be laundered because it also contains metal thread, and the bast fiber probably would not survive even a gentle wash.

Anne Summerfield, John Summerfield

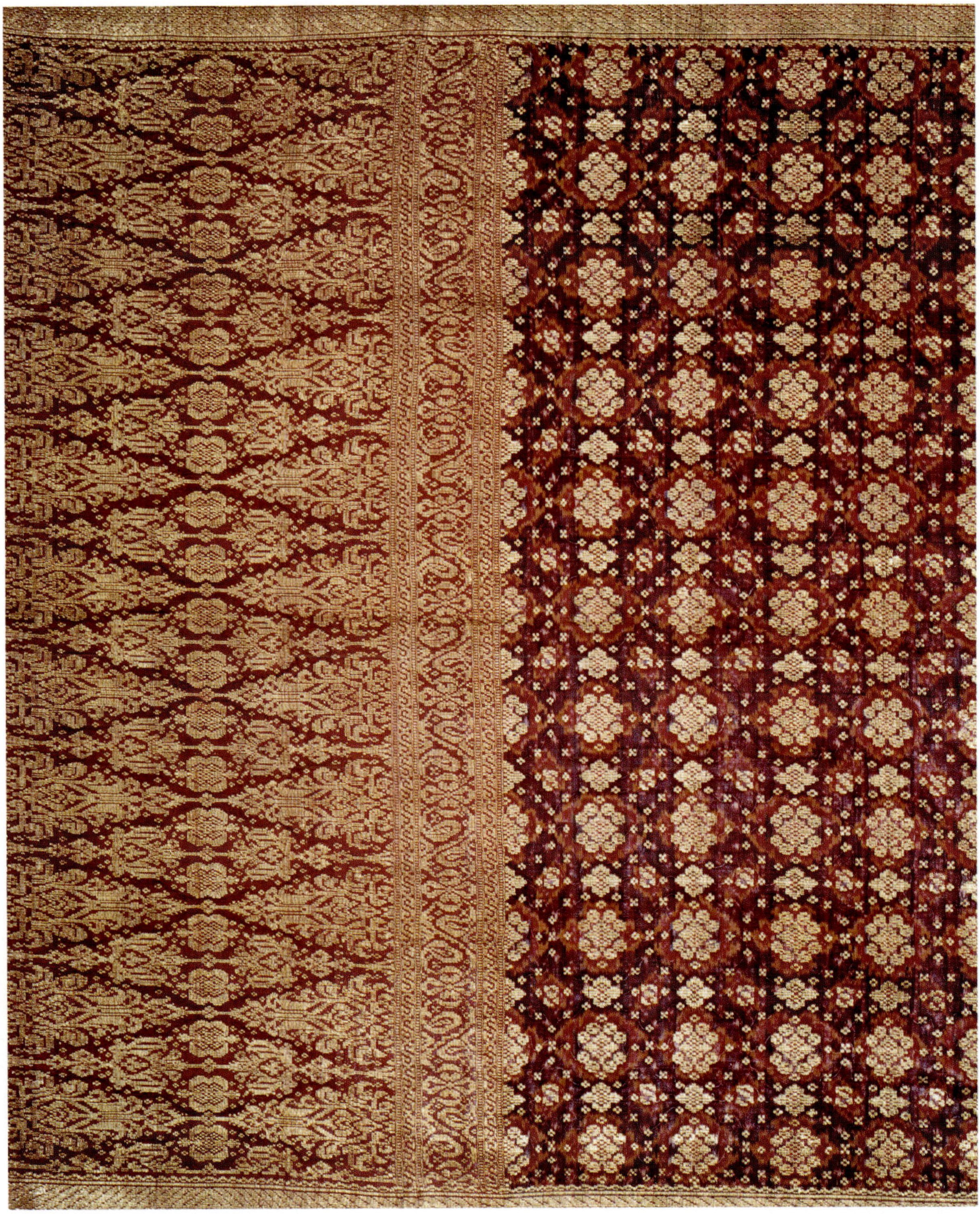

Fig. 6.16. Man's sarong with elaborate gold center panel (kepala) that stretches from waist to ankle at center front. Palembang, circa 1800.

Fig. 6.17. The large sarong at its fullest extent.

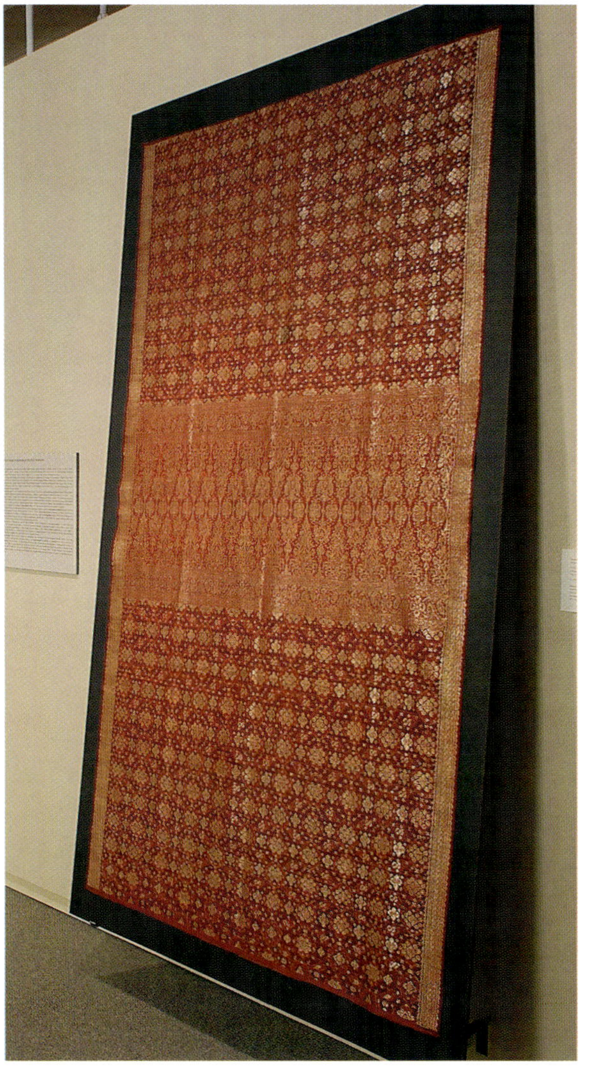

Figure 6.16
Sarong, circa 1800
Palembang, South Sumatra
Silk, gold-wrapped thread
Plain weave, supplementary weft, weft ikat
87-1/2 x 42 in., 222.2 x 107.7 cm

Two or three centuries ago an aristocratic man or a member of royalty would have worn a sarong like this to important ceremonies in Palembang, a city on the Musi River in southeast Sumatra, some sixty miles inland from the Straits of Malacca. The history of Palembang is rich in stories of aggressive warring kings, the exotic lore of the now-mysterious kingdom of Srivijaya, the hurly-burly of international trade, and the extended visits of foreign traders either waiting for the trade winds' seasonal change of direction or needing a safe harbor from vicious piracy. Not surprisingly, Palembang's extraordinary textile culture is deeply cosmopolitan.

Srivijaya was probably founded sometime around the late 600s or early 700s C.E. The capital of the kingdom has been variously placed at Palembang, Jambi, or even Thailand. Statuary and stone inscriptions support all three locations. There is ample information to support the view that the capital moved from place to place as the reigning monarchs saw fit. Although gold thread was found buried in the bowels of Srivijaya ruins in Sumatra along with unpolished rubies and pieces of gold plate (Suwati Kartiwa, personal communication), there is no corroborating evidence that local weavers used gold thread at that early date.

Malaysian weavers in the district of Terengganu, one of Malaysia's two great weaving regions, attribute the introduction of songket weaving into Malaysia to Sumatra, and especially to Palembang. This is partly because of the history of early (that is, Srivijaya-era) weaving in the Palembang area (Selvanayagam 1990: xviii). Some say that the word *songket* was derived from songka, a Palembang cap in which gold threads were first woven (Kartiwa 1986: 11).

Textiles made in Palembang up to the time of World War II (when weaving materials became unavailable in Japanese-occupied Indonesia) have been noted for their beauty, the excellence of their materials, and the skill of their weavers. Extensive experience over centuries with different types of thread, but especially with silk, gave Palembang weavers knowledge of how best to use different threads to make superior textiles. Centuries of weaving songket also led to the development of a style unique to Palembang, which incorporated but adapted influences from other parts of the world. According to Suwati Kartiwa, the lavish and expensive Palembang songkets are passed down through generations as heirlooms (Kartiwa 1986: 11). Care of songkets is considered as important as care of the family's money. The prestige associated with fine ceremonial textiles gave weavers the incentive to develop the skills necessary to produce these cloths. A case in point is the special gold thread once made for use in songkets.

When gold was plentiful in the area, pure gold was exported to be extruded into fine filaments and spun into fine gold thread, which was then returned to Palembang. These gold threads were stripped from damaged textiles to be used in the production of new songkets. Long after pure gold was no longer converted into gold thread, even as late as the 1980s, it was customary to strip commercially made gold thread from damaged weavings if it was thought to be superior to what was available in the marketplace.

At the beginning of Palembang's long history of weaving with silk, the thread was imported from China. But in the fifteenth century the first mulberry tree in the Indonesian Archipelago was planted at Palembang, and silkworm cultivation began (Kartiwa 1986: 6). Other areas of Indonesia, including other parts of Sumatra and Sulawesi, soon followed.

Songket weaving in nearby Malaysia, unlike songket weaving in most of Sumatra, currently is bound by strict rules (Selvanayagam 1990: xv). The supplementary gold thread may not be passed over or under an arbitrary number of warps to execute the weaver's designs. The path of the gold supplementary thread must lie over three, five, or seven warps and under only one. This requirement is known as the Malaysian Convention.

In this magnificent sarong the paths of the gold threads in the body of the textile are mostly over five warps, under one, over five, under one, and so on. A few are over three, under one. In the ornate central panel (the head, or kepala, of the sarong), all paths are over three, under one, over three, under one, and so on. The effect of this path restriction is easily seen in the accompanying photograph. Even though the warps cannot be counted without the aid of a magnifier, the restricted structure of the thread paths gives a modular, geometric appearance to the motifs.

The body of the sarong is further decorated with weft ikat patterning. The piece was purchased in Palembang, but on comparison we find that the pattern of the ikat is similar to ikats in Malaysian songkets. That and the fact that the gold thread follows the Malaysian convention raises the question of whether this textile was made in Malaysia or in Palembang. Either could be the place of origin.

Anne Summerfield, John Summerfield

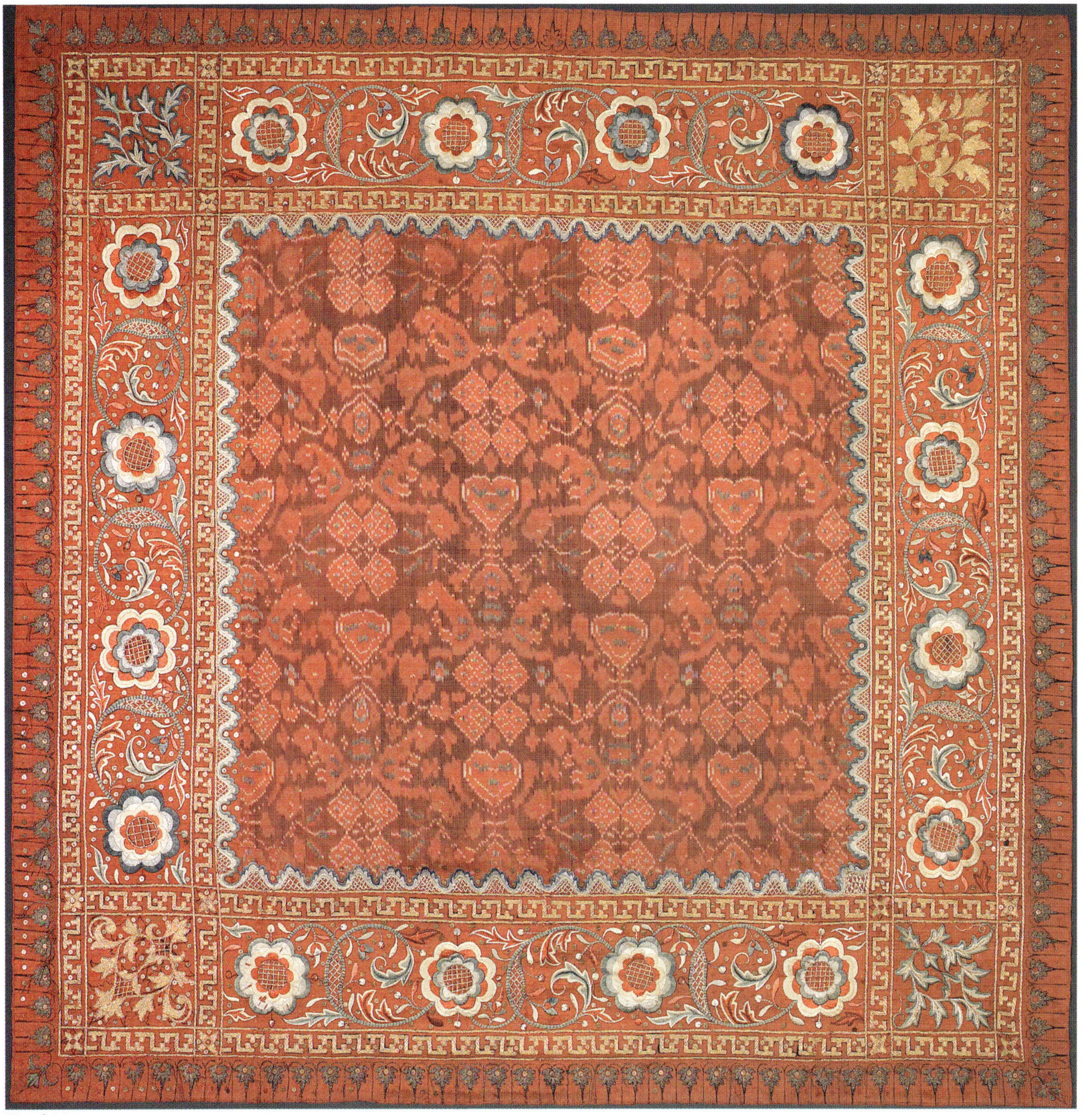

Fig. 6.18

Figure 6.18.
Kain kepala (headcloth), 1875
Palembang, South Sumatra
Silk, silk embroidery floss, gold-wrapped thread, silver-wrapped thread
Plain weave, supplementary weft, couching, satin stitch embroidery, weft ikat, appliqué
37-1/2 x 37-1/2 in., 95.2 cm square

This resplendent headcloth is distinguished by the fact that six different techniques were employed in its manufacture and embellishment:
*The ground cloth is woven in plain or tabby weave.
*The geometric pattern that borders the center panel is formed by the addition of gold supplementary weft to the ground fabric.
*Alternate corners are decorated with vines and leaves couched in gold-wrapped thread. Couching is an embroidery technique.
*The other two corners contain blossoms made in silk satin-stitch embroidery, with couched crosshatched centers of corroded silver-wrapped thread.
*The silver-wrapped blossoms on stems that frame the entire textile are embellished with a hand-appliquéd sequin at each center. Adding extra material to the surface of a textile is called appliqué.
*The center portion of the headcloth is patterned with weft ikat. The pattern is tied and dyed in the weft threads before the textile is woven.

To make a tabby weave, the weft is passed over one warp, under the next, over one, under one, and so on. On the return pass of the weft, the thread takes the opposite path: where it went under a warp, it now goes over, and where it went over a warp, it now goes under. This weave is commonly found on simple baskets.

Supplementary weft weaving is a technique that allows the weaver to float a gold, silver, or silk supplementary thread over as many warps as are required to form the selected pattern, rather than being restricted to over one, under one, used for the ground fabric. For a full explanation of the technique, see chapter 4.

Couching is an embroidery technique that allows for the addition of metallic thread patterns on an already woven textile. Metal-wrapped thread cannot be embroidered as silk is embroidered on a finished cloth. The narrow strips of metal that are spiraled around the core would be stripped from the core as the thread was pulled through the cloth. Metal-wrapped thread may be used to embellish an already woven cloth, however, if it is placed on the cloth in the desired position and sewn to the textile with small inconspicuous stitches. This technique is called couching. The process is tedious and unexpectedly demanding of the sewer's skills and stamina. On some complicated designs, the couching threads may be placed so that they form an additional pattern.

Satin stitch embroidery is used to produce blocks of color on the surface of a textile. The embroiderer pushes her needle from the underside of the cloth to the top and returns the needle to the underside from an appropriate point across that element of the design. A series of such floats, stitched closely parallel to one another, produces a block of color on both the front and back of the original cloth. The embroidery thread floats from one edge of the design to the other, essentially filling in the outlined design on the front of the cloth and on the back. Juxtaposing such blocks of different colors can produce a solid multihued pattern on the surface of a fabric. Embroidery was probably introduced into the Indonesian archipelago and the Malay peninsula by Chinese immigrants.

The pattern in the center section of the headcloth is produced by the dyeing technique called weft ikat. As noted earlier in this volume, the word ikat comes from the Indonesian and means "to tie." See chapters 3 and 4 for detailed discussions of the techniques of tying and dyeing threads for weft ikat. Materials as different as banana fiber and Mylar strips have been used for tying thread bundles in sections not to be dyed. The tied wefts are placed in the dye bath. When dyeing is complete, the threads are stretched out to dry. Ties are removed from the dry threads, and the wefts are made ready for weaving. If more than one color is to be dyed, the process must be repeated for each color: protect the threads not to be dyed or redyed, dye, dry, unwrap. This is a time-consuming and laborious process.

The pattern intended for the center portion of this headcloth is the heart motif. On close examination we see that the pattern is imperfectly executed. In one place the top of the heart is not rounded but is nearly flat, a fault in the tying. The heart motif appears frequently in the highly prized Indian textile called the *patola*. As mentioned in earlier chapters, patolas were brought to Southeast Asia by Arab and Indian traders, who gave them to high officials in the hope of receiving economic favors. These silk cloths were so popular throughout the area that inhabitants who could not afford to buy them started producing a much less expensive domestic cotton version called a *sarassa*.

This beautiful, heavily embellished cloth is made for display not on a wall but on the head of a wealthy and important man. The cloth is not tied directly on the head but is draped and shaped over a small hat, thus protecting it somewhat from perspiration and hair oil. Most Palembang headcloths are embellished with some gold-wrapped thread but are not nearly as sumptuous as this example. This piece has survived in unusually good condition, thanks in part to the Palembang tradition of protecting family heirloom textiles.

Anne Summerfield, John Summerfield

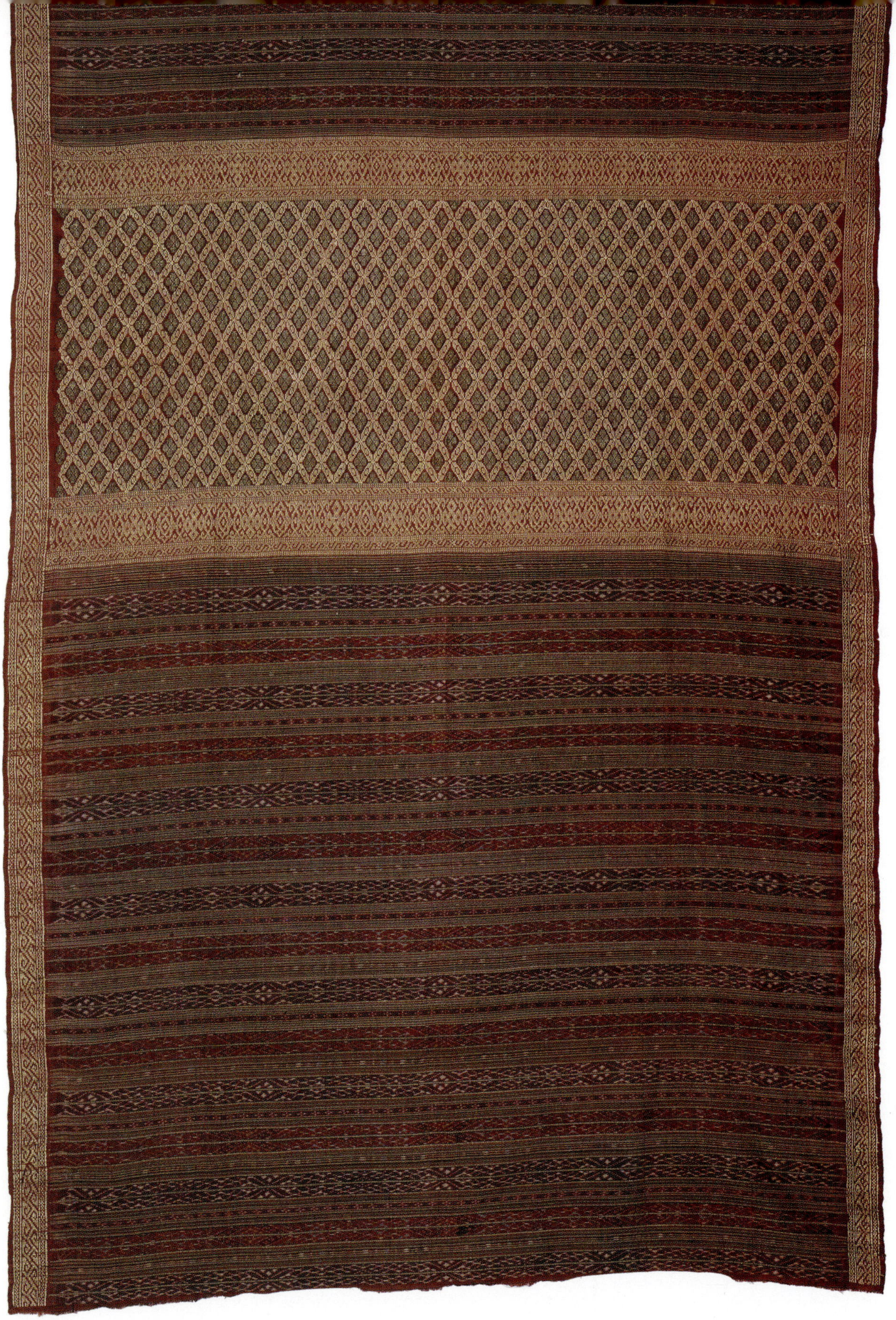

Fig. 6.19

Figure 6.19
Woman's sarong, circa 1800
Terengganu, Malaysia
Silk, silk floss, gold- and silver-wrapped thread
Plain weave, supplementary weft (gold and silk), weft ikat
86 x 40 in., 218.7 x 101.5 cm

This Malaysian woman's elegant sarong is patterned with a dyeing technique, weft ikat, and a weaving technique, metal-wrapped thread supplementary weft. According to the rather restrictive Malaysian convention, when the supplementary weft metallic threads are woven into the fabric, they are limited in terms of the paths they can follow—that is, they may pass over only three, five, or seven warps and under one. The pass is called the weft float. This convention produces a highly distinctive design but one that is less fluid than the typical Sumatran songket motif.

The somewhat somber colors, dark red and dark purple, suggest a strong Islamic element. They lend great dignity to this garment. The decorated *kepala*, or head, of the sarong is densely packed with gold and silver motifs called *bunga pecah empat*, a four-petaled flower. The intersecting diagonal lines that form enclosures for the motif are called *rantai* (a generic Indonesian word for "chain"). These appear in many Malaysian songkets and take varied forms. The rantai here are formed of individual vine and leaf clusters. Four clusters constitute a diamond-shaped enclosure for the four petals.

The fineness of the motifs in this sarong and their density, which required a large amount of metallic thread, suggest that the expensive garment was made for an aristocrat. Close inspection of the metallic thread in the supplementary weft shows that much of the gold has worn off the gold-wrapped thread. This has exposed a paper base, to which gold leaf had been affixed. The silver-wrapped thread in the kepala is in nearly perfect condition. Abrasion of gold from thread wrapped with strips of gold leaf on a paper base regularly occurs over years of use.

Weft ikat as a patterning technique is confined to the body of the textile, where a combination of ikat and gold appear in stripes of three different widths. Weft ikat patterns in Malaysian songkets in general are thought to have been adapted from the patterns in Indian patola cloths.

Songket weaving in Malaysia originally flourished in two main weaving regions, Terengganu and Kelantan, provinces on the east coast of peninsular Malaysia. Trading with India and Arabia was active and weavers were exposed to patterned and embellished weavings from these areas. There are two different assumptions about how making songkets became a part of the Malaysian weavers' skills. The Kelantanese believe that songket came from around Cambodia and Thailand and worked its way down the peninsula. People from Terengganu say that songket came from India through the Sumatran centers of Palembang and Jambi. They base their argument on the fact that songket weaving existed in the kingdom of Srivijaya, which was physically closer to areas of Malaysia than was Cambodia or Thailand. Also, there was intermarriage between royals of Malaysia and Sumatra to achieve political alliances. The Sumatran brides undoubtedly brought their songkets to their new homes and may have also brought weavers (Selvanayagam 1990: xviii)

Palembang weavers have always used backstrap looms to weave their songkets. With a backstrap loom, tension on the warp threads is controlled by the thrust of the weaver's back against a wooden or leather strap that is tied to the breast beam of the loom. Contemporary Malaysian weavers use frame looms, in which tension on the warps is controlled entirely within the loom. For gold-thread weaving Indian traders probably introduced the backstrap loom to Malaysia initially, but it was eventually replaced by the slightly more complex frame loom.

Grace Impam Selvanayagam writes (1990: xv) that the supplementary-weft patterns on ancient songkets lay higher above the ground cloth than songket patterns of today because the metallic thread was of larger diameter. Contemporary thread is made of a flat strip of metal or of gold leaf on paper, which is wound around a core usually made of plied cotton or plied silk thread. The original Malaysian gold thread was made of round filaments of gold wrapped around a large core. It was larger in diameter and therefore more apparent.

Motifs in the kepala of the Malaysian woman's sarong pictured here resemble the motifs in the ikatted body of the man's sarong from Palembang (fig. 6.16). Both contain the bunga pecah empat, the four-petalled flower, but they differ in the rantai. This similarity adds to the confusion over whether the sarong was woven in Palembang or in Malaysia.

Anne Summerfield, John Summerfield

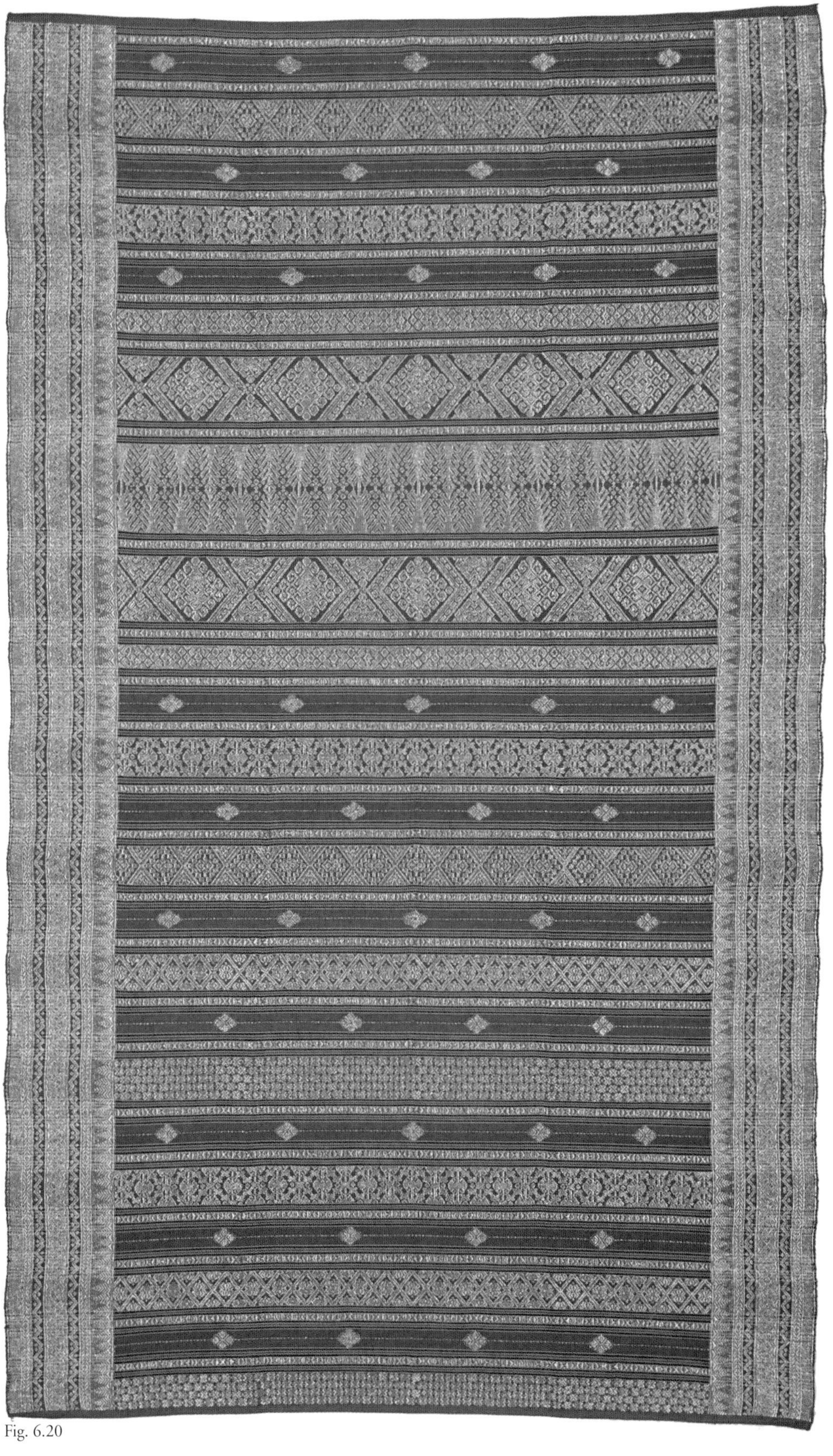

Fig. 6.20

Figure 6.20
Sarong, 2005
Minangkabau people
Pandai Sikek, West Sumatra
Polyester, gold wrapped thread, supplementary weft
64 x 38 in., (162.6 x 96.5 cm)
Iris and B. Gerald Cantor Art Gallery Study Collection

The brokers who marketed this lively sarong and its accompanying shoulder cloth in 2006 in a shop in Bukittinggi cheerily told me that this songket textile set was a *kreasi baru*-style cloth. That is, it is a "new creation" sort of songket in the sense that the weaver was pursuing innovation in design (along with a hint of that Sumatran favorite, the modern). And this is indeed so. This songket's overall format, made up of motif bands interspersed with plain ones, was held to be the latest style in 2005. In truth this alternation of bands is a historical pattern. In Pandai Sikek, however, now West Sumatra's main weaving village, the bands-on-bands approach was thought to be "the latest thing."

Another innovative, creative aspect of this particular songket was said (by the textile dealers) to be its use of this particular tone of clear, bright red. Along with aqua, peach, lime green, and light pink, this tone of red was thought to be up to date and modern. Minangkabau weavers have been engaged in a romance with commercial dyes since at least the early 1900s, and this interpretation of red as new is part of that trend. Ironically, red tones have been the basic color for Southeast Asian status textiles in mercantile Muslim societies for centuries.

Perhaps most important, in terms of this particular songket's cachet as something new and creative, was the identity of the weaver: he was a man. The handlooming of special fabrics in Indonesian societies is stereotypically regarded as a feminine endeavor. In many Indonesian societies outside Indic Java and Bali, weaving a cloth on a backstrap loom is metaphorically linked to pregnant women's work in growing their fetuses. Sometimes the female reproductive body images for cloth are quite explicit, as when the knife used to cut a completed ikat textile off the loom is likened to the blade used to sever a newborn's umbilical cord. In village societies in parts of eastern Indonesia, Kalimantan, and the Batak regions of Sumatra, relatively lightweight, pliable, soft handwoven textiles are often thought to be products of women's hands and, by extension, women's bodies. Correspondingly, heavy, dense, sharp metal objects such as swords and daggers and iron tools are thought to be the products of men's hands. The textiles/femininity pair is further linked in many of the idea systems of these societies to life and growth: to babies, but also to agricultural bounty in the rice fields. The metal goods/masculinity pair in these schemes of thought reference warfare and death (See Mattiebelle Gittinger, *Splendid symbols; Textiles and tradition in Indonesia,* 1990, for rewarding discussions of these themes. See also Susan Rodgers, 1985, *Power and gold; Jewelry from Indonesia, Malaysia, and the Philippines*, on gold and metal exchange).

The measured interaction of the two opposed sides establishes world order and the continuity of generations through time. For example, in a process of gift exchange found in some societies in Sumba, an exchange of metalwork bridewealth payments from the bridegroom's side for textiles brought into the union by the bride ritually completes and empowers the marriage (Adams 1969). The balanced sets of gifts and countergifts make the pairing fertile and foster good order in the village as a whole. Associations between women and weaving are foundational to many Indonesian village epistemologies in such ways.

Songket weaving has historically proved to be more of a cosmopolitan craft linked to international markets and Muslim courts than it has been to village worldviews per se. But women have been the typical weavers of songkets throughout Sumatra. In Minangkabau textile memories, for instance, the great weavers of the early twentieth century were older women. Throughout the history of songket weaving in Palembang and Jambi it has been older girls and women who weave gold cloths. In Pandai Sikek today, however, without much apparent ideological crisis, adolescent boys and younger men (to about age forty) are sitting at looms and producing excellent textiles.

The red-banded songket set in fig. 6.20 was woven in 2005 by a young male college student. His family resides in Pandai Sikek, and as is usual there, numerous women and girls in his immediate and extended family weave. Pandai Sikek older weavers estimate that some 75 percent of homes there have songket looms; sometimes these frame looms are in a downstairs room near a window, while in other homes a group of looms is placed upstairs for several adolescent girls to weave upon. The young man attends college in a university in Padang, the West Sumatran capital. His tuition fees and room and board costs at a boarding house are high for a person of modest means. It is commonly understood in Pandai Sikek that fine songket sets of this one's quality sell for the rupiah equivalent of $75 to $125. And he is aware that the weaver's take of that sum is ready cash and more in many instances than the income he could get from odd jobs. So he has become a songket weaver, with little apparent embarrassment.

The phenomenon of Pandai Sikek men weaving songkets has been especially marked in the years since the Southeast Asian currency crisis of 1997–98. Indonesia's national economy has encountered numerous problems in bounding back from the rupiah's loss of value in 1998. West Sumatran villages such as Pandai Sikek have had abundant agricultural output to help tide them over, but cash sources are few. The songket market is a strong part of the luxury goods sector for middle-class and upper-class Minangkabau. So, doing the laborious work of weaving songkets over many weeks and months makes sense for some Pandai Sikek men in this context. Some college students from Pandai Sikek have assembled frame looms in their lodgings in Padang so that they can work away at their songkets little by little in their off hours from study.

Though still young, the weaver of this cloth already has a signature style. He combines classic Pandai Sikek motifs and design formats (such as the row of interlocked zigzag patterns along the selvedge edges here) with motifs from other old village traditions throughout Minangkabau. He likes and admires these motifs and enjoys combining them with Pandai Sikek styles in new ways. In its overall conceptualization his red songket is traditionalist yet new, heritage-conscious yet stylish—and easily sellable, to boot. His broker has a hard time keeping this college student's weavings in stock.

Susan Rodgers

Fig. 6.21

Figure 6.21
Selendang (shoulder cloth), 2006
Minangkabau people
Halaban neighborhood, Payakumbuh, West Sumatra
Polyester, silver-wrapped thread, supplementary weft
57-1/2 x 13-1/4 in., 146 x 38 cm
Iris and B. Gerald Cantor Art Gallery Study collection

The Minangkabau songket set of which this shoulder cloth is a part is densely woven with silver-wrapped thread. The piece is unusual, even unorthodox. This is so in several ways. First, in Minangkabau, silver thread for the supplementary wefts is less common than is gold-wrapped thread, although both have a long history in West Sumatran weaving. Secondly, and perhaps more importantly, this weaver has combined motif bands in ways that the majority of Pandai Sikek craftswomen would not do. Why is this so? Therein lies a story.

Recall that Pandai Sikek is West Sumatra's sole remaining great songket-weaving village. The town of Silungkang also produces good songket cloth today, but most weavers there use fly-shuttle looms and do not show the extremely high level of technical skill found in abundance in the other village. There is also some songket weaving done in the towns of Payakumbuh and Batu Sangkar, but again—surely in the eyes of Pandai Sikek weavers—their cloths are not to the high standard of Pandai Sikek songkets in terms of tightness of weaving, numbers of threads per pattern stick, and comprehensive knowledge of Minangkabau motif repertoires. The weaver of this black-and-silver-thread textile has created an ambitious, shimmery, intensely detailed songket, yet some Pandai Sikek older weavers disparage the quality of this cloth. The selvedge bands are well-executed in typical Pandai sikek motifs. But, the weaver has jumbled motifs bands together in the center field in ways that strike some Pandai Sikek purists as odd and laughable. The weaver "at fault" has herself been encouraged by her boss to draw on Pandai Sikek craft traditions. What is wrong? The problem is that this weaver is not living and working in the village of Pandai Sikek itself but is operating under her boss' tutelage in distant Payakumbuh.

Most troubling, in this rhetoric of blame about "bad weaving" (or rather, morally problematic weaving), is the fact that this weaver's boss has engineered this whole situation for profit making in an unorthodox geographic locale. Place is indeed crucial to this dispute.

Pandai Sikek weavers often trace their craft's history back to the great women weavers of Pitalah Village, a settlement that was associated (as noted) in the 1800s with exquisitely fine songket ceremonial belts and head ties. As older Pandai Sikek weavers tell the history today in interviews, Pitalah women brought their demanding weaving techniques and certain motifs to Pandai Sikek in the early 1800s. Pandai Sikek women drew on these and perfected them (the tale goes). A rule of residence after marriage ensued: Pandai Sikek women with weaving knowledge are ideally supposed to stay in their home village throughout their lives so as not to allow their great skills to be disseminated to other villages. As the number of songket-weaving villages constricted to just a few, this idealized rule of residence for textile craftswomen began to make even more sense in terms of village pride and sheer economics.

Daughters from Pandai Sikek families may certainly move away to other villages and cities to marry and work in fields such as teaching, health care, shopkeeping, government positions, and so on. But if they intend to weave songkets, they must stay in the village itself.

In actual practice, this idealized rule of residence for Pandai Sikek women is sometimes broken. This silvery textile is one result. What happened is the following. An expert and admired Pandai Sikek weaver married a man from the town of Payakumbuh and moved there.

She continued to weave songkets, and "what is worse," say detractors back in her home village, she established a songket-weaving business there, training Payakumbuh women in the old Pandai Sikek techniques. Objective observers might say that songkets such as this one are delightful, but the renegade business manager/weaving entrepreneur is currently a target of opprobrium from some of her home village colleagues.

"Bad songket weaving" at the simplest level is often talked about in Pandai Sikek in terms of skipped patterns, rough weave, or off-kilter motifs. Older weavers tut-tut that such errors can be made by inexperienced younger weavers. This black and silver Payakumbuh piece has been woven at a high level of technical brilliance, and the supposed faults here lie in the moral domain of breaking tradition. Creative, lovely textiles can evidently come from that.

Susan Rodgers

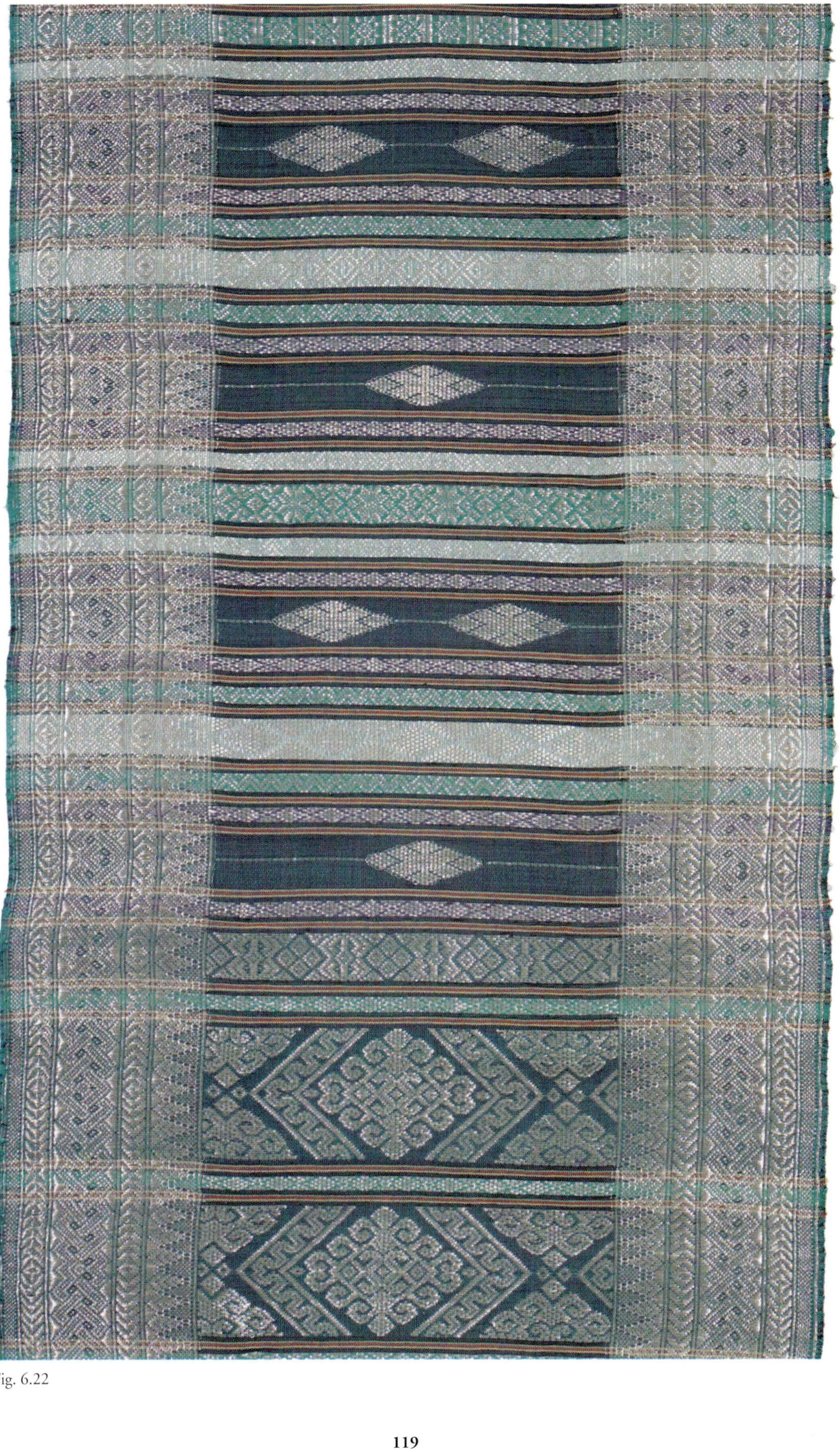

Fig. 6.22

Figure 6.22.
Selendang (shoulder cloth), 2005
Minangkabau people
Pandai Sikek
Silk and polyester blend, gold-wrapped thread
Supplementary weft
67-3/4 x 13 in., 172 x 33 cm
Iris and B. Gerald Cantor Art Gallery Study Collection

This dramatic songket shoulder cloth, shown here in detail, uses a tone of aqua from commercially dyed threads that has enjoyed much popularity over the last couple of years. The textile was woven in Minangkabau's Pandai Sikek Village or in the nearby neighborhood of Tanjung. The latter small settlement of wood and concrete houses is located a bit up the mountain slopes from Pandai Sikek proper.

Weavers in both places revel in the color choices provided by commercial dyes: green, a large blue palette, cream, deep red, several striking purples, yellows, tans, black, purple-brown, and a current favorite, "peach" (the English word is used). Much is going on in Sumatran songket color aesthetics.

Aniline dyes became available to ikat weavers in Kalimantan by 1890. By the mid-twentieth century at the latest, Minangkabau songket weavers were also relying on commercial dyes for some of their work. Today factory-produced and dyed thread is the overwhelming norm for weavers in West Sumatra. This is true for all fibers. Some Pandai Sikek weavers take much care in selecting their own dye lots of thread, traveling to the Silungkang market specially for this on a regular basis.

In part, a globalized fashion market determines a weaver's selection of aqua threads such as those used here. Colors that become popular in international couture fashion (such as the lime green of a few seasons ago) affect ready-to-wear manufacture worldwide. The colors used in these everyday fashions in turn shape the international thread market for weavers. This influences a Pandai Sikek weaver's color choices when she shops at the Silungkang thread market.

In the Dutch East Indies the choice of the color red for ritual textiles was sometimes inflected by politics. Sandra Niessen reports, for instance, that Karo Batak in highland villages in the 1820s wore blue textiles, dyed with indigo (Niessen 2003: 53-61). This color was thought to be the distinctively Karo one. Yet by the twentieth century Karo ulos textiles were deep red; by the 1950s onward, Karo ulos were shot through with gold threads. Niessen explains that when Karo began moving down out of the highlands to plantation-belt Deli around the turn of the twentieth century they encountered new textile universes that proved to be immensely attractive to weavers. In Deli, Karo newcomers saw the red status textiles of coastal Malay sultanate peoples. Karo sometimes attempted to "become Malay" in Deli in order to better their chances of being accepted as responsible, civilized people (as opposed to pagan highlanders, a constant slur against the Batak). Shifting the Karo ritual textile color palette was part of this process. In Deli Karo immigrants also encountered "the clothing and textile ferment found in the East Indies" (Niessen 2003: 54). Karo saw high-status Western dress and prestigious Malay songkets as well. Supplementary wefts of gold-wrapped thread began to infiltrate Karo "traditional textiles." The diagnostically Karo ulos today is a dark red with highlights of gold thread.

Susan Rodgers

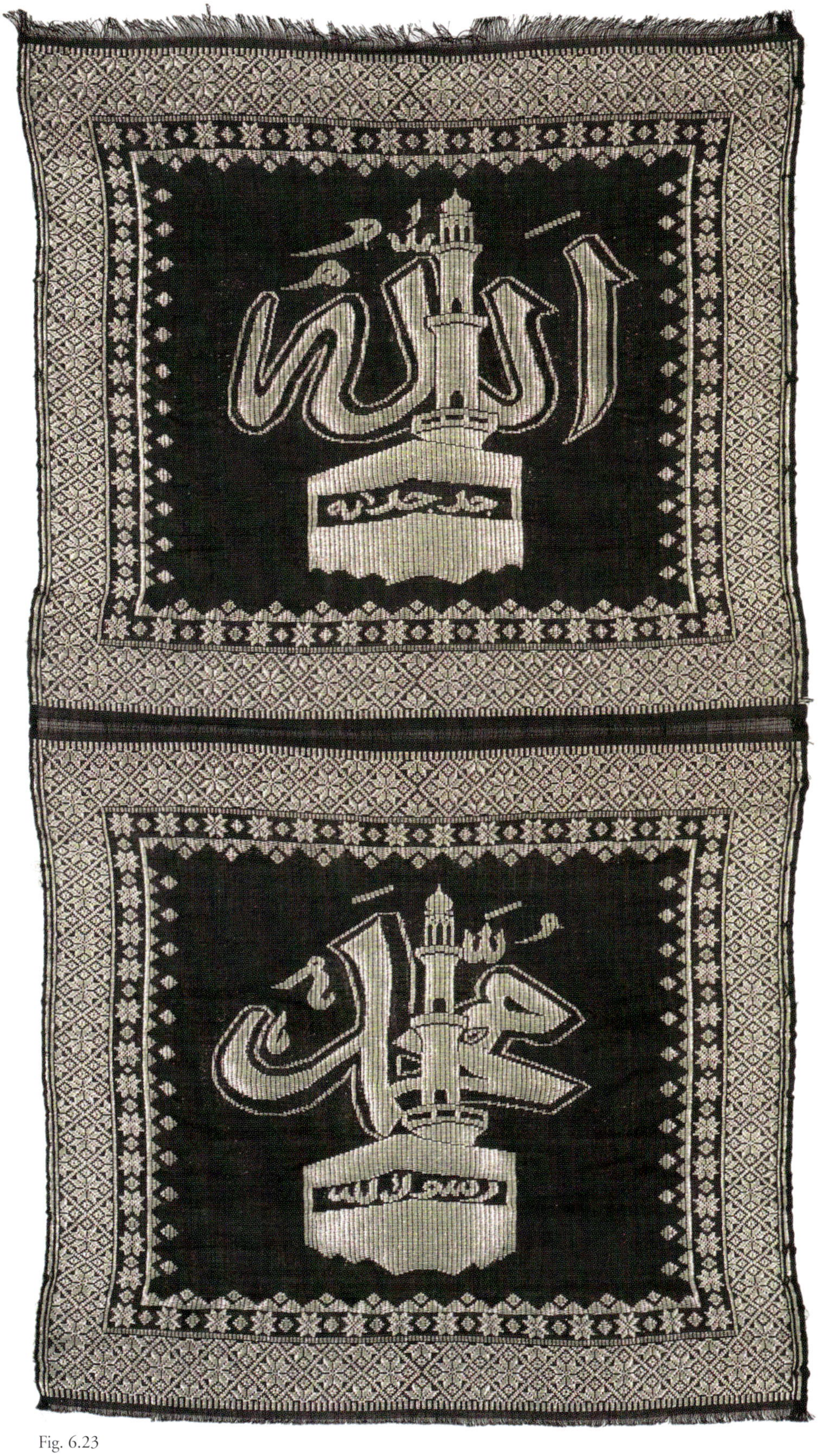

Fig. 6.23

Figure 6.23
***Wall hanging*, 2006**
Minangkabau people
Pandai Sikek, West Sumatra
Cotton-blend, silver-wrapped thread, supplementary weft
22 x 13 in., 56 x 33 cm
Iris and B. Gerald Cantor Art Gallery Study Collection

Like the three contemporary songket sets discussed previously, this double-panel piece was woven in Pandai Sikek. It shows Arabic calligraphy: the letters for Allah, at the top, and then for Mohammad, in the next panel down. Images of minarets are also worked into the letters, forming a prime representation of Muslim piety for the Sumatran and Jakarta families who typically buy these pieces today. This set, designed to be used together or separately as wall hangings for a family home, cost about the rupiah equivalent of $50 in 2006. The relatively high cost, dealers say, is due to the difficulty of weaving curvilinear shapes in songket. These panels come in a choice of several dark colors, with either gold or silver supplementary wefts. Pandai Sikek men do some of this specific type of songket weaving

This style is fairly new to the Pandai Sikek market and seems to be a local response to a widespread Sumatran phenomenon: the production of popular religious objects incorporating Arabic letters for display as wall hangings. In Palembang songket shops customers often find sayings from the Koran laid out in prada gold-leaf work on felt; in Bukittinggi shoppers have an array of beaten aluminum plaques to choose from. All these products are for display on walls. Traditional marketplaces throughout Sumatra have stalls chock-a-block with Arabic calligraphy trinket-type wall hangings, some in cloth, some in metal, some in carved wood. This Pandai Sikek songket is a particularly upmarket instance of this phenomenon

Contemporary Minangkabau songkets are woven in tense interrelationship with Muslim cloths of many sorts, and this calligraphic metal-thread textile may represent an attempt on the part of weavers and brokers to capture some market space and in effect "control the competition." Busana Muslim or modern Muslim fashions are extremely popular among Minangkabau town and city middle-class adolescent girls and women today. These clothing styles consist of long polyester or cotton-blend straight skirts, long-sleeved tunics, and various versions of the *jilbab*, the throat, forehead, and head covering now demanded by modern Indonesian Islam. Middle Eastern styles of head coverings are also present in West Sumatran busana Muslim (the effect, probably, of the Java-based and Malaysia-based busana Muslim couture market). Beyond considerations of piety, these Muslim fashions are washable, unlike songket. The more practical Muslim clothes for women do seem to be pushing songket formal wear into constricted areas of purchase and use. Many women in Bukittinggi are today electing to wear elaborate, elegant busana Muslim suits of clothing to formal events. The Pandai Sikek weavers' Arabic calligraphy wall hangings seem to have sprung from this increasingly competitive ritual clothing area.

Susan Rodgers

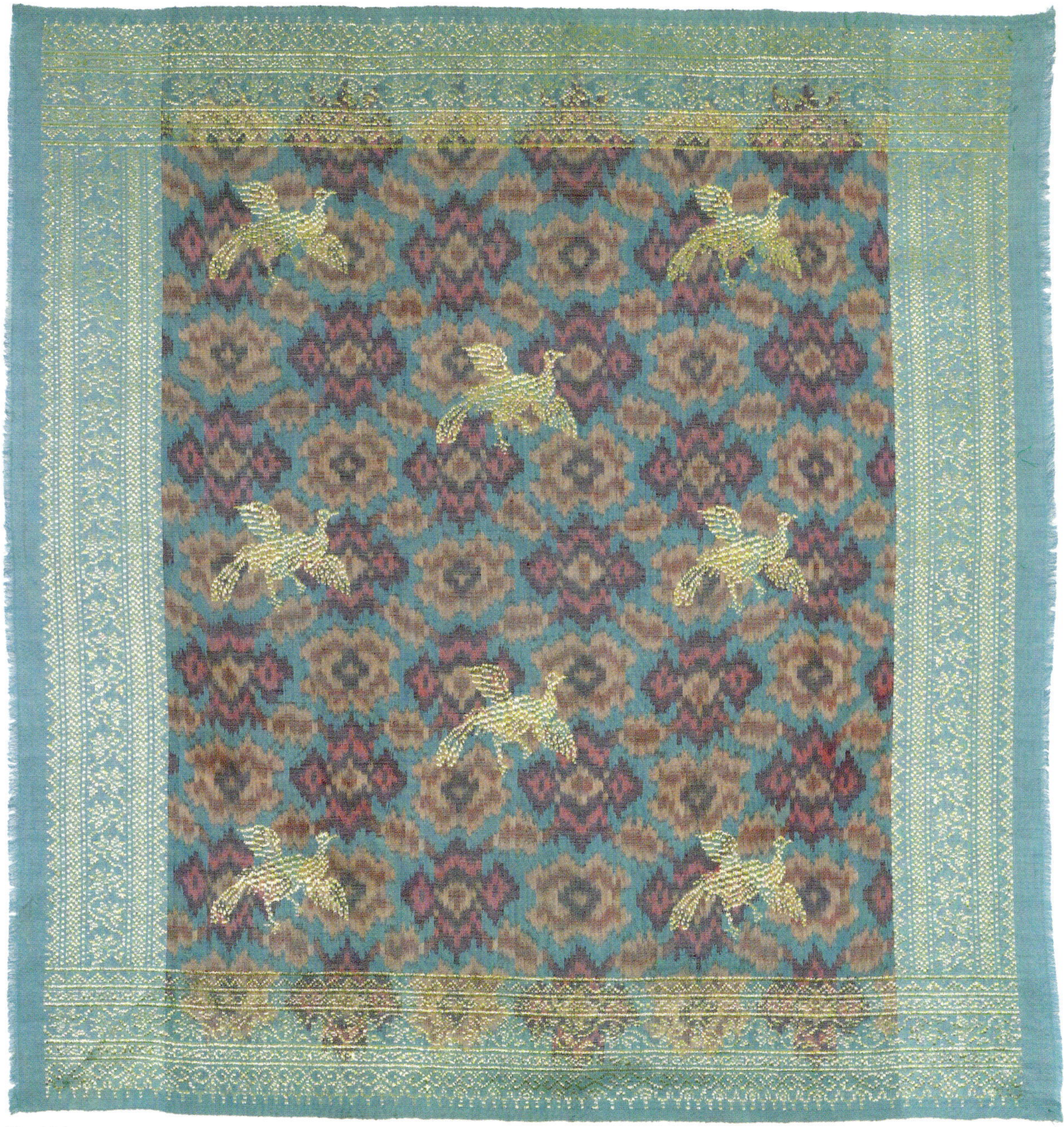

Fig. 6.24

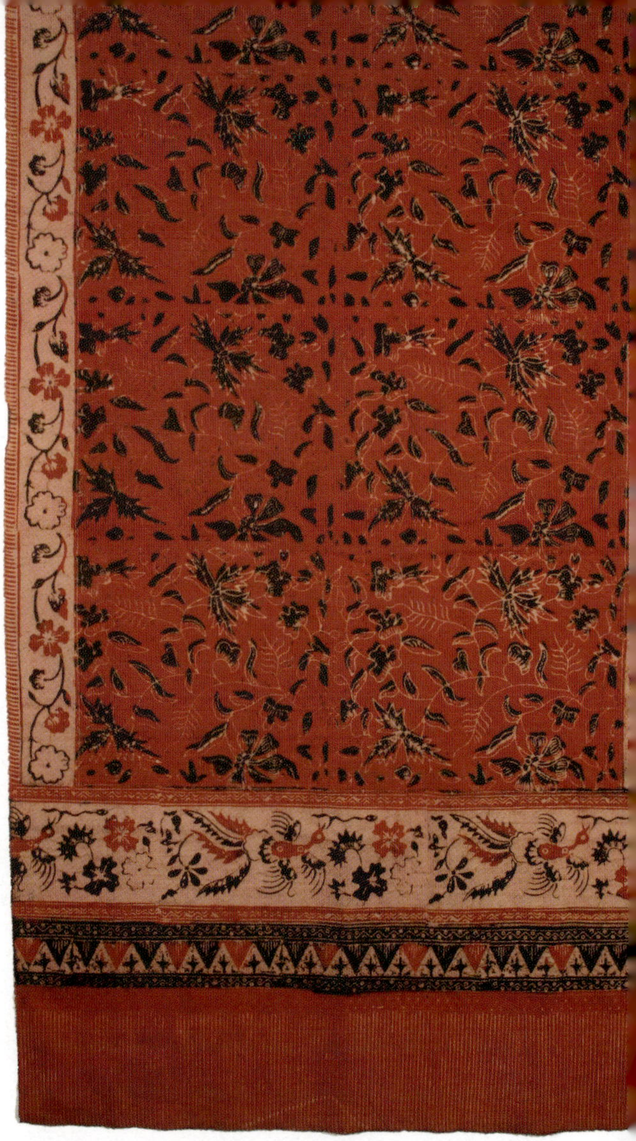

Fig. 6.25. A batik from Jambi, circa 2000.

Figure 6.24
Man's head tie, *kain limar* style, 2005
Jambi, southern Sumatra
Silk blend, gold-wrapped thread, supplementary weft, ikat
28 x 27-1/2 in., 71 x 70 cm
Iris and B. Gerald Cantor Art Gallery

Jambi is a modern commercial city built along one of Sumatra's great flat, brown eastern rivers, the Batang Hari. All these wide, muddy watercourses meander from the island's central uplands toward the Straits of Malacca, the entire region's commercial lifeblood. Jambi arts have long participated in the Straits' and the wider Malay world's riverine cosmopolitanism.

Jambi's strategic position—near Sumatra's resource-rich hinterlands yet easily accessible to regional trade in the Straits of Malacca—have given this river port its historical importance and resilience. Nearby downriver was the site of the Malayu Kingdom, a Hindu-Buddhist trade state that thrived circa 1000 C.E. Malayu was a successor state to mighty Srivijaya, which was a classic Southeast Asian Buddhist center of commerce and religious learning located somewhere near present-day Palembang (as noted above, the exact heart of Srivijaya is in dispute among archaeologists). Srivijaya elites were in partial control of the southern Sumatran end of China-to-India trade contacts from the 700s C.E until the era of the rise of Malayu, whose nobles may have been ethnically and linguistically Malay. Temple complex ruins in Muara Jambi (twenty-six kilometers downstream from the modern city) indicate a mix of Hindu and Buddhist heritage. Candi (temples) there date from the ninth to the thirteenth centuries. The Dutch colonial period was an era of competition among South Sumatra's small pepper-growing kingdoms for European favor and for regularized access to international markets.

All these geographical, political, commercial, and religious conditions over the course of Jambi's long history as a trade hub have shaped the region's remarkable textiles. Jambi is perhaps best known among textile scholars today for its distinctive cotton batiks (fig. 6.25). These differ from the more familiar batik traditions of central and north coast Java. Court-influenced batiks from the sultans' circles in Yogyakarta and Surakarta tend toward browns and blacks, with geometric patterns. North coast Javanese batiks exult in brighter colors and draw on bird, animal, and cloud motifs popular with the Indonesian Chinese merchant class (the peranakan Chinese in towns such as Cirebon). Jambi batiks are produced with the same technology of plain cotton cloth, hot wax styluses, dye baths, and successive boilings as is found in Java. But in Jambi cloth the textile field is often treated almost like a painter's canvas, with large, ambitious "drawings." Jambi batiks also use signature colors,

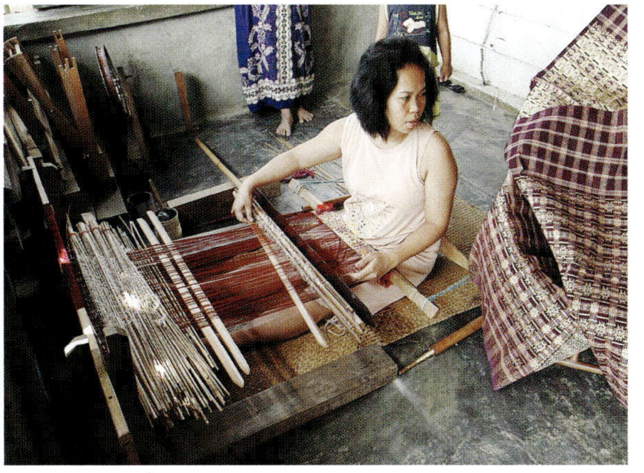

Fig. 6.26. Ny. Mania Ali weaving a plaid songket. Jambi, 2005.

which include deep blues and rusty reds, greens for foliage, muted tans, and black. Florals and animal designs are popular (see Fiona Kerlogue 1999, 2005, for extensive discussion of Jambi batiks).

Jambi's other great, if somewhat lesser-known, textile type is songket woven with gold-wrapped threads. With Jambi's old Malay kingdom antecedents, it is no surprise that the city and its riverine villages have strong songket-weaving heritages. After all, songket is the prototypical Malay Muslim court status cloth.

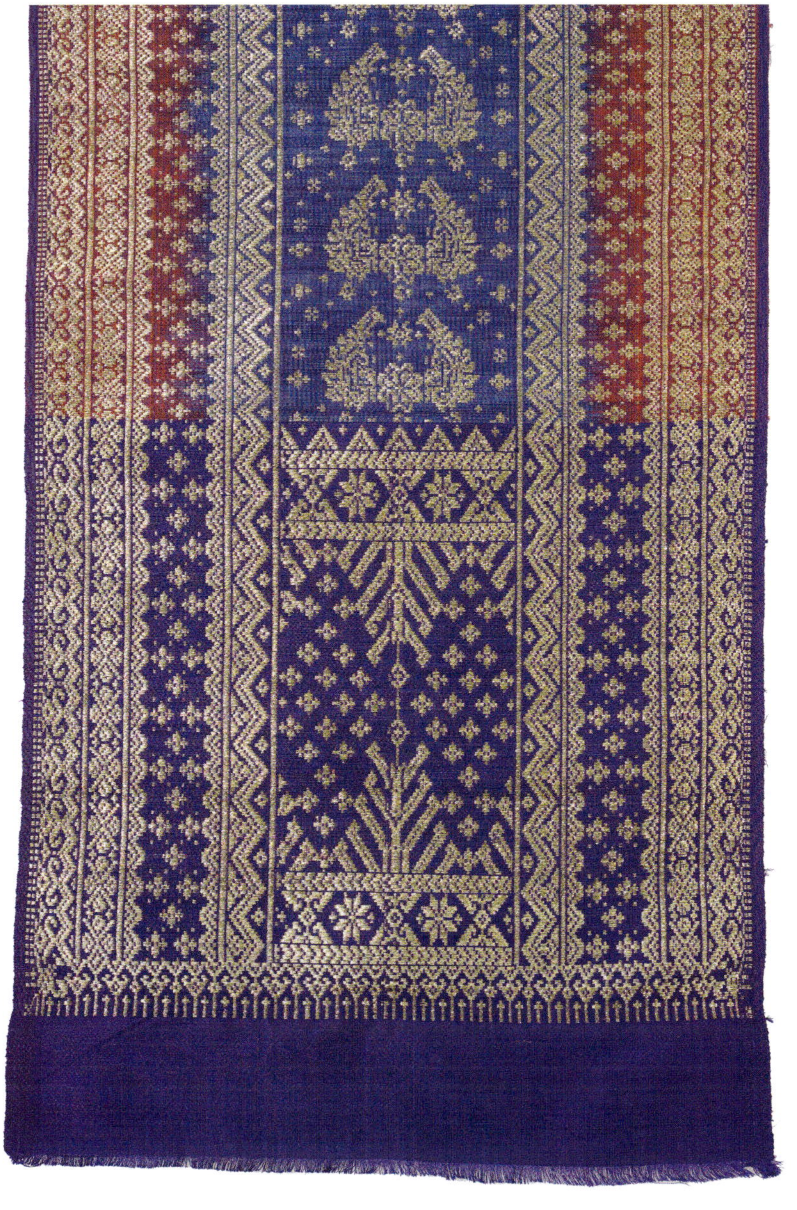

Fig. 6.27. Jambi songket, 2005.

In Jambi, songket wear is used for the expected range of Islamized adat occasions, but the textile is also pushing into new fashion domains. The songket shown here illustrates the latter trend. It is at base a traditional textile for ritual wear in adat and Islam. In trendy aqua, this man's head tie has fairly standard motif bands along its edges. Yet jaunty peacocks gambol across the central field. Jambi batik imageries indeed do cross over into Jambi songket manufacture. Jambi mainstream society is devoutly Muslim, yet animal figuration like that shown here animates many quite acceptable local songkets for luxury and ceremonial wear. Another Jambi songket type also thrives: gorgeous plaids, like that shown to the right of Ny. Mania Ali's backstrap loom (fig. 6.26). A third type of Jambi songket closely resembles the stately cloths from Palembang (fig.6.27).

Susan Rodgers

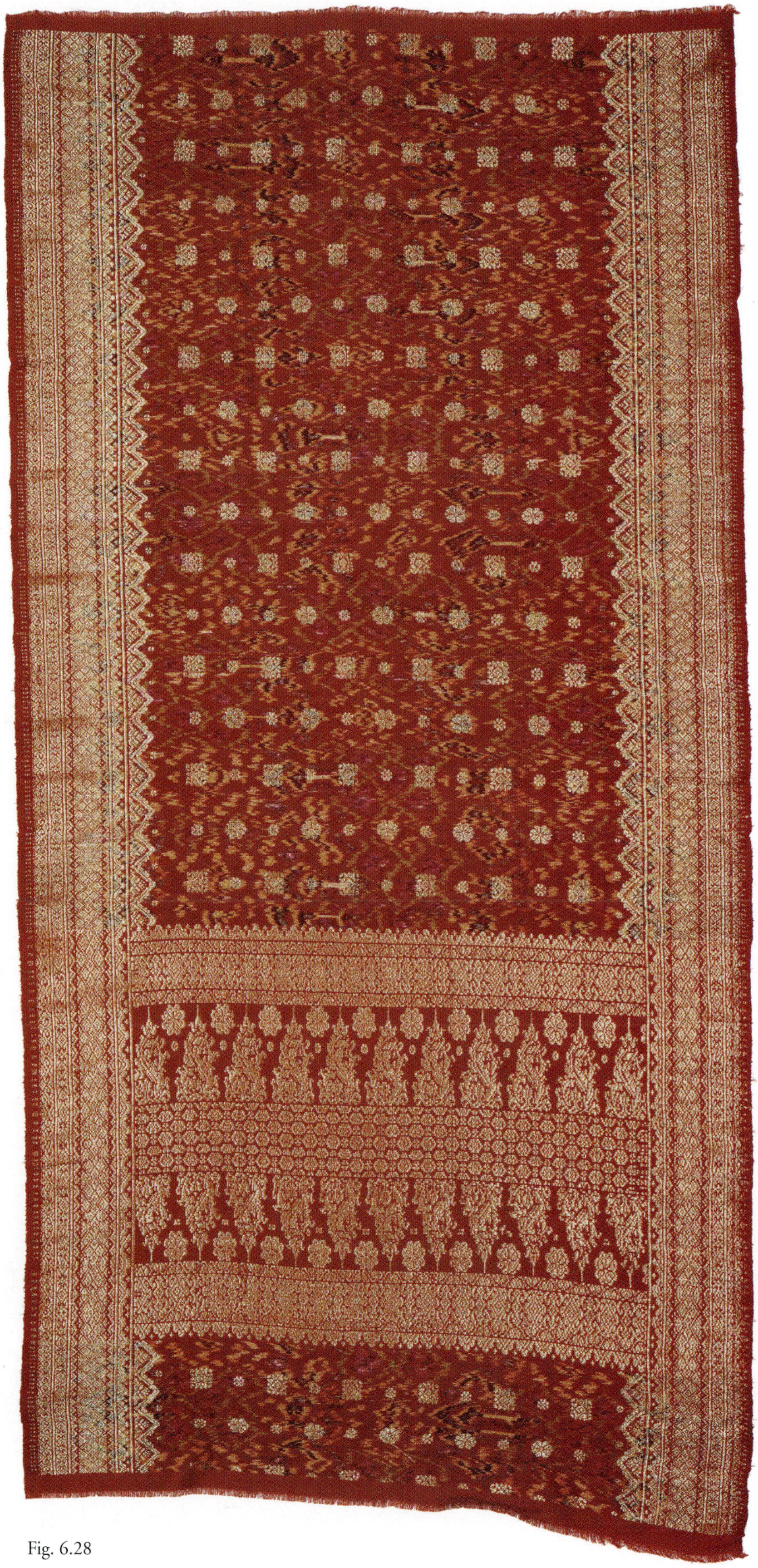

Fig. 6.28

Figure 6.28
Sarong, *kain limar* style, 2005
Palembang, South Sumatra
Silk blend, gold-wrapped thread, supplementary weft, ikat
70-1/2 x 33 in., 179.1 x 84 cm
Iris and B. Gerald Cantor Art Gallery Study Collection

This red silk kain limar was purchased in 2005 from an old-line Malay textile dealer family in the main songket-weaving neighborhood of the southern Sumatran city of Palembang. The shop is called the Fikri Koleksi, and this emporium for all types of Palembang Malay specialty cloths is part of a far-flung set of family songket businesses managed by the seven sons and daughters of Agus Haji Hussein Rahmat. The Fikri Koleksi designer/managers (discussed at length in chapter 5) ask their women weavers to produce both classic and new-style Palembang songkets. Although some of the gold-thread cloths are innovative in terms of dye color and motifs, all conform to the Palembang standards: a long length for sewing or folding into a sarong or waistcloth, the shoulder cloth, the square head tie for men, the pair of baby coverings to be used to enfold the infant when he or she is given a name (as noted in chapter 5, Barbara Andaya 1989 and Megumi Uchino 2005 provide excellent historical analysis of southern Sumatran songket handloom industries).

Kain limar is a specific form of southern Sumatran silk songket that includes ikat work. It has heavy bands of songket decoration along all four sides and a spray of songketted blossoms or stars in the central field, which is done in ikatted silk. This textile conforms to that standard. The silk threads are imported to Palembang via Singapore; the gold thread used in the Fikri Koleksi often comes from Japan.

The luxuriant dark red used in this textile is Palembang's signature color for songket. Silk, distant lands for materials, ceremonial wear for elites, lush reds and golds: the brokers of fine Palembang songkets like this one and its antique antecedents traffic quite consciously in such icons of the exotic. Palembang is known throughout Indonesia as a songket-weaving center for Malay heritage wear. The geography of textiles like this one is complex, however.

In the late 1800s these Palembang kain limar were carried in trader's packs to regions throughout highland and coastal Sumatra. Many of these areas did no songket weaving of their own. Weavers and the local wealthy classes likely marveled at the beauty and technical intricacy of these shining cloths. In Sipirok, a southern Batak weaving town far to the north of Palembang, the distinctive local *ulos* (ceremonial cloak) is formatted in pattern bands and edge designs so that it resembles a Palembang songket. Yet the Sipirok ulos is executed in rough, nubby cotton thread, dyed black and red. The designs on Sipirok ulos bear little resemblance to the starker abstractions found in Toba Batak ulos. It seems possible that a Palembang cloth wandered north, inspired local weavers, and sparked a new heritage textile tradition. Sipirok's ulos inspiration could also have come from Minangkabau songkets. Both regional types show up in sacred house treasures of Sipirok nobility.

Much the same process of encountering a foreign textile, studying it carefully, and executing it with local materials through domestic aesthetics yielded Palembang songkets in the first place. These showy cloths and southern Sumatra's larger array of gold costumes for aristocrats drew in part on encounters with Indian trade cloths.

Since at least the 1920s Palembang's silk songkets have gone on other journeys too. The old silk head tie shown here (fig. 6.29) was woven in the city's distinctive dark red silk and is decorated with the expected deep bands of songket work along the edges. This head tie doubtless started its life as a ceremonial piece for a Palembang grandee, but it was purchased many years later in an antique shop in Jakarta. The store is located in the Jalan Jaksa area, a rather notorious backpacker haven of cheap hotels and beery eateries. Located among these establishments are some of the capital city's most historic antiquities shops.

The store in question was established by a Minangkabau trader family extraordinaire. They stock all manner of Sumatran antiques: Dutch-era ceramic lamps and knickknacks, Bengkulu wedding finery, Pitalah ritual belts, and Palembang songkets from the 1800s. The shop is also a prime place to purchase old north coast Javanese batiks. The kain limar head tie fit right in, in the shop's glass-fronted, carved-wood cabinets jam-packed with folded cloths from past decades. How did this family obtain these goods for sale? They started out as tinkers and tinsmiths in the West Sumatran village of Sungai Puar. In the 1910s and 1920s resident Dutch officials in Bukittinggi were starting private collections of Minangkabau antiquities, including old songkets. The Sungai Puar itinerant peddlers circulated from village to village fixing pots and pans and in the process noticed which great houses had especially stunning stockpiles of "antiquities," at the time emerging as such for educated Minangkabau onlookers as well as Dutch connoisseurs. Voilà: the Sungai Puar tinkers began reinventing themselves as antiques dealers. The illustrious Jakarta shop Toko Djody is one offshoot of that business.

Susan Rodgers

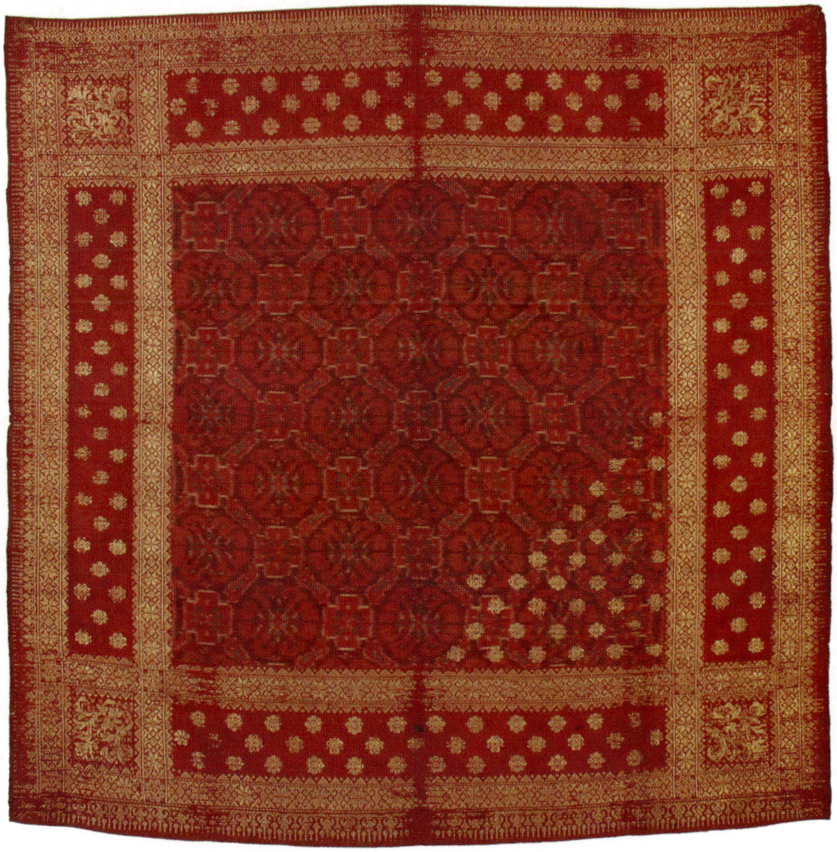

Fig. 6.29 A man's ceremonial headtie, Palembang, early 20th century.

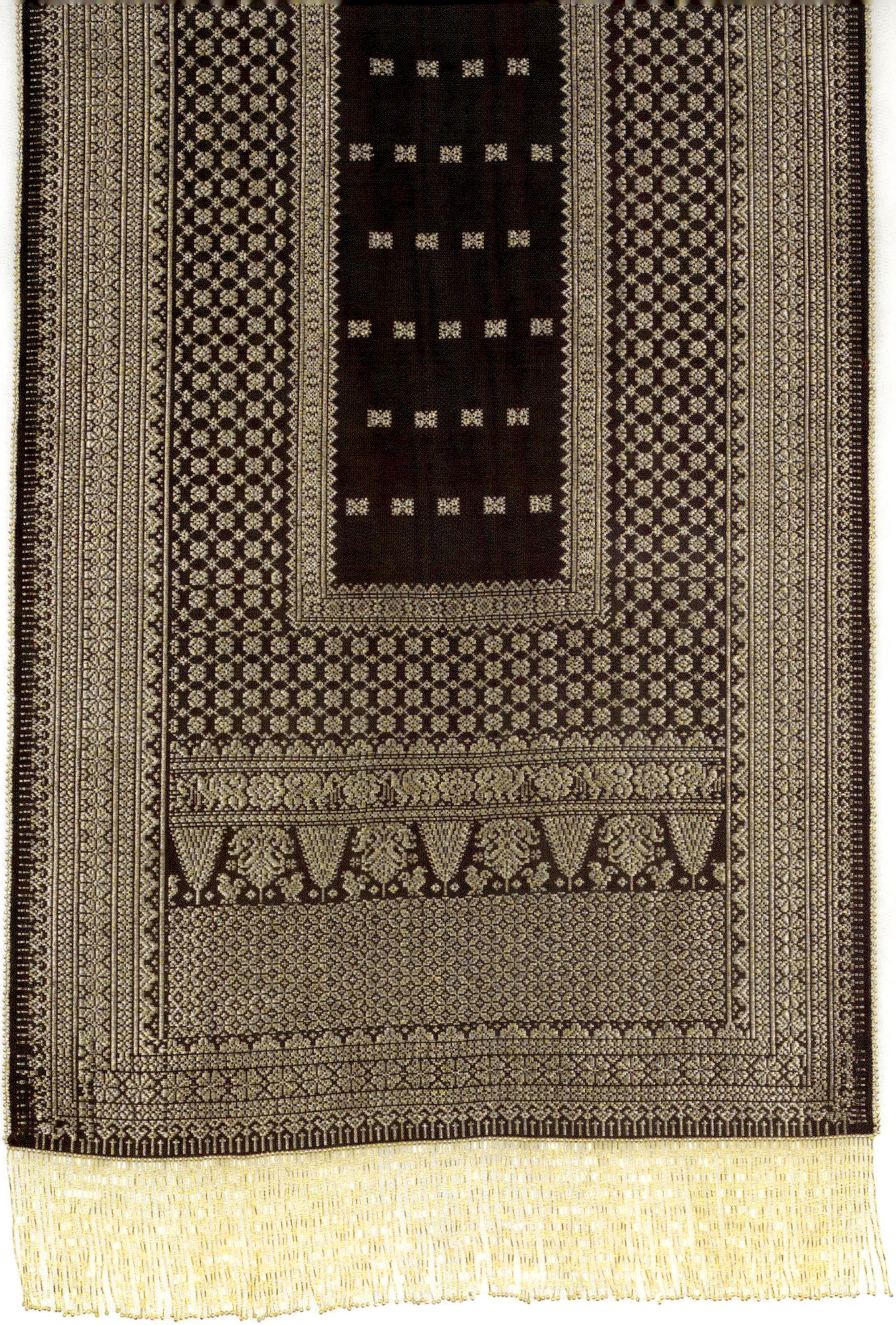

Fig. 6.30

Fig. 6.31. Pelangi cloth, silk, Fikri Koleksi, Palembang. 2006.

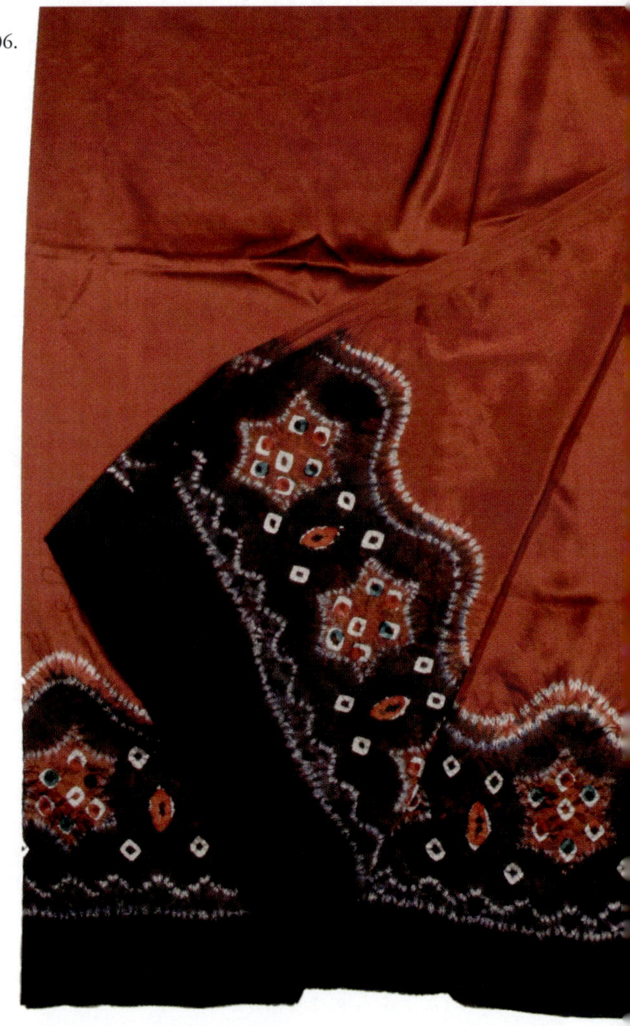

Figure 6.30
Selendang (shoulder cloth), 2005
Palembang, South Sumatra
Cotton blend, gold-wrapped thread, glass beads and fringe, supplementary weft
82 x 23-1/4 in., 208 x 59 cm
Iris and B. Gerald Cantor Art Gallery Study Collection

While Palembang songkets are most immediately identified with the rich red silk kain limar varieties just discussed, metallic-thread supplementary weft weaving in this southern Sumatran oil city is far more extensive today. There has long been a good deal of family wealth in this town; songket luxury wear has had the opportunity to diversify over the last forty years (Uchino 2005). Today customers who visit the songket shops in the 30 Ilir neighborhood of Palembang (the old Malay quarter) will be offered fine examples of the standard red silks. But they will also have the happy task of choosing from among innumerable silk, silk-polyester, and polyester-blend songkets in lime green, purple, baby pink, blue, orange, and peach. Another eye-catcher: black songkets like this one, studded to within an inch of its life with gold beads.

Songket sarong and shoulder cloth sets in black or dramatic purples (done without ikatting) have been staples of the Palembang trade since at least the 1970s. Such songkets were particular favorites at the time among upscale southern Batak families, far to the north in South Tapanuli and in émigré neighborhoods in the city of Medan. Yet the black songket shown here, made in 2005 and sold in 2006, is something different. As discussed in chapter 5, Pak Zainal, the designer/proprietor of the shop from which this cloth set came, often seeks to make his songkets distinctive in a wide market of similar goods by adding extra elements of shininess and glamour. The gold beads that weigh down this shoulder cloth exemplify that effort.

Palembang's contemporary songkets may range far afield in color and thread type, but they still hew to convention when it comes to issues of basic shape and size. As mentioned, these are the standard sarong and shoulder cloth lengths, the infant coverings, and the ceremonial head tie. Palembang's other heritage cloths (most notably, silk pelangi) are veering away from strict adat use into fashion's yard-goods needs. Pelangi forms part of the costume of the bride's attendants in traditional Palembang Malay weddings, but this tie-dyed cloth is also making serious inroads in Indonesian high fashion. Pelangi has an advantage there over metal-thread songket: a soft, lightweight glamour fabric, pelangi can be cut by seamstresses for use in other garments (fig. 6.31).

Despite these incursions into high fashion for "cuttable" cloths, Palembang's basic weaving technology for songkets per se has remained relatively staid. The backstrap loom is the foundation for Palembang gold-thread supplementary-weft work. Songket weaving in another corner of the Malay world, in Terengganu state in peninsular Malaysia, differs from this. Some handlooming is still done in Terengganu, but government subsidies are pushing the craft toward higher production rates. This has resulted in the establishment of virtual songket factories, with dozens of weavers at work. As well, the state government's craft board is exploring the use of computer-programmed looms (retooled for turning out acceptable Malay songket cloth). These looms come from the United States.

As high-end Malaysian songket is extremely expensive (at times up to $1,000 for a fairly simple bridal set of sarong and shoulder cloth), other globalization processes are vigorously at work elsewhere in the region. Along one of Singapore's main old cloth brokerage streets, Arab Street, some shops sell cheap facsimiles of Malaysian songkets factory-produced in Pakistan.

Susan Rodgers

LIST OF REFERENCES

Adams, Kathleen M.
2006 *Art as politics; Re-crafting identities, tourism, and power in Tana Toraja, Indonesia.* Honolulu: University of Hawai'i Press.

Adams, Marie Jeane
1969 *System and meaning in East Sumba textile design.* New Haven: Yale University Southeast Asia Studies Center Monograph.

Andaya, Barbara Watson
1989 'The cloth trade in Jambi and Palembang during the seventeenth and eighteenth centuries', *Indonesia* 48:26-46.
1993 *To live as brothers; Southeast Sumatra in the seventeenth and eighteenth centuries.* Honolulu: University of Hawai'i Press.

Bellwood, Peter
1979 *Man's conquest of the Pacific; The prehistory of Southeast Asia and Oceania.* New York: Oxford University Press.

Benda-Beckmann, F. von
1979 *Property in social continuity; Continuity and change in the maintenance of property relationships through time in Minangkabau.* The Hague: Nijhoff. [KITLV, Verhandelingen 86.]

Blackwood, Evelyn
1995 'Senior women, model mothers, and dutiful wives; Managing gender contradictions in a Minangkabau village', in: Aihwa Ong and Michael Peletz (eds), *Bewitching women, pious men; Gender and body politics in Southeast Asia*, pp. 124-58. Berkeley and Los Angeles: University of California Press.
1999 *Webs of power; Women, kin, and community in a Sumatran village.* Lanham, MD: Rowman and Littlefield.

Brenner, Suzanne A.
1996 'Reconstructing self and society; Javanese Muslim women and "the veil"', *American Ethnologist* 23:673-97.

Bruner, Edward M. and Judith O. Becker
1979 *Art, ritual, and society in Indonesia.* Athens: Ohio University, Center for International Studies.

Bühler, Alfred, and Eberhard Fischer
1979 *The patola of Gujarat; Double ikat in India.* Basle: Krebs. Two vols.

Casey, Margaret
1987 'Female work patterns in Silungkang, West Sumatra; Preliminary observations', *Indonesia Circle* 43:41-9.

Causey, Andrew
2003 *Hard bargaining in Sumatra; Western travelers and Toba Bataks in the marketplace of souvenirs.* Honolulu: University of Hawai'i Press.

Conway, Susan
2001 *Silken threads lacquer thrones; Lan Na court textiles.* Art Media Resources.

Dobbin, Christine E.
1974 *Islamic revivalism in a changing peasant economy; Central Sumatra, 1784-1830.* London/Malmö: Scandinavian Institute of Asian Studies. [Reprinted 1984.]
1977 'Economic change in Minangkabau as a factor in the rise of the Padri movement, 1784-1830', *Indonesia* 23:1-38.

Drakard, Jane
1999 *A kingdom of words; Language and power in Sumatra.* New York: Oxford University Press USA.

Encyclopedia Brittanica.
1974 'Micropedia', in Vol. 3. 15th edition. Chicago/London: Encyclopedia Brittanica. Exhibition Catalogue.
1949 *2000 years of silk weaving.* New York: Weyhe.

Feldman, Jerome
1979 'The house as world in Bawamatuluo, South Nias', in: Edward M.
Bruner and Judith O. Becker (eds), *Art, ritual, and society in Indonesia*, pp. 127-89. Athens: Ohio University, Center for International Studies.

Fielder, Conrad
1949 *On judging works of visual art.* Berkeley/Los Angeles: University of California Press.

Forshee, Jill
2001 *Between the folds: Stories of cloth, lives, and travels from Sumba.* Honolulu: University of Hawai'i Press.

Fox, James (ed.)
1980 *The flow of life; Essays on eastern Indonesia.* Cambridge, MA: Harvard University Press.

Fraser-Lu, Sylvia
1990 *Handwoven textiles of South-East Asia*. Second edition. Singapore: Oxford University Press.

Gibson, Thomas
2005 *And the sun pursued the moon; Symbolic knowledge and traditional authority among the Makassar*. Honolulu: University of Hawai'i Press.

Gittinger, Mattiebelle
1980 (ed.) *Indonesian textiles; Irene Emery roundtable on museum textiles, 1979: Proceedings*. Washington, DC: Textile Museum.
1989 (ed.) *To speak with cloth; Studies in Indonesian textiles*. Los Angeles: Museum of Cultural History, University of California.
1990 *Splendid symbols; Textiles and tradition in Indonesia*. Second edition. Singapore: Oxford University Press.
2005 *Textiles for this world and beyond; Treasures from insular Southeast* Asia. London: Scala.

Gittinger, Mattiebelle and H. Leedom Lefferts, Jr.
1992 *Textiles and the Tai experience in Southeast Asia*. Washington, DC: Textile Museum.

Graves, Elizabeth E.
1981 *The Minangkabau response to Dutch colonial rule in the nineteenth century.* Ithaca, NY: Cornell Modern Indonesia Project, Southeast Asia Program, Cornell University.

Green, Gillian
2003 *Traditional textiles of Cambodia; Cultural threads and material heritage*. Chicago: Buppha Press.

Hauser-Schäublin, Brigitta, Marie-Louise Nabholz-Kartaschoff and Urs Ramseyer
1991 *Balinese textiles*. London: British Museum Press.

Harper, Donald J. et al.
2000 *Javanese and Sumatran batiks from courts and palaces; Rudolf G. Smend Collection.* Köln: Galerie Smend.

Heringa, Rens
1993 *Een schitterende geschiedenis; Weefsels en batiks van Palembang en Djambi*. Den Haag: Museon.

Hitchcock, Michael
1985 *Indonesian textile techniques*. Aylesbury: Shire.

Hoskins, Janet
1989 'Why do ladies sing the blues?; Indigo, cloth production, and gender symbolism in Kodi', in: Annette B. Weiner and Jane Schneider (eds), *Cloth and human experience*, pp. 142-73.Washington, DC: Smithsonian Institution Press.
1998 *Biographical objects; How things tell the stories of people's lives*. New York/London: Routledge.

Indictor, Norman
1986 'The identification and characterization of metal wrappings in historic textiles using microscopy and energy dispersive x-ray spectrometry', *Scanning electron microscopy* 2:491-7.
1999 'Metallic threads in Minangkabau textiles', in: Anne Summerfield and John Summerfield (eds), *Walk in splendor; Ceremonial dress and the Minangkabau*, pp. 225-37. Los Angeles: UCLA Fowler Museum of Cultural History. [Textile Series 4.]

Jasper, J.E. and Mas Pirngadie
1916 *De inlandsche kunstnijverheid in Nederlandsch Indië. Vol. 3. De* batikkunst. 's-Gravenhage: Mouton.

Jessup, Helen Ibbitson
1990 *Court arts of Indonesia*. New York: Asia Society Galleries/Abrams.

Jones, Carla and Ann Marie Leshkowich
2003 'Introduction; The globalization of Asian dress; Re-orienting fashion or re-orientalizing Asia', in: Sandra Niessen, Ann Marie Leshkowich, and Carla Jones (eds), *Re-orienting fashion; The globalization of Asian dress*, pp. 1-48. Providence, RI: Berg.

Kahlenberg, Mary Hunt
1977 *Textile traditions in Indonesia.* Los Angeles: Los Angeles County Museum of Art.

Kahn, Joel S.
1980 *Minangkabau social formations; Indonesian peasants and the world economy*. Cambridge: Cambridge University Press. [Cambridge Studies in Social Anthropology 30.]
1992 *Constituting the Minangkabau; Peasants, culture, and modernity in Colonial Indonesia*. Providence, RI: Berg.

Kartiwa, Suwati
1980 'The social functions of kain songket Minangkabau', in Mattiebelle Gittinger (ed.), *Indonesian textiles; Irene Emery roundtable on museum textiles, 1979: Proceedings*, pp. 56-80. Washington, DC: Textile Museum.
1986 *Kain songket Indonesia (Songket weaving in Indonesia)*. Jakarta: Djambatan.

Kato, Tsuyoshi
1982 *Matriliny and migration; Evolving Minangkabau traditions in Indonesia.* Ithaca, NY: Cornell University Press.

Keane, Webb
2007 *Christian moderns; Freedom and fetish in the mission encounter*. Berkeley/Los Angeles: University of California Press.

Kerlogue, Fiona
1995-96 *Scattered flowers—Textiles from Jambi, Sumatra.* Hull: University of Hull, Centre for Southeast Asian Studies.
1999 'Perceptions and problems in cataloguing; The case of Jambi Batik', *Journal of Museum Ethnography* 11:79-93.
2005 'Jambi batik; A Malay tradition?', *Indonesia and the Malay World* 33-96:183-204.

Kipp, Rita Smith
1990 *The early years of a Dutch colonial mission; The Karo field.* Ann Arbor: University of Michigan Press.

Krier, Jennifer
1994 *Displacing distinction; Political processes in the Minangkabau backcountry.* PhD thesis, Department of Anthropology, Harvard University, Cambridge, MA.
1995 'Narrating herself; Power and gender in a Minangkabau woman's tale of conflict', in: Aihwa Ong and Michael Peletz (eds), *Bewitching women, pious men; Gender and body politics in Southeast Asia,* pp. 51-75. Berkeley/Los Angeles: University of California Press.

Kusmayadi, Taruna
2005 *Busana pengantin Muslim.* Jakarta: Gramedia Pustaka Utama.

Leigh, Barbara
1989 *Hands of time; The crafts of Aceh.* Jakarta: Djambatan.
2000 *The changing face of Malaysian crafts; Identity, industry, and ingenuity.* Kuala Lumpur/New York: Oxford University Press.

Locher-Scholten, Elsbeth
2004 *Sumatran sultanate and colonial state; Jambi and the rise of Dutch imperialism, 1830-1907.* Ithaca, N.Y.: Southeast Asia Program, Cornell University.

Marsden, William
1811 (1986)
The history of Sumatra. Reprint of the third edition 1811. Singapore/London: Oxford University Press.

Maxwell, Robyn
2003 *Textiles of Southeast Asia; Tradition, trade, and transformation.* Revised edition. Singapore: Periplus.
2004 *Sari to sarong; 500 Years of Indian and Indonesian textile exchange.* Canberra: National Gallery of Australia.

Mohamad, Maznah
1996 *The Malay handloom weavers; A study of the rise and decline of traditional manufacture.* Singapore: Institute of Southeast Asian Studies.

Museum Adityawarman.
1998 *Kain songket Pandai Sikek.* Padang: Bagian Proyek Pembinaan Permuseuman Sumatera Barat.

Niessen, Sandra
2003 'Three scenarios from Batak clothing history; Designing participation in the global fashion trajectory', in: Sandra Niessen, Ann Marie Leshkowich and Carla Jones (eds), *Re-orienting fashion; The globalization of Asian dress,* pp. 49-78. Providence, RI: Berg.

Niessen, Sandra, Ann Marie Leshkowich, and Carla Jones (eds)
2003 *Re-orienting fashion; The globalization of Asian dress.* Providence, RI: Berg.

Ng, Cecilia
1987 *The weaving of prestige; Village women's representations of the social categories of Minangkabau society*. PhD thesis, Australian National University, Canberra.

Ong, Aihwa and Michael Peletz (eds)
1995 *Bewitching women, pious men; Gender and body politics in Southeast Asia*. Berkeley/Los Angeles: University of California Press.

Othman, Dato' Haji Sulaiman et al.
1994 *The crafts of Malaysia*. Singapore: Didier Millet.

Oxford Asian Textile Group
1996 *Oxford Asian Textile Group Newsletter* no. 3 (February).

Pemberton, John
1994 *On the subject of 'Java'*. Ithaca, NY: Cornell University Press.

Provincial Tourism Office, Special Province of Jambi
n.y. *Jambi at glance*. Jambi: Dinas Pariwisata Propinsi Jambi.

Radjilis, Elly
1995 *Tata rias dan upacara adat pernikahan, pengantin daerah pesisir (Padang) Sumatera Barat*. Jakarta: Carina Indah Utama.

Razni, Sita Dewi, M.J. Juni and Rebecca Dahlan
2005 *Pakaian tradisional Kotogadang*. Bukittinggi: Yayasan Kerajinan Amai Setia.

Reid, Anthony
1988 *Southeast Asia in the age of commerce, 1450-1680. Volume One, The lands below the winds*. New Haven: Yale University Press.
1995 (ed.) *Witnesses to Sumatra; A traveler's anthology*. New York/London: Oxford University Press.
2005a *An Indonesian frontier; Acehnese and other histories of Sumatra*. Singapore: Singapore University Press.
2005b 'The Turkish connection', in: Anthony Reid, *An Indonesian frontier; Acehnese and other histories of Sumatra*, pp. 69-93. Singapore: Singapore University Press.

Reid, Anthony and Lance Castles (eds)
1975 *Pre-colonial state systems in Southeast Asia*. Kuala Lumpur: Malaysian Branch of the Royal Asiatic Society.

Rodgers, Susan
1985 *Power and gold; Jewelry from Indonesia, Malaysia, and the Philippines*. Geneva: Musée Barbier-Mueller/Prestel.
1995a *Telling lives, telling history; Autobiography and historical imagination in modern Indonesia*. Berkeley/Los Angeles: University of California Press.
1995b *Weaving life, weaving wealth; Sumatran textiles in transition*. Worcester, MA: Iris and B. Gerald Cantor Art Gallery.
2003 *Keris/Cloth; Sacred metal and textile arts of Indonesia*. Worcester, MA: Iris and B. Gerald Cantor Art Gallery.
2005 *Print, poetics, and politics; A Sumatran epic in the colonial Indies and New Order Indonesia*. Leiden: KITLV Press. [Verhandelingen 225.]

Sanday, Peggy Reeves
2004 *Women at the center; Life in a modern matriarchy*. Ithaca, N.Y.: Cornell University Press.

SarDesai, D.R.
2003 *Southeast Asia: Past and present*. Boulder, CO: Westview Press.

Schefold, Reimar and Han F. Vermeulen (eds)
2002 *Treasure hunting? Collectors and collections of Indonesian artefacts*. Leiden: CNWS.

Schnitger, F.M.
1989 *Forgotten kingdoms of Sumatra*. New York/London: Oxford University Press. [Originally published 1939.]

Sears, Laurie J.
1996 *Shadows of empire; Colonial discourse and Javanese tales*. Durham, NC: Duke University Press.

Selvanayagam, Grace Impam
1990 *Songket – Malaysia's woven treasure*. Singapore: Oxford University Press.

Steedly, Mary M.
1996 'The importance of proper names; Language and "national" identity in colonial Karoland', *American Ethnologist* 23:447-75.

Summerfield, Anne
1999 'Women's ceremonial dress and related textiles', in: Anne Summerfield and John Summerfield (eds), *Walk in splendor; Ceremonial dress and the Minangkabau*, pp. 105-70. Los Angeles: UCLA Fowler Museum of Cultural History. [Textile Series 4.]

Summerfield, Anne and H.A. Sutan Madjo Indo
1999 'Motifs and their meaning', in: Anne Summerfield and John Summerfield (eds), *Walk in splendor; Ceremonial dress and the Minangkabau*, pp. 171-200. Los Angeles: UCLA Fowler Museum of Cultural History. [Textile Series 4.]

Summerfield, Anne and John Summerfield
1990 *Trailing the tiger to golden cloths of Sumatra's Minangkabau; Exhibition guide*. Washington, DC: Textile Museum.
1991 *Fabled cloths of Minangkabau*. Santa Barbara, CA: Santa Barbara Museum of Art.
1999 (eds) *Walk in splendor; Ceremonial dress and the Minangkabau*. Los Angeles: UCLA Fowler Museum of Cultural History. [Textile Series 4.]

Summerfield, John
1999a 'Men's ceremonial dress', in: Anne Summerfield and John Summerfield (eds), *Walk in splendor; Ceremonial dress and the Minangkabau*, pp. 79-104. Los Angeles: UCLA Fowler Museum of Cultural History. [Textile Series 4.]
1999b 'Fibers and patterning techniques', in: Anne Summerfield and John Summerfield (eds), *Walk in splendor; Ceremonial dress and the Minangkabau*, pp. 201-24. Los Angeles: UCLA Fowler Museum of Cultural History. [Textile Series 4.]

Sweeney, Amin
1987 *A full hearing; Orality and literacy in the Malay world*. Berkeley/Los Angeles: University of California Press.

Taylor, Jean Gelman
2003 *Indonesia; Peoples and histories*. New Haven: Yale University Press.

Taylor, Paul M. (ed.)
1994 *Fragile traditions; Indonesian art in jeopardy*. Honolulu: University of Hawai'i Press.

Taylor, Paul M. and Lorraine V. Aragon (eds)
1991 *Beyond the Java Sea; Art of Indonesia's Outer Islands*. Washington, DC: National Museum of Natural History, Smithsonian Institution, New York: Abrams.

Uchino, Megumi
2005 'Socio-cultural history of Palembang Songket', *Indonesia and the Malay World* 33-96:205-23.

Van Gelder, Lydia
1980 *Ikat*. New York: Watson-Guptill Publications.

Wahyono, M.
1981 *Lurik; Suatu pengantar*. Jakarta: Wastraprema.

Warming, Wanda and Michael Gaworski
1981 *The world of Indonesian textiles*. Tokyo: Kodansha International.

Weiner, Annette B. and Jane Schneider (eds)
1989 *Cloth and human experience*. Washington, DC: Smithsonian Institution Press.

Wolters, O.W.
1967 *Early Indonesian commerce; A study of the origins of Srivijaya*. Ithaca, NY: Cornell University Press.

Yogi, Olga
1980 'Lurik, a traditional textile in Central Java', in: Mattiebelle Gittinger (ed.) *Indonesian textiles; Irene Emery roundtable on museum textiles, 1979; Proceedings*, pp. 282-5. Washington, DC: Textile Museum.

Young, Ken
1994 *Islamic peasants and the state; The 1908 tax rebellion in West Sumatra*. New Haven: Yale University Center for International and Area Studies. [Yale Southeast Asia Studies Monograph 40.]

GOLD CLOTHS IMAGE/PHOTOGRAPHY CREDITS

Cover
Frank E. Graham

Map
Sharon Matys

ix
Susan Rodgers

Ch 1

Frank E. Graham	1.0, 1.3, 1.5, 1.7, 1.8, 1.9, 2.0
Susan Rodgers	1.1, 1.2a, 1.2b, 1.4, 1.6

Ch 2

Frank E. Graham	2.0, 2.8, 2.9, 2.11
Roger Hankins	2.7, 2.15, 2.16, 2.17
Susan Rodgers	2.1, 2.2, 2.3, 2.4, 2.5, 2.6, 2.10, 2.12, 2.13, 2.14

Ch 3

Frank E. Graham	3.3, 3.7, 3.9, 3.10, 3.15
Roger Hankins	3.5, 3.6, 3.8, 3.9, 3.11, 3.12, 3.14, 3.22
Susan Rodgers	3.0, 3.1, 3.2, 3.4, 3.13, 3.16, 3.17, 3.18, 3.19, 3.20, 3.21

Ch 4

Anne and John Summerfield	4.1, 4.2, 4.3, 4.4, 4.5, 4.6, 4.7, 4.9, 4.10, 4.11, 4.12, 4.13, 4.14, 4.15, 4.16, 4.17
Roger Hankins	4.0, 4.8
Frank E. Graham	4.18

Ch 5

Frank E. Graham	5.1, 5.2, 5.9, 5.11, 5.12, 5.13, 5.16, 5.18, 5.23, 5.26, 5.27
Roger Hankins	5.10, 5.14, 5.15, 5.17, 5.19, 5.20, 5.23, 5.24, 5.28
Susan Rodgers	5.0, 5.3, 5.4, 5.5, 5.6, 5.7, 5.8, 5.21, 5.22, 5.25, 5.29
Anne and John Summerfield	5.3

Ch 6

Frank E. Graham	6.1, 6.5, 6.6, 6.7, 6.8, 6.12, 6.13, 6.14, 6.15, 6.16, 6.17, 6.18, 6.19, 6.20, 6.21, 6.22, 6.23, 6.24, 6.26, 6.27, 6.28, 6.30
Roger Hankins	6.25, 6.29, 6.31
Susan Rodgers	6.0, 6.26
Anne and John Summerfield	6.2, 6.3, 6.4, 6.9, 6.10, 6.11, 6.13

TEXTILE COLLECTIONS

Anne and John Summerfield Indonesian Textile Study Collection,
Iris and B. Gerald Cantor Art Gallery, College of the Holy Cross

1.5., 1.8, 2.7., 2.15., 2.16., 2.17., 3.3., 3.5., 3.6., 3.7., 3.8., 3.9., 3.10., 3.11., 3.12., 3.14, 3.22., 4.0., 4.18., 5.9., 5.10., 5.11, 5.17., 5.20., 5.23., 5.24., 5.26., 5.28., 6.6., 6.7., 6.20., 6.21., 6.23., 6.25., 6.27., 6.28. foreground, 6.29., 6.30., 6.31.

Collection of Anne and John Summerfield

1.0., 1.3., 1.9., 2.0., 2.8., 2.11., 3.15., 4.4., 4.8., 4.10., 4.11., 4.12., 4.13., 4.17., 5.18., 5.19., 6.1., 6.3., 6.5., 6.8., 6.10., 6.11., 6.12., 6.14., 6.15., 6.16., 6.17., 6.18., 6.19., 6.28. background

Private Collection

1.7., 2.9., 5.12., 5.13., 5.14., 5.15., 5.16., 5.27., 6.22., 6.24.